America: Past and Present

Volume III: The Continuing Quest

KATHERINE L. HARRINGTON

America
Past & Present

SECOND EDITION

VOLUME III

THE CONTINUING QUEST

HEINLE & HEINLE PUBLISHERS

A Division of Wadsworth, Inc.
BOSTON, MASSACHUSETTS 02116

Publisher: Stanley J. Galek
Editor: Erik Gundersen
Associate Editor: Lynne Telson Barsky
Editorial Production Manager: Elizabeth Holthaus
Production Editor: Kristin M. Thalheimer
Photo Coordinator: Martha Leibs-Heckly
Manufacturing Coordinator: Jerry Christopher
Project Manager: Ros Herion Freese
Interior Design: Ros Herion Freese
Composition: A+ Publishing Services
Cover Design: Hannus Design Associates
Map Illustrations: Leslie Genser Design

America: Past and Present
Volume III: The Continuing Quest

Heinle & Heinle Publishers is a division of Wadsworth, Inc.

Manufactured in the United States of America

Photograph credits appear on p. xvii, which constitutes a part of this copyright
page.

Library of Congress Cataloging in Publication Data

Harrington, Katherine L. (Katherine Lancelot), 1943–
    America, past & present / Katherine L. Harrington.
      p.   cm.
    Rev. ed. of: America, past and present. 1981–1985.
    Contents: v. 1. The exploration of a continent. -- v. 2. The
challenge of new frontiers -- v. 3. The continuing quest.
    ISBN 0-8384-3439-8 (v. 1). -- ISBN 0-8384-3440-1 (v. 2). -- ISBN
0-8384-3441-X (v. 3)
      1. Readers--United States. 2. English language--Textbooks for
foreign speakers. 3. United States--History--Problems, exercises,
etc. I. Harrington, Katherine L. (Katherine Lancelot), 1943–
America, past and present. II. Title. III. Title: America past and
present.
PE1127.H5H3   1993   92-31762
428.6'4--dc20   CIP

ISBN 0-8384-3441-X

10 9 8 7 6 5 4 3

Dedication

America: Past and Present is dedicated,
with much affection,
to Joey and Chris.

Contents

Preface to the Second Edition

RATIONALE

America: Past and Present is a comprehensive cultural history of the United States for students of English as a Second Language or Foreign Language. It has also been used effectively by native-speaking students enrolled in English or Social Studies developmental programs. The texts are especially suited for university pre-university, or secondary school curricula, where students must acquire good English language skills as well as a fundamental knowledge of American social and cultural history.

Taken as a series, the three volumes trace the origin and growth of American social, political, and cultural traditions from colonial times through the twentieth century. Though designed for the English language student, these volumes follow the content-based sequence of mainstream American Social Studies programs, covering all of the major topics presented in the basic curriculum. Volume I begins with a discussion of Native American culture, continues through the Age of European Discovery and the Revolutionary Era, and concludes with Jefferson at the dawn of the nineteenth century. Volume II offers an overview of key developments and personalities in nineteenth-century America, beginning with the Age of Jackson and ending with an analysis of the Civil War and of the effects of that tragic struggle on the nation as a whole. In Volume III, the most important events and leading personalities of twentieth-century American history are analyzed. Although the volumes follow one another in historical sequence, each is a separate and independent text and can be used effectively either as part of a series or in isolation.

ORGANIZATION OF THE TEXT

This second edition of *America: Past and Present* retains the many key features that were judged highly effective by teachers and program coordinators over the past ten years. Thus, each volume in the series remains a combination reader, anthology, and language skills workbook, with the twelve units in each volume divided into three major parts.

The first part, a **Historical Background** reading, offers an overview of the leading personalities and main events of each period. Following the background summary is a short illustrative anthology **Selection**. These original selections, taken from the works of famous writers and thinkers, serve to introduce students to some of the most important representatives of America's literary, political, social, and philosophical heritage. They also offer important primary-source commentary on the historical background readings, putting students in touch with *original* material from each of the main historical periods. In addition, by continuing the themes of the historical background readings, these anthology selections serve to review vocabulary, idiomatic expressions, and grammatical structures introduced in the historical surveys.

Both in the background summaries and in the anthology selections, the cultural and ethnic diversity in America's developing history continues to be emphasized. Volume I, for example, focuses on the extensive Hispanic contributions to the development of America and the shaping of its traditions. The contributions of Native American cultures—from the magnificent Aztec civilization to the rich Pacific Northwest heritage—are also discussed, with photographs, maps, and original Native American and Spanish selections supporting historical summaries and providing topics for discussion.

The role of women in American history remains central to this second edition of *America: Past and Present*. From colonial times to the present, both the ongoing contributions of women and their continuing struggle for equality have been emphasized, with selections from the works of great female poets, novelists, explorers, and reformers enhancing the historical background summaries. Also of major significance in the series is the critical role of African-American history. Here again, photographs, maps, and original selections from the works of famous African-American writers, educators, and political leaders support the historical narrative and provide opportunities for discussion and composition.

Coordinated **Exercises**, reflecting an integrated task-oriented approach to language study, comprise the third section of each unit in the series. All exercises are designed to develop reading, writing, and oral skills by means of interactive processes that invite creative student participation. Throughout, the underlying principle is the belief that reading, writing, and speaking skills are closely interrelated, and that a variety of exercises reflecting this interconnection can best help students maintain interest, develop confidence, and improve oral and written language proficiency.

For purposes of classroom organization, the exercises have been grouped into five general categories:

1. *Reading Comprehension*   In every unit, there is a variety of exercises designed to teach—and not merely test—such critical reading skills as making inferences, summarizing, sequencing, finding the main topic, identifying cause and effect, comparing, contrasting, and drawing conclusions. To provide further practice in the techniques of information gathering, some of these exercises are keyed to the maps, graphs, and time-lines in each volume.

    Prereading exercises, corresponding to the photographs or illustrations that introduce each unit, are a new feature of this second edition. These exercises encourage students to interact with new material in terms of information and vocabulary already learned. They also provide the context for creative class discussion, inviting shared student responses to each historical period as it is introduced.

2. *Vocabulary and Idiomatic Expressions*   Reflecting a belief that good vocabulary skills are critical to the study of both history and literature, the exercises in this section serve to introduce new vocabulary and to review words and idioms learned in previous chapters. Again, to avoid tedious repetition, there is a wide variety of exercise types, helping students to guess meaning from context, to supply appropriate words in cloze paragraphs, to practice with synonyms, antonyms, phrasal verbs, prefixes and suffixes, and to expand vocabulary

through related word formation. As in the *Reading Comprehension* section, these exercises are devised to go over the historical content *as they review* the target language skills. In that way, students are constantly expanding their familiarity with both American cultural history and American English.

3. *Structures* Exercises designed to review key grammatical structures follow the vocabulary section in each unit. These exercises have been graded so that students can progress to a review of increasingly difficult structures as they progress chronologically across the panorama of American history. The underlying principle has been to engage students interactively with both historical *and* grammatical content by providing the opportunity for creative response to structural models.

4. *Topics for Composition* In every unit, there are several opportunities for written evaluations of historical content. Instead of asking students merely to summarize, however, these questions encourage creative, personal responses. For example, students may be asked to write a personal opinion letter, to make a character sketch, to agree or disagree with received historical judgment, to design an interview, to analyze time-lines, graphs, and photographs, to draw conclusions, to make comparisons and contrasts, or to expand upon well-known proverbs in analyzing historical facts and figures. Throughout, the operating principle has been to engage the student's enthusiastic involvement, and not just to elicit a repetition of facts.

5. *Questions for Class Discussion* Many of the exercises in this section involve pairing or small group discussion as well as task-oriented activities. They include directives for interviewing, decision making, role playing, reporting, opinion gathering, description, and persuasion. Students are also encouraged to share their own personal experiences and to relate the customs and traditions of their own families and cultures to the historical content presented in each unit.

At the end of each unit is a list of **Some Interesting Places to Visit.** These may include museums, libraries, battlefields, historical houses, national memorials, universities, and state and national parks. Also included are new photographs in all three volumes of this second edition. Where needed, information contained in statistical graphs has been updated. Appendix C, the list of American Presidents at the end of each volume, has also been updated, and Appendix D, a list of American states and their abbreviations, has been included. Appendix A, The Declaration of Independence, and Appendix B, The Constitution of the United States of America, have been retained in all three volumes. In some units, students have been asked to refer to these documents as they prepare their responses to discussion or composition questions. For example, in Volume I, prereading questions on the development of slavery are used to direct students to a specific analysis of the Declaration of Independence. In Volume II, students are again referred to the Declaration of Independence as part of a larger analysis of Elizabeth Stanton's Seneca Falls Declaration. As part of a creative interpretation of the Jacksonian Era, students are also directed to the American Constitution, specifically to a comparison of Article 1, Section 7, with the significance of a well-known political cartoon.

Teachers should feel free to make further reference to these documents as time and needs dictate. For example, a discussion of the First Amendment to the Constitution could follow the analysis of the quest for religious freedom as presented in Units 4 and 5 of Volume I. A reading of Articles 1–8 of the Constitution could underscore the analysis of the Constitutional Convention as presented in Unit 8 of Volume I. In Volume II, a discussion of the contributions of Susan Anthony and Elizabeth Stanton could be followed by a reference to the 19th Amendment to the Constitution. Similarly, a reading of Amendments 13–15 to the Constitution might be assigned after Units 10–12 of Volume II, while a discussion of Amendments 18 and 21 could follow the Jazz Age presentation of Unit 7 of Volume III.

Throughout, teachers should also feel free to use all or part of the exercises in each volume. The units have been designed with enough flexibility to fit the concentrated format of intensive programs as well as the extended syllabus of longer semesters. They have also been designed to allow for paired student work and small group activities if teachers so choose. In each volume, however, the readings should be assigned in order, as both the historical background and the primary source selections often build upon information given in previous readings. Several exercises refer directly to previous units, so that students can learn to place new information in meaningful relation to knowledge already learned. The total effect of each text in the series, then, is greater than the sum of its parts. As students gain skills in making comparisons and contrasts, as they learn to recognize subtle relationships of cause and effect, and as they begin to make their own considered historical judgments, the panorama of American culture as it has evolved will sharpen in focus and significance.

CONCLUSION

In conclusion, I am grateful to the many teachers and students, both in the United States and abroad, who have continued to find *America: Past and Present* an effective and informative series throughout the years. I am thankful, too, for their generous comments and insightful suggestions, which I have attempted to incorporate into this new edition. In so doing, I hope that I have brought an in-depth knowledge of American culture—too often reserved for the advanced history student—well within the range of intermediate-language students.

Katherine L. Harrington

Acknowledgments

It is a pleasure to acknowledge the debt of gratitude I have incurred in the writing of this second edition of *America: Past and Present*. For their expert advice throughout all phases of this project, I am grateful to Erik Gundersen, Lynne Telson Barsky, and Kristin Thalheimer of Heinle & Heinle Publishers. I am also indebted to Rosalie Herion Freese, who coordinated all aspects of production for the series; Terry Eppridge, whose original maps have remained an inspiration to me; and Leslie Genser, who provided new maps for this second edition.

As always, I am especially indebted to my family. For their continuing encouragement, I wish to thank my parents, Dolores and Milton Lancelot. For their generous enthusiasm, I remain grateful to my sons, Joey and Chris. Finally, for his unfailing personal and professional support, I wish to thank my husband, Joe.

About the Author

Katherine Harrington took her M.A. and Ph.D. in Comparative Literature at Harvard University, where she entered as a Woodrow Wilson National Fellow in 1965. She has lectured widely in European and American cultural history, and has taught Western Cultural History, Spanish, and English at the university level.

In 1977, Dr. Harrington founded the Scarsdale Institute, a private academy for intercultural exchange and language study. In addition to *America: Past and Present*, she is the author of *O Susannah!*—an award-winning drama about Susan Anthony and Elizabeth Cady Stanton and their struggle for human rights.

Credits

Cover: Art by Edward Hopper. Courtesy of the Fogg Art Museum, Harvard University Art Museum, Louise E. Bettens Fund.

p. ii: UN Photo 165054 / Lois Conner. (Doc. 1005L)

p. 2:   Museum of the City of New York, The Byron Collection.

p. 9:   Courtesy of the Library of Congress.

p. 10:   Edith Wharton Restoration.

p. 19:   Solomon D. Butcher Collection, Nebraska State Historical Society.

p. 21:   Union Pacific Museum Collection. Photo by A.J. Russell. H-1-23

pp. 37 and 42:   Hawaii State Archives.

pp. 53, 59, and 61:   U.S. Department of the Interior, National Park Service, Edison National Historic Site.

p. 71:   Museum of the City of New York.

p. 74:   Museum of the City of New York. The Jacob A. Riis Collection, #502. Photo by Jessie Tarbox Beals.

p. 78:   University of Illinois at Chicago, The University Library, Jane Addams Memorial Collection.

p. 89:   Courtesy of the Library of Congress.

p. 95:   National Archives. Photo No. 111-SC-27410.

p. 107:   Culver Pictures.

p. 112:   Courtesy of the Library of Congress.

p. 125:   Franklin D. Roosevelt Library. Photo by Fechner.

p. 133:   Franklin D. Roosevelt Library. Photo by Dorothea Lange.

p. 143:   National Archives. Photo No. 26-C-2402.

p. 148:   National Archives. Photo No. 111-SC-340762.

p. 159:   ST No. 22-1-62. 8/62. In the John F. Kennedy Library.

p. 162:   UN Photo 165054 / Lois Conner. (Doc. 1005L)

p. 165:   United Press International Photo.

p. 181:   UPI/Bettmann.

pp. 188–189:   From *The Bonfire of the Vanities* by Tom Wolfe. Copyright © 1987 by Tom Wolfe. Reprinted by permission of Farrar, Straus, & Giroux, Inc.

p. 201:   Courtesy of AmeriCares.

p. 211:   National Aeronautics and Space Administration.

America: Past and Present

Volume III: The Continuing Quest

1

Money and Magnificence

The Gilded Age

PREREADING

Look at the photograph below. Then, working in pairs or small groups, answer these questions.

1. Pictured on the corner of Fifth Avenue and 65th Street is the Manhattan mansion built for Mrs. Caroline Astor in 1893. The fashionable homes of other wealthy New Yorkers can be seen farther up Fifth Avenue. Describe the Astor home with as much detail as possible. What rooms do you think occupied the first floor? The second? Who might have lived on the top floor? Why do you think the home was designed to resemble a French castle?

2. Turn to the photograph on p. 71. Pictured is Hester Street, Manhattan, 1899. Although it was taken about the same time as the photograph of Mrs. Astor's house, the scene is a very different one. Would you say New York in the 1890s was a city of enormous contrasts? How do you think some of these contrasts developed?

New York, Fifth Avenue and 65th Street, at the turn of the twentieth century

1   In 1876, as Americans celebrated their nation's centennial, there was a lingering[1] sadness throughout the country. Only a decade earlier, in 1865, a long and terrible civil war had ended.* Four years of fighting between the North and the South had taken the lives of half a million Americans. And although Northern victory had ultimately preserved the American Union, vivid[2] memories of a ghastly[3] war still lingered. Southern states had been devastated[4] by constant invasion. In fact, in 1876, they were still under the burden[5] of postwar martial rule. Northern states had escaped complete destruction, but thousands of their soldiers, too, had died. For both sides, therefore, the war between the states had been a shattering experience, an overwhelming[6] sorrow which America had to bear in order to end the injustice of slavery.

THE RISE OF BIG BUSINESS

2   Thus, at the end of their first century, the people looked ahead with mixed emotions. As in many postwar periods, there remained bitterness and self-doubt. But as often happens after a major conflict, there was also a new commitment to prosperity. For the war had brought expansion as well as disaster. It had created new social patterns and a vast new technology—advances that made it possible for America to realize its fullest economic potential.

3   The federal government, for example, had greatly developed during the years of military crisis. To provide effective leadership, it had become a complex, centralized, and powerful organization. So after 1865, Americans increasingly looked to the government for assistance and support. Business leaders, consumers, pioneers, and workers all demanded attention. They learned to lobby,[7] to apply pressure on the government, to use all of the government's new powers. With more and more help from Washington, therefore, they were able to promote[8] the settlement of land, the development of industry, and the extension of investment opportunities.

4   Like the expanded role of government, the military campaigns of the Civil War also advanced the American economy. For in order to carry on the enormous struggle, there were continuous developments in industry, communication, agriculture, banking, and marketing. Railroad lines were extended and farm machinery improved. Medicine advanced, the telegraph spread, and publicity methods for wartime propaganda developed. Indeed, in almost every area of national production, there were technical and professional improvements to meet the emergency needs of war.

5   Finally, the Civil War turned out to be a testing ground for talent. On the battlefields, during strategy[9] sessions, at supply lines, and in hospitals, only one thing

---

1. linger: remain, continue
2. vivid: strong, very real
3. ghastly: horrible
4. devastate: destroy completely
5. burden: heavy load

6. overwhelming: very powerful
7. lobby: attempt to influence political policy
8. promote: encourage
9. strategy: detailed plan

* In the second volume of *America: Past and Present,* Units 10 through 12 offer an analysis of the American Civil War.

mattered: success. Those who could do their job well were acknowledged and advanced. Those who failed were replaced and forgotten. Thus, when the fighting was over, there were tough, experienced managers among the war's survivors. These directors were the future leaders of America's peacetime development.

THE GILDED AGE

6   As its second century dawned, therefore, the United States was just beginning its greatest period of expansion. Government assistance, improved technology, and aggressive leaders were transforming[10] the country's economy, and a war-weary nation turned in relief to the steady pursuit of wealth. Fortunes were made and millions invested as the people developed their land, their natural resources, and their manufacturing capacity. So by World War I—fifty years after the Civil War—a remarkable[11] transformation had taken place. America had conquered a continent to become the leading nation of an emerging modern age.

7   But the quality of life in that half-century did not quite match the nation's wealth. Power, too often, led to corruption.[12] And the chance for a fortune brought greed and unrest to the souls of ambitious achievers. For this reason, the decades that followed the Civil War became known as America's Gilded[13] Age. On the surface there appeared rapid growth and great technological achievement. Sometimes, however, beneath the prosperity, there was a deeper reality of dishonesty and fraud.[14]

8   And yet, despite its darker side, the Gilded Age was a memorable period in the American experience. As symbolized by its ragtime music, it was an age of tremendous[15] energy. From the fields of oil in Pennsylvania to the cattle ranches of Texas, from Rocky Mountain silver mines to the avenues of Manhattan, there was constant, creative activity. There was also a new elegance, as fabulous houses and fashionable clothes replaced the simplicity of a pioneer past. Above all, of course, there were the millionaires themselves—those brilliant[16] investors and extraordinary business leaders who shaped the miracles of America's new economy.

FOCUS ON ANDREW CARNEGIE

9   Among these figures, the most famous, perhaps, was Andrew Carnegie. Born in Scotland in 1835, Carnegie spent his childhood in the romantic and picturesque[17] countryside around the ancient town of Dunfermline. With its fine old abbey[18] and its palace ruins, the area was rich in Scottish history, and young Andrew—sensitive and proud—soon learned to treasure his national heritage.[19] He thrilled to family stories of legendary heroes. He took delight in the folklore and tradition of Scotland's past. Indeed, from the land and from its people, Carnegie seemed to get a special strength— a sense of comfort, an identity that linked him to the glory of a vanished[20] epic[21] age.

---

10. transform: change
11. remarkable: extraordinary
12. corruption: evil, dishonesty
13. gilded: covered with a thin
     layer of gold
14. fraud: trick, dishonesty
15. tremendous: great, very large

16. brilliant: very intelligent
17. picturesque: charming
18. abbey: church, monastery
19. heritage: traditions
20. vanish: disappear
21. epic: great, heroic

10   Suddenly, however, this security was rudely shaken. The Industrial Revolution was sweeping across Britain, and Dunfermline, too, began to change. One after another, its artisans were replaced by the new machinery of a growing factory system. And even Carnegie's father—a prosperous and respected weaver—could not escape. He struggled hard to keep his regular customers, but it was no use. Machines could make his cloth much faster and cheaper. There would soon be no more work for him, he realized sadly. But in America, toward the western frontiers, there would at least be a chance for his children.

11   So in 1848, after selling the family possessions to pay for their passage, the Carnegies sailed away from Scotland. For little Andrew— then only thirteen—this departure from Dunfermline was traumatic.[22] Again and again he turned toward the abbey, fading symbol of a world that had crumbled[23] and a peace that was gone forever. Ahead lay America—continent of opportunity. But Carnegie's roots, and his heart, remained in the Scottish hills.

12   After arriving in New York, the Carnegie family moved on to Pittsburgh, Pennsylvania. There, relatives had told them, new industries and spreading railroad connections had created employment opportunities. But as the newcomers discovered, conditions in Pittsburgh soon proved disappointing. Carnegie's father found few customers for his lovely handmade cloths, and the only employment his mother could find was some part-time work as a shoemaker's assistant. Before long, "the prospect[24] of want[25] had become to me a frightful[26] nightmare," Carnegie confessed. More than anything else, the proud boy who had cherished[27] Scotland's heroes now longed to become his family's savior. If only he could restore the days of Dunfermline's plenty. If only he could ease the pain of poverty in America.

13   Determined, Andrew Carnegie found some work in a nearby cotton factory. Then, for better pay, he quickly changed to another mill. By day, he spent long hours amid the sickening odors[28] of the oil vats.[29] At night, he studied the latest methods of accounting. Finally, the chance for advancement appeared. A messenger boy was needed at the local telegraph office, and Carnegie was hired. At last he had an opportunity to meet the business leaders who sent and received the city's wires.

14   Indeed, it was from the telegraph office that Carnegie's rise began. He was only fifteen, but he quickly absorbed all the business information that passed over the wires to this office. After a year, he learned to operate the telegraph machine itself. Then, with his speed and skill, he soon impressed all the merchants and bankers who needed the information he received.

15   One of these businessmen was Mr. Thomas Scott, superintendent of the western division of the Pennsylvania Railroad. On his frequent visits to the telegraph office, he often observed its clever young operator. So when the expanding railroad needed its own operator, Scott insisted on Carnegie. In this way, Andrew Carnegie entered the fast-paced,[30] multimillion-dollar railroad industry.

---

22. traumatic: very upsetting
23. crumble: break into many small pieces
24. prospect: possibility
25. want: poverty
26. frightful: terrible

27. cherish: treasure
28. odor: smell
29. vat: large container for liquids
30. fast-paced: competitive, growing

16   Here again, he quickly mastered the details and techniques of a complex organization. From telegraph operator he became Scott's assistant. Then, after Scott was promoted to vice president of the line, Carnegie himself became the division superintendent. It was a position of immense responsibility and countless[31] managerial duties, for railroads were quickly becoming the first great corporations in America. They invested vast amounts of capital in machinery, maintenance, land, construction, and supplies. They depended on the flawless[32] operation of long-range communication systems. And they needed a carefully coordinated staff of thousands in order to operate successfully.

17   From 1859 to 1865—years which spanned the Civil War—Carnegie directed his division with energy and skill. Thus, at a time when railroads were under tremendous wartime pressures, he became an expert in corporate finance, personnel management, marketing, promotion, and large-scale business operations. He was also able to make shrewd[33] personal investments, since he was in constant touch with the economic and political leaders of the nation.

A NEW INDUSTRIAL TECHNOLOGY

18   When Carnegie left the railroad, therefore, he was already a wealthy man. Although only twenty-nine, his dreams of saving the family from want had long since been fulfilled. But greater achievements still lay ahead. During his years on the railroad, Carnegie had realized that steel, not wood or iron, was destined to become the modern world's construction material. He had heard about the new Bessemer process for converting iron to steel and was determined to utilize[34] this process in steel plants of his own. So by means of brilliant investments, and drawing upon[35] all his railroad experience, he began the systematic expansion of one of his earliest companies—the Keystone Bridge Company—into a vast corporation: Carnegie Steel. For almost forty years, he devoted himself with customary energy to the management of this corporation. And in the process, he perfected techniques of corporate management that are still central to international business today. He expanded his facilities, updated machinery, and coordinated a huge staff. He also managed to keep his prices competitive while aggressively seeking world-wide markets.

19   Unfortunately, this brought Carnegie to a tragic confrontation with labor in 1892. When workers at his Homestead Plant went out on strike against a pay cut, Carnegie's partner—Henry Frick—responded with a call for hundreds of guards. In the violence that quickly developed, many guards and several strikers were killed or wounded.

20   In 1901 Carnegie finally sold his company to the world-famous banker, J. P. Morgan. The price agreed upon was $480 million—and a new corporation was reorganized as United States Steel.

21   By this time, Carnegie was already involved in an organized program of philanthropy,[36] for he had determined to give away much of his fortune to those who needed it. He established libraries, supported churches, built public buildings, and created pensions. While establishing trusts for future projects, he also founded universities and supported education in both Europe and America. Indeed, by

---

31. countless: many
32. flawless: without mistakes
33. shrewd: very clever

34. utilize: use
35. draw upon: use as a source
36. philanthropy: helping humanity

mastering the system that had mastered his father, Carnegie triumphed completely over the villains[37] of his youth. He had, of course, paid a high price for success. He had made enemies as well as admirers, for especially after the Homestead Strike, there were critics who had attacked him for having used ruthless[38] business procedures. Yet, like the heroes of his childhood fantasies,[39] he had emerged victorious. Like them, his name was legend. Tycoon[40] of the Gilded Age, his exploits,[41] too, would live on forever in the shadows of Dunfermline's abbey.

---

37. villain: evil person
38. ruthless: cruel, unjust
39. fantasy: dream

40. tycoon: wealthy industrialist
41. exploit: notable deed

✠ SELECTION I

The following selection is from Carnegie's *Autobiography*. Written after he had become a famous industrialist, it describes the childhood traumas of unexpected poverty, departure from Scotland, and emigration to America.

from
Autobiography of Andrew Carnegie

With the introduction and improvement of steam machinery, trade grew worse and worse in Dunfermline for the small manufacturers, and at last a letter was written to my mother's two sisters in Pittsburgh stating that the idea of our going to them was seriously entertained—not, as I remember hearing my parents say, to benefit their own condition, but for the sake of their two young sons. Satisfactory letters were received in reply. The decision was taken to sell the looms[1] and furniture by auction. And my father's sweet voice sang often to mother, brother, and me:

> "To the West, to the West, to the land of the free,
> Where the mighty Missouri rolls down to the sea;
> Where a man is a man even though he must toil
> And the poorest may gather the fruits of the soil."

The proceeds[2] of the sale were most disappointing. The looms brought hardly anything, and the result was that twenty pounds more were needed to enable the family to pay passage to America. Here let me record an act of friendship performed by a lifelong companion of my mother— ... She boldly ventured to advance the needful twenty pounds, my Uncles Lauder and Morrison guaranteeing repayment. Uncle Lauder also lent his aid and advice, managing all the details for us, and on the 17th day of May, 1848, we left Dunfermline. My father's age was then forty-three, my mother's thirty-three. I was in my thirteenth year, my brother Tom in his fifth year—a beautiful white-haired child with lustrous[3] black eyes, who everywhere attracted attention....

---

1. loom: machine for weaving   2. proceeds: money collected   3. lustrous: shiny

Andrew Carnegie

On the morning of the day we started from beloved Dunfermline, in the omnibus that ran upon the coal railroad to Charleston, I remember that I stood with tearful eyes looking out of the window until Dunfermline vanished from view, the last structure to fade being the grand and sacred old Abbey. During my first fourteen years of absence my thought was almost daily, as it was that morning, "When shall I see you again?" … All my recollections[4] of childhood, all I knew of fairyland clustered[5] around the old Abbey and its curfew[6] bell, which tolled at eight o'clock every evening and was the signal for me to run to bed before it stopped ….

The arrival at New York was bewildering.[7] I had been taken to see the Queen at Edinburgh, but that was the extent of my travels before emigrating. Glasgow we had not time to see before we sailed. New York was the first great hive[8] of human industry among the inhabitants of which I had mingled,[9] and the bustle[10] and excitement of it overwhelmed me….

---

4. recollection: memory
5. cluster: gather
6. curfew: time when people must return to their homes

7. bewildering: completely confusing
8. hive: habitat for bees
9. mingle: mix
10. bustle: constant activity

Unlike Andrew Carnegie, Edith Newbold Jones grew up in the privileged world of New York society during America's Gilded Age. She traveled often, even in childhood, visiting elegant resorts with her wealthy parents and friends. She began to develop a keen interest in literature and writing, but her enthusiasm, considered improper for a young lady, was firmly discouraged by her parents. Dutifully, in 1885, she married Edward Wharton, a prominent[1] member of Boston society. Before long, however, she suffered a mental collapse, torn between her duties as a fashionable young hostess and her desire to find a deeper, more meaningful life. After a slow and painful period of recovery, she published a book of short stories in 1899. Three years later came her first novel, *The Valley of Decision,* followed by one of her best works, *The House of Mirth,* in 1905. When her marriage, strained to the breaking point, came to an end in 1913, Edith Wharton had already settled in Paris, determined to continue her career as an author. *The Custom of the Country,* another of her great novels, appeared that same year; six years later, she was awarded[2] the Pulitzer Prize for her masterpiece of fiction, *The Age of Innocence.* Surrounded by a brilliant circle of artists, she continued to write until her death in 1937, publishing over fifteen novels, several volumes of short stories, plays, poetry, and travel books.

Edith Wharton

---

1. prominent: well-known

2. to award: to give a prize

Following is a selection from *The House of Mirth*.[3] Set in the fashionable New York world Wharton had known as a girl, the novel describes the struggles of the beautiful, ambitious, and intelligent Lily Bart. Once wealthy, Lily's parents have suffered financial disaster, leaving their daughter to make her own way in society. The only solution, Lily knows, is to marry a rich man, but she repeatedly turns away from the wealthy, foolish bachelors who surround her. She is attracted to Lawrence Selden, a gifted[4] and handsome young lawyer of modest financial means.[5] Torn between her ambition and a desire for independence, she makes a tragic mistake that destroys her only chance for true love. It is a typical theme in Wharton's novels, where women must sacrifice their own fulfillment and obey society's rules, or else face certain destruction.

In the following selection, Lily and Selden have an honest discussion during afternoon tea.

from
The House of Mirth

by EDITH WHARTON

"Don't you ever mind," she asked suddenly, "not being rich enough to buy all the books you want?"

He followed her glance about the room, with its worn furniture and shabby[6] walls.

"Don't I just? Do you take me for a saint on a pillar[7]?"

"And having to work—do you mind that?"

"Oh, the work itself is not so bad—I'm rather fond of the law."

"No; but the being tied down: the routine—don't you ever want to get away, to see new places and people?"

"Horribly[8]—especially when I see all my friends rushing to the steamer."

She drew a sympathetic breath. "But do you mind enough—to marry to get out of it?"

Selden broke into a laugh. "God forbid![9]" he declared.

She rose with a sigh, tossing her cigarette into the grate.

"Ah, there's the difference—a girl must, a man may if he chooses." She surveyed him critically. "Your coat's a little shabby—but who cares? It doesn't keep people from asking you to dine. If I were shabby no one would have me: a woman is asked out as much for her clothes as for herself. The clothes are the background, the frame, if you like: they don't make success, but they are a part of it. Who wants a dingy[10] woman? We are expected to be pretty and well-dressed till we drop—and if we can't keep it up alone, we have to go into partnership."

Selden glanced at her with amusement: it was impossible, even with her lovely eyes imploring him, to take a sentimental view of her case ...

---

3. mirth: joy; laughter; happiness
4. gifted: very intelligent, talented
5. of modest financial means: not wealthy
6. shabby: worn out; old; dirty

7. pillar: stone column
8. horribly: very much
9. God forbid!: certainly not!
10. dingy: shabby

Reading Comprehension

A.   Choose the best answer for the following:

1. As Americans celebrated their nation's centennial,
    a. they looked back with pride at the country's first century.
    b. they felt only bitterness.
    c. they had mixed emotions.
2. The Civil War advanced America's economy for all of the following reasons *except*
    a. a strong federal government developed.
    b. southern states were completely destroyed.
    c. experienced managers emerged from the years of fighting.
3. In American history, the decades after the Civil War are called the Gilded Age because
    a. there was increasing prosperity.
    b. there was increasing poverty.
    c. beneath the great prosperity, there were sometimes corruption and greed.
4. All of the following are characteristic of the Gilded Age *except*
    a. ragtime music.
    b. fabulous houses.
    c. a lower standard of living throughout America.
5. Based on the information in paragraph 9, we may suppose that
    a. Carnegie's childhood was secure and happy.
    b. Carnegie was a lonely and disturbed child.
    c. Carnegie did not easily make friends.
6. In paragraph 10, the author gives
    a. the reasons for Carnegie's departure from Scotland.
    b. the results of Carnegie's departure from Scotland.
    c. a description of Carnegie's departure from Scotland.
7. When Carnegie's parents arrived in Pittsburgh, they found
    a. more than they had hoped for.
    b. less than they had hoped for.
    c. exactly what they had imagined.
8. "When Carnegie left the railroad, therefore, he was already a wealthy man." The reasons for this statement in paragraph 18 are given in
    a. paragraph 18.
    b. paragraphs 16 and 17.
    c. paragraph 19.
9. Put the following in the correct order.
    a. Carnegie developed his own steel company.
    b. Carnegie worked for the telegraph company.
    c. Carnegie worked for the Pennsylvania Railroad.

10. In paragraph 21, the reader can find examples of
    a. Carnegie's executive skills.
    b. Carnegie's investments.
    c. Carnegie's generosity.

B. **Write *true* or *false* next to the following statements.**

1. Americans celebrated their nation's centennial in 1976.
2. After the Civil War, the federal government gave increased support to the economy.
3. America's economy was stimulated by military campaigns of the Civil War.
4. The Gilded Age refers to the decades immediately preceding the Civil War.
5. The Civil War gave valuable experience to many of the leaders of the Gilded Age.
6. The Gilded Age was a materialistic era in America.
7. Because he became ill, Carnegie's father could not find work in Scotland.
8. Andrew Carnegie was anxious to go to America.
9. Carnegie gained extensive executive experience in the railroad industry.
10. Carnegie left all of his money to his family.

C. **Choose the answers that best explain the word or words in italics below.**

1. After the Civil War, groups in Washington began *to lobby* with great success.
    a. to register voters
    b. to influence political policies
    c. to restore historical buildings
2. As a child, Carnegie *took delight in* the traditions of Scotland.
    a. enjoyed
    b. understood
    c. explained
3. More than anything, he wanted *to ease the pain* of poverty in America.
    a. to forget
    b. to reduce the suffering of
    c. to endure in spite of
4. To build up his own steel company, Carnegie *drew upon* his railroad experience.
    a. made a summary of
    b. tried to remember
    c. took advantage of

D. **Which of the following happened first? Circle the correct answer in each pair.**

1. a. Americans celebrated their nation's centennial.
    b. The American Civil War came to an end.
2. a. The government of the United States rapidly expanded.
    b. Civil War between the North and the South broke out.
3. a. The Industrial Revolution spread throughout the British Isles.
    b. Carnegie's father faced unemployment.
4. a. Carnegie became a superintendent on the Pennsylvania Railroad.
    b. Carnegie worked as a telegraph operator.
5. a. Carnegie Steel was founded.
    b. United States Steel was founded.

Vocabulary

A. Word Forms. Choose the correct word form for each of the following. Make all necessary changes.

1. to conflict, conflicting, conflict
   a. The Civil War was a major national _____ in nineteenth-century America.
   b. The goals of Northern people _____ with those of the Southerners.
   c. Until the telegraph was improved, there were often _____ reports from many battlefields.

2. prosperity, prosperous, to prosper
   a. During the Gilded Age, there was mounting _____ throughout America.
   b. While working for the railroad, Carnegie soon became a _____ executive.
   c. He continued _____ when he formed his own company.

3. assistance, to assist, assistant
   a. Carnegie began his rise to power as a telegraph _____ .
   b. Impressed by his ability, Scott asked Carnegie _____ him on the railroad.
   c. With government _____ , the railroad industry quickly developed.

4. capacity, capable, capably
   a. Scott soon discovered that Carnegie was a _____ assistant.
   b. He managed his division of the railroad very _____ .
   c. His _____ for shrewd investments was extraordinary.

5. symbol, to symbolize, symbolic
   a. For Andrew Carnegie, Dunfermline's abbey was _____ of childhood's security.
   b. It _____ a quiet and peaceful time in his life.
   c. It remained a cherished _____ throughout his lifetime.

6. thrill, thrilling, to thrill
   a. It was a _____ sight to see the tall new buildings.
   b. Carnegie always _____ to the stories of Scotland's legendary past.
   c. It was a _____ for him to return to his home town once again.

7. destined, destiny, destination

    a. The train's _____ was Portland, Oregon.

    b. Carnegie realized that steel was _____ to become a major construction material.

    c. His _____ , he felt, was to restore the family's position and pride.

8. to convert, convert, conversion

    a. After reading the reports, he became a _____ to the modern methods.

    b. He was _____ by the forceful arguments of his associates.

    c. The Bessemer _____ process was essential to the new industry.

B.   Match the words in column A with those in column B.

A	B
ghastly	change
burden	dishonesty
overwhelming	huge
devastate	horrible
promote	plan
strategy	powerful
transform	load
remarkable	destroy
corruption	encourage
tremendous	extraordinary

C.   From the list below, choose the word that is closest in meaning to the word or phrase in italics. Make any necessary changes.

vivid	*abbey*	*traumatic*	*odor*
brilliant	*heritage*	*cherish*	
fraud	*vanish*	*frightful*	

1. By means of *very intelligent* investments, Carnegie made a fortune.
2. His departure from Scotland was *extremely upsetting*.
3. Throughout his life, Carnegie *treasured* his Scottish traditions.
4. Throughout his life, Carnegie treasured his Scottish *traditions*.
5. He was especially attracted to the picturesque *monastery*.
6. Somehow, he was able to endure the sickening *smell* of the oil vats.
7. Fear of poverty became a *terrible* nightmare for Carnegie.
8. His comfortable childhood had *disappeared*.
9. In the 1870s, *very real* memories of a terrible war still lingered throughout America.
10. Unfortunately, the Gilded Age was a time of both prosperity and *dishonesty*.

Structures

A. In the paragraph below, fill in the blanks with the correct preposition.

When Carnegie left the railroad, therefore, he was already a wealthy man. Although only twenty-nine, his dreams _____ saving the family _____ want had long since been fulfilled. But greater achievements still lay ahead. He had heard _____ the new Bessemer process _____ converting iron _____ steel and was determined to utilize this process _____ steel plants _____ his own. So _____ means _____ brilliant investments, and drawing _____ all his railroad experience, he began the systematic expansion _____ one _____ his own first companies—the Keystone Bridge Company—into a vast corporation: Carnegie Steel. _____ almost forty years, he devoted himself _____ customary energy _____ the management _____ this corporation.

B. Following the model, supply the comparative forms of the italicized words.

Model: (long, experienced) The *longer* the war was, the *more experienced* people became.

1. *(large, powerful)* The _____ the government became, the _____ it was.
2. *(rich, greedy)* The _____ some people got, the _____ they became.
3. *(hard, few)* The _____ his father tried, the _____ customers he found.
4. *(much, wealthy)* The _____ Carnegie worked, the _____ he became.
5. *(old, much)* The _____ he got, the _____ he loved his native land.

Composition

Write a paragraph on the topic of one of the following.

A. Reread paragraphs 3–6 in the Historical Background. Then in your own words, tell how the tragedy of the American Civil War resulted in a great period of national expansion.

B. When Carnegie came to America, he found opportunities for employment, self-improvement, and self-fulfillment. According to Lily Bart, in the selection from *The House of Mirth,* did women have the same chances? In one brief paragraph, summarize Lily's position.

C. "Absence makes the heart grow fonder." According to this well-known proverb, we often value something more when we can no longer have it. Summarize the selection from Carnegie's *Autobiography* to illustrate the truth of this proverb.

D. Carnegie loved the historical buildings and ruins of his ancient home town. They were scenes, for him, of cherished childhood memories. Was there a place that was very meaningful to you as a child? Does it still remain vivid in your memory? Describe it in detail and tell why it meant a lot to you.

Topics for Class Discussion

Interviewing a partner or small group of your classmates, talk about the following.

A. After the Civil War, railroads became a major industry in nineteenth-century America. What are the major industries in your country? Are there enough trained persons to work in these industries? Are too many people going into these fields? Do men and women have an equal opportunity to get jobs and advance in these industries? Are certain key industries located in particular areas of the country? Is any one city famous for any one industry?

B. As both philanthropist and industrialist, Carnegie became world-famous. Is there anyone in your country's history who is well-known for philanthropic achievements? Please describe this person.

C. Carnegie's departure from Scotland was traumatic. Do you remember a particularly difficult parting in your childhood? Leaving home for school or camp? Moving away to a different city, a different state, a new country? Please share your memories of this occasion.

D. When Carnegie arrived in America, he found New York unlike anything he had ever experienced in Scotland. Have you ever traveled to a city that was totally different from your usual environment? In what way was it different? Has your opinion ever changed about that place?

❈ SOME INTERESTING PLACES TO VISIT ❈

New England Area

Edith Wharton Restoration (The Mount)
Lenox, Massachusetts

The Breakers, The Elms, Rosecliff, Marble House,
Belcourt Castle, and Astors' Beechwood
Newport, Rhode Island

Middle Atlantic Area

Cooper-Hewitt Museum (former Carnegie
mansion)
New York, New York

Carnegie Hall
New York, New York

The Frick Collection
New York, New York

The Pierpont Morgan Library
New York, New York

Sleepy Hollow Cemetery (grave of Andrew
Carnegie)
Tarrytown, New York

Vanderbilt Mansion National Historic Site
Hyde Park, New York

Gateway Center,
Pittsburgh, Pennsylvania

Historical Society of Western Pennsylvania
Pittsburgh, Pennsylvania

Carnegie Mellon University
Pittsburgh, Pennsylvania

Clayton House, Henry Frick's home
Pittsburgh, Pennsylvania

2

Conquest of the Prairies

One Last Frontier

PREREADING

Look at the photograph below. Then, working in pairs or small groups, answer these questions.

1. Describe the prairie house in the picture. How many rooms might it have? What do you think it is made of? Why? What is the area around the house like? How would you describe the pioneer family in the photograph? What do you think the man's occupation might be? Does he have any helpers? What are the woman's duties? Does she have anyone to help her? What dangers might threaten this family? Why do you think they have moved to this land?

2. Turn to the illustration on p. 21. Captured in a photograph is a great moment in American history—the completion of the country's first transcontinental railroad at Promontory Point, Utah, on the tenth of May, 1869. How did this railroad affect the development of nineteenth-century America? In what ways did it change the lives of pioneer families on the prairies? In what ways did it change the lives of the Native Americans on the prairies?

Nebraska, 1889

1   When the United States became a nation in 1776, it was composed of thirteen Atlantic states. In a short time, however, new states were formed as pioneers moved west across the Appalachians. The soil was rich, the rivers were good, and the supply of wood for fuel and construction was abundant.[1] So when the Civil War started in 1861, all American territory east of the Mississippi was settled. There were large farms, growing cities, spreading railroads, and increasing opportunities for industry and trade.

2   Out west beyond the Rocky Mountains, United States territory was also settled by Americans before the Civil War. In the 1840s, pioneers had followed earlier missionaries to the fertile land of Oregon. At the same time, Brigham Young had led Mormon settlers across the plains to Utah. Then, gold had been discovered near San Francisco. Hoping for a fortune, thousands of prospectors[2] had rushed to California, making that territory a state of the union as early as 1850.

3   Thus, by the middle of the nineteenth century, there were American states throughout the East and on the nation's Pacific coast. But in between, from Missouri to the Rockies, few pioneers had stopped to settle. For in between were the endless prairies, the vast and windy flatlands of the continent's interior.

4   Treeless and dry, these central plains stretched out for hundreds of miles. In the summer they burned under the steady glare[3] of a merciless midwestern sun. In winter they froze as mountains of snow drifted[4] eastward over the Rockies. So only the prairie grass—sturdy[5] and thick—had been able to flourish[6] there. From Texas to Canada, it was food for the buffalo that roamed[7] in vast herds over the hard and stubborn[8] ground.

5   These animals, in turn, provided Native Americans with meat, warm blankets, and skins for clothing and tents. So in spite of the climate and forbidding[9] terrain, the Native Americans on the plains had prospered. They had become remarkable hunters of courage and endurance—the great and dreaded masters of America's landlocked center.

6   Thus, when the Civil War ended, the interior prairies were America's last frontier. Lonely and wild, they beckoned to[10] only the hardiest[11] pioneers—those who could endure isolation, a harsh[12] environment, and tragic conflicts with Native Americans.

MEETING THE CHALLENGE OF THE INTERIOR PLAINS

7   It was in the Gilded Age, as the nation expanded, that determined settlers decided to take up this challenge. They were encouraged, in part, by political and technological

---

1. abundant: plentiful
2. prospector: person who looks for precious metals
3. glare: very bright light
4. drift: float, move slowly
5. sturdy: strong
6. flourish: grow successfully, prosper
7. roam: wander
8. stubborn: unbending, not flexible
9. forbidding: very frightening
10. beckon to: attract
11. hardy: tough, strong
12. harsh: rough, unpleasant

Promontory Point, Utah, on the 10th of May, 1869

developments that had taken place during the Civil War. In 1862, for example, a strengthened wartime government had passed the Homestead Act. According to this law, 160 acres of free public land could be given to any adult settler; in exchange, the settler had to live on this land and improve it for a period of at least five years.

8   A cross-country railway system was also begun during the Civil War, for under pressure from business as well as the army, Congress had agreed to support long-range transportation. So in 1862, it passed the Pacific Railway Act, offering land grants and subsidies[13] to western railroad lines. Seven years later, at Promontory Point, Utah, the nation's first transcontinental line was completed. And by the 1890s, there was a total of five cross-country routes. Both the Northwest and the Southwest were linked to the East, all principal cities in the country were connected, and all major areas of the land could be reached. The American prairies were no longer inaccessible.[14]

CONFLICT WITH NATIVE AMERICANS

9   For the Native Americans, however, this spectacular[15] development brought swift[16] and final disaster. Railroad lines gave important advantages to hunters in search of the buffalo herds. They made it easier to reach the animals; they provided an efficient system for the transportation of buffalo hides.[17] So in a short time, the plentiful herds disappeared. And with them vanished the way of life of the Native Americans on the plains. Their sources of food, shelter, and clothing diminished,[18] making resistance to

---

13. subsidy: financial support
14. inaccessible: unable to be reached
15. spectacular: very impressive

16. swift: rapid
17. hide: animal skin
18. diminish: decrease

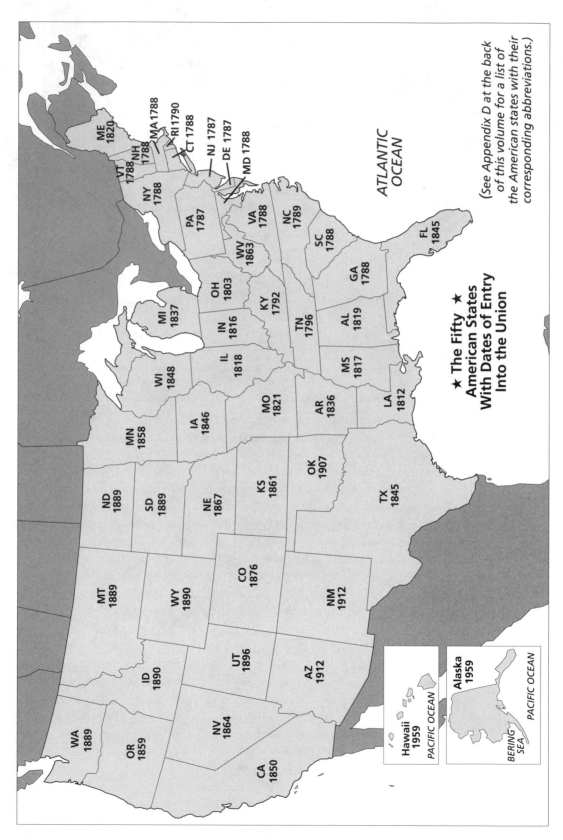

★ The Fifty ★
American States
With Dates of Entry
Into the Union

(See Appendix D at the back
of this volume for a list of
the American states with their
corresponding abbreviations.)

ATLANTIC OCEAN

ME 1820
VT 1788
NH 1788
MA 1788
RI 1790
CT 1788
NY 1788
NJ 1787
DE 1787
MD 1788
PA 1787
VA 1788
WV 1863
NC 1789
SC 1788
FL 1845
GA 1788
OH 1803
KY 1792
TN 1796
AL 1819
MI 1837
IN 1816
MS 1817
IL 1818
WI 1848
LA 1812
MO 1821
AR 1836
IA 1846
MN 1858
OK 1907
KS 1861
ND 1889
SD 1889
NE 1867
TX 1845
MT 1889
WY 1890
CO 1876
NM 1912
ID 1890
UT 1896
AZ 1912
WA 1889
OR 1859
NV 1864
CA 1850

Hawaii 1959
PACIFIC OCEAN

Alaska 1959
BERING SEA
PACIFIC OCEAN

the settlers impossible. After a few stunning[19] victories over the American armies, therefore, the Plains people were steadily subdued.[20] In 1890, there was one last confrontation[21]—a tragic massacre of the Sioux at Wounded Knee, South Dakota. After that, as the twentieth century dawned, the epic struggle between settlers and Native Americans was over. Confined[22] to reservations of poor and unsuitable land, the broken tribes were no longer an obstacle[23] to the pioneer conquest of the prairies.

10   In addition to the Homestead plan, railroad expansion, and destruction of the Native American threat, there was one more development which encouraged emigration to the prairies. New machines had replaced the men who had gone off to battle in the Civil War. Thus, better plows, reapers,[24] harvesters, and threshers[25] were available after 1865. Without this machinery, it would have been impossible to break the rock-hard ground of the plains. But with its help, the richness that lay beneath the surface of the prairies was brought up in great harvests of corn and wheat.

11   The conquest of the prairies, of course, was not accomplished overnight. It took three decades—from the Civil War to the turn of the twentieth century—for settlers to unearth the treasures of the plains. During that time, there were setbacks[26] to be endured and countless obstacles to overcome. Alone on the plains, surrounded by wind and the limitless horizon, homesteaders had to face illness, accident, and death. There were winter storms, summer droughts,[27] insect plagues,[28] and prairie fires. And above all, always, there was the tough, unpredictable land itself. To tame that land, to cultivate its glory, required indomitable courage, enormous strength, and unshakable faith in the future of the plains.

FOCUS ON WILLA CATHER

12   No one understood this better than the American novelist Willa Cather. Born in Virginia after the Civil War, she moved with her family to the Nebraska frontier in 1883. In contrast to the settled world of southern civilization, this midwestern wilderness was rugged[29] and raw. Its little towns had only recently appeared along the new transcontinental railroad routes. Beyond these towns, on the solitary[30] prairies, struggling settlers were still fighting for survival. Like the Cathers, some of these settlers had come from eastern states. But many others were European. From Scandinavia, Germany, Switzerland, and Bohemia, they had followed their dreams of land and opportunity to America's distant interior. There they had built their caves of sod,* determined to master both a defiant land and the bewildering culture of a strange new world.

---

19. stunning: spectacular
20. subdue: conquer
21. confrontation: argument; battle
22. confine: restrict to a certain area
23. obstacle: barrier
24. reaper: machine for cutting and gathering crops

25. thresher: machine for removing seeds
26. setback: disappointment, difficulty
27. drought: very dry season
28. insect plague: enormous numbers of harmful insects
29. rugged: tough, uncivilized
30. solitary: lonely, isolated

* These houses, called *soddies,* were built of dried earth (sod), since there was very little wood for construction on the prairies.

13   Willa Cather was soon attracted to the untamed life of the prairies. Its lonely grandeur[31] and the courage of its people suited her strong and independent spirit. Indeed, within a very short time, neighboring settlers were well-acquainted with the bright little girl from the Cather farm. For although many Americans avoided the Europeans, Willa Cather was different. She was fascinated by their unusual customs and the wealth of their old world traditions. She loved to hear the music of their strange, foreign speech. Most of all, she admired their energy, their remarkable endurance. Like the land itself, they were proud, vigorous,[32] full of life and strength and mystery. More than anyone, Cather thought, they had the pioneer spirit, the unbending will that refused to be defeated by a lonely and hostile world.

14   Unlike these settlers, Cather's father soon left his farm and moved to Red Cloud, the nearest little town. Here the family had some of the comforts they had always had back East; but for Willa Cather, the change was unsettling.[33] Instead of free and hardy pioneers, this new place had merchants, bankers, and railroad employees—middle-class townspeople of conventional traditions and strict social codes. Among them, Cather was sometimes uncomfortable. She refused to adopt the submissive[34] manner considered correct for proper young ladies. She was too inquisitive,[35] too energetic. So many times, she would escape from the little world of Red Cloud society to the free and open spaces of the prairies. There she would wander with joy over the waving grass, past golden cornfields, to the pioneers on their farms. No detail of their heroic struggles, no incidents of their intense existence, escaped her notice. From them, the future writer received deep and lasting impressions that were later transformed into the unforgettable scenes of her finest novels.

15   In 1890, Willa Cather left Red Cloud to enter the University of Nebraska. As she began to write essays, reviews, and short stories, her extraordinary writing talent became apparent. Thus, after her graduation in 1895, she was offered a job as a journalist for a new Pittsburgh publication. Within a few years, she was in New York, writing for *McClure's,* a famous magazine. Brilliant and hardworking, she was soon a respected editor of power and prestige.[36] Yet in 1912, at the height of her editorial career, she resigned from *McClure's.* For after twenty-two years away from Red Cloud, she realized that Nebraska burned in her memories as the subject of the stories she was ready to write. So she returned through her art to her youth on the prairies; and within a year, her first great novel appeared.

O PIONEERS!

16   Entitled simply *O Pioneers!,* it was Willa Cather's homage[37] to the struggling families she had once known on the plains. Very appropriately,[38] therefore, it opens with a magnificent description of Nebraska in the 1880s. It is wintertime—a period of incredible isolation on the vast and frozen land. Exhausted settlers, faced with dwindling[39] supplies and ever-mounting piles of snow, are desperately trying to survive

---

31. grandeur: greatness
32. vigorous: strong and healthy
33. unsettling: disturbing
34. submissive: humble
35. inquisitive: curious

36. prestige: social importance
37. homage: words of praise
38. appropriate: correct, fitting
39. dwindle: decrease, diminish

until spring. But for some pioneers, the effort becomes impossible. They are broken in body and spirit by the hostile world around them.

17   John Bergson, a Swedish immigrant, is one of these settlers. For eleven years, he has fought to subdue the land and build a prosperous farm for his growing family. But in vain; illness and misfortune have repeatedly destroyed his attempts. So in profound[40] despair, he gives up the struggle, preferring death to a bitter life on the plains.

18   Bergson's daughter, Alexandra, is different. She is a fighter, a striver,[41] a woman of extraordinary energy and common sense. She is also an individualist. She is willing to experiment and defy the forces of convention if she believes her own values and opinions are correct. Thus, as old Bergson dies, he entrusts[42] the homestead to his capable daughter, for he knows that Alexandra, among all his children, has the courage and skill to carry on.

19   As the novel progresses, John Bergson's estimate of Alexandra proves correct. In contrast to her older brothers, she accepts her new responsibilities with joy. She travels for days over the windy plains, visiting homesteads and getting advice from every possible source. Open-minded and aggressive, she listens to anyone who has a proven[43] new method, even if she must discard[44] traditional farming techniques. For in Alexandra's mind, the prairies are not an enemy to be feared. They are rather a mysterious ally—a benefactor[45] who will someday reward the creative pioneers who have been able to endure.

20   Alexandra's vigorous management steadily brings results. Her farm continues to prosper until finally she is one of the wealthiest and most respected settlers on the Divide.* Yet the novel does not end in happy contemplation[46] of Alexandra's success. For as she tells her heroine's tale, Willa Cather brilliantly introduces the tragic story of Alexandra's brother. Emil is the youngest Bergson child and Alexandra's favorite relative. It is for him that she has struggled year after year, hoping to be able to give him an education and knowledge of the world beyond the farms of Nebraska. At first, Alexandra's efforts, like her activities on the farm, bring results. Emil goes away to school, travels, and returns to the Divide a young man of promise and charm. So proud of him, in fact, is Alexandra that she cannot see the inner[47] torment[48] that begins to destroy him. For Emil has fallen in love with Alexandra's dearest friend, Marie. Marie is attractive and full of life, like Alexandra and Emil. But she is a married woman, linked forever in a loveless match to an unhappy and violent man.

21   While Alexandra's life bears the rich fruits of success, Emil's fatal attachment grows. His love for Marie is at last returned, and the desperate lovers manage to share a summer of stolen joy. Their happiness, however, is brief. Discovered together, they are shot by Marie's husband and left to die under the pitiless stars of the cloudless prairie sky.

---

40. profound: deep
41. strive: work with ambition
42. entrust: place in someone's care
43. proven: tested
44. discard: throw away

45. benefactor: someone who gives help, especially money
46. contemplation: quiet observation
47. inner: beneath the surface
48. torment: extreme pain

* The Divide—an area of Nebraska between the Republican and Little Blue rivers where Willa Cather's family had their farm.

22   As Alexandra struggles to accept her brother's death, the principal themes of the novel emerge. In his own way, she realizes, Emil has shared in the life of the prairies as fully, as intensely as she has. Her destiny was to love the land, to conquer it by respecting its grandeur. His fate was to reflect, in human terms, the terrible power and beauty of that land. Thus, the lovers—generous and noble and driven by tragic forces—become symbols of the great earth that receives them. And at the same time, the prairies—fierce and magnificent—remain an image of all that is eternal in youth and passion and unyielding determination. In the end, therefore, there is a final bittersweet[49] unity—one which forever joins those who understand the land, and the land itself, and the people who live with a passionate[50] intensity that mirrors the power of the land.

23   Willa Cather underscores[51] this central theme as the novel closes. Alexandra and a dear old friend are walking away from the fields toward her home. "They went into the house together," the author says, "leaving the Divide behind them, under the evening star. Fortunate country, that is one day to receive hearts like Alexandra's into its bosom,[52] to give them out again in the yellow wheat, in the rustling corn, in the shining eyes of youth!"

24   *O Pioneers!* is one of America's greatest novels. It explores, in superbly[53] lyrical[54] prose, the great human mysteries of love and death, hatred and desire, ambition and revenge. At the same time it celebrates the majestic land of America's Middle West and the unconquerable spirit of the pioneers who chose to live there. Among all her novels, it is perhaps the fullest expression of Willa Cather's genius—a genius that shaped American history into timeless and exquisite forms of art.

---

49. bittersweet: something that is both sad and beautiful
50. passion: strong emotion
51. underscore: emphasize; give importance to
52. bosom: breast
53. superb: excellent
54. lyrical: musical

In the following selection, John Bergson—ill and discouraged—looks out over the savage land that has defeated him. Then, after her father's death, Alexandra Bergson turns toward a similar landscape, but in her gaze is the love and determination of a true pioneer.

from
O Pioneers!

by WILLA CATHER

In eleven long years John Bergson had made but little impression upon the wild land he had come to tame. It was still a wild thing that had its ugly moods; and no one knew when they were likely to come, or why. Mischance[1] hung over it. Its Genius[2] was unfriendly to man. The sick man was feeling this as he lay looking out of the window, after the doctor had left him, on the day following Alexandra's trip to town. There it lay outside his door, the same land, the same lead-colored miles. He knew every ridge and draw and gully[3] between him and the horizon. To the south, his plowed fields; to the east, the sod stables, the cattle corral, the pond—and then the grass....

Alexandra and Emil spent five days down among the river farms, driving up and down the valley. Alexandra talked to the men about their crops and to the women about their poultry. She spent a whole day with one young farmer who had been away at school, and who was experimenting with a new kind of clover[4] hay. She learned a great deal. As they drove along, she and Emil talked and planned. At last, on the sixth day, Alexandra turned Brigham's[5] head northward and left the river behind....

When the road began to climb the first long swells of the Divide, Alexandra hummed[6] an old Swedish hymn, and Emil wondered why his sister looked so happy. Her face was so radiant that he felt shy about asking her. For the first time, perhaps, since that land emerged from the waters of geologic[7] ages, a human face was set toward it with love and yearning.[8] It seemed beautiful to her, rich and strong and glorious. Her eyes drank in the breadth of it, until her tears blinded her. Then the Genius of the Divide, the great, free spirit which breathes across it, must have bent lower than it ever bent to a human will before. The history of every country begins in the heart of a man or a woman....

---

1. mischance: trouble
2. genius: spirit
3. draw and gully: long deep holes in the earth
4. clover: small plant

5. Brigham: Alexandra's horse
6. hum: sing with the lips closed
7. geologic: pertaining to very ancient times
8. yearning: intense desire

EXERCISES

Reading Comprehension

A. Choose the best answer for the following:

1. The main topic of paragraph 1 is
   a. reasons for the rapid settlement of America's Pacific territory.
   b. reasons for the rapid settlement of America's eastern territory.
   c. the difficulties involved in settling some Atlantic states.
2. All of the following are reasons for the settlement of Pacific states *except*
   a. the California gold rush.
   b. missionary activity.
   c. border wars with Canada.
3. "Thus, when the Civil War ended, the interior plains were America's last frontier." The reasons for this statement in paragraph 6 are given in
   a. paragraphs 1 and 2.
   b. paragraphs 4 and 5.
   c. paragraph 7.
4. In paragraph 7, the Homestead Act is introduced as an example of
   a. political developments that helped in the settlement of the Great Plains.
   b. technological developments that brought new methods of farming to the plains.
   c. railroad expansion legislation.
5. Paragraph 9 presents
   a. a contrast to what was previously discussed.
   b. a continuation of what was previously discussed.
   c. a completely new topic.
6. From what is said in paragraph 9, we may assume that the author
   a. is pleased about the rapid destruction of the Native American way of life.
   b. regrets this destruction.
   c. is uninterested in this aspect of American history.
7. Paragraph 11 presents
   a. the suffering of Native Americans on the plains.
   b. the advantages enjoyed by the settlers on the plains.
   c. the suffering of American settlers on the plains.
8. Unlike most American settlers, Willa Cather
   a. hated the foreign pioneers.
   b. feared the foreign pioneers.
   c. was attracted to the foreign pioneers.
9. From what we are told in paragraph 14, we may assume that Willa Cather
   a. was a strong-willed youngster.
   b. was deeply religious.
   c. was a conformist.

10. *O Pioneers!* is the story of
    a. America's first Europeans in Jamestown, Virginia.
    b. the Pilgrims in Plymouth, Massachusetts.
    c. Scandinavian settlers on America's Great Plains.

B. **Match the items in column A with the definitions in column B.**

A	B
Homestead Act	place where first cross-country railroad was finished
Pacific Railway Act	scene of Willa Cather's childhood memories
buffalo herds	classic American novel
Wounded Knee, South Dakota	houses of dried earth on the prairies
Promontory Point, Utah	land grants and subsidies for cross-country transportation
soddies	free land for Americans on the plains
Red Cloud, Nebraska	scene of final confrontation with Native Americans
O Pioneers!	source of life's essentials for the Plains people

C. **Study the map on p. 30. Then answer the following:**

1. America's first transcontinental line ran from Sacramento to Omaha, Nebraska. Two famous railroads were involved in the building of this route. One began in Omaha and advanced westward over the plains and the Rockies. The other started in Sacramento and continued eastward across the Sierras. They met at Promontory Point, Utah, in 1869. What two lines were these?
2. To go from New Orleans to Los Angeles—a journey over the Rocky Mountains and across southwestern deserts—what new railroad could you have taken at the end of the nineteenth century?
3. To go from Kansas City to Santa Fe—a challenging trip across the Great Plains and into the Rocky Mountains—which line would you have chosen?
4. Duluth, Minnesota, is on Lake Superior. What railroad line connected this waterway to Seattle on the Pacific?
5. Which line ran parallel to the Canadian border across the great northern plains to the Pacific?

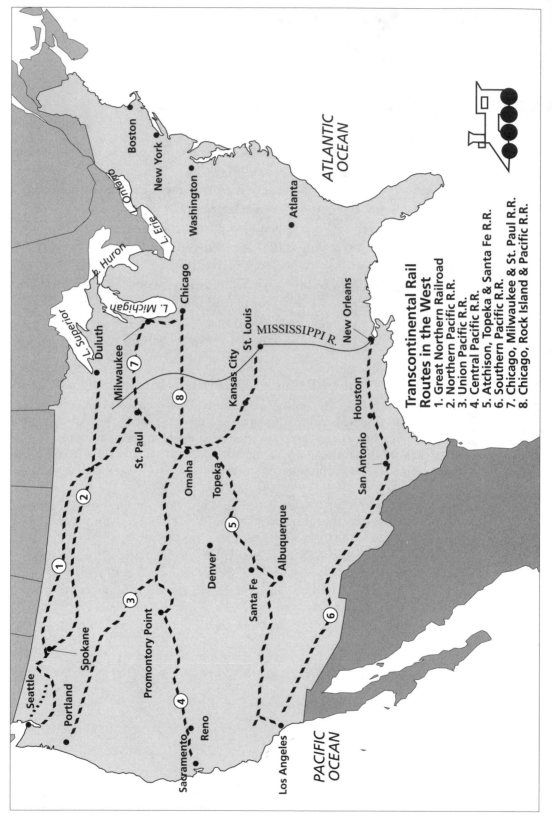

Transcontinental Rail Routes in the West
1. Great Northern Railroad
2. Northern Pacific R.R.
3. Union Pacific R.R.
4. Central Pacific R.R.
5. Atchison, Topeka & Santa Fe R.R.
6. Southern Pacific R.R.
7. Chicago, Milwaukee & St. Paul R.R.
8. Chicago, Rock Island & Pacific R.R.

Vocabulary

A. Word Forms. Choose the correct word form for each of the following. Make all necessary changes.

1. to dread, dreadful, dreaded

   a. At the middle of the nineteenth century, Native Americans were still the _____ masters of America's landlocked center.

   b. Unfortunately, there was a _____ massacre at Wounded Knee.

   c. Very soon, Native Americans began _____ the coming of the railroads.

2. resistance, irresistible, to resist

   a. It was difficult _____ the settlers once the buffalo were gone.

   b. For Willa Cather, the unrestricted freedom of the prairies was _____ .

   c. Native American _____ to the pioneers diminished.

3. to predict, prediction, unpredictable

   a. The weather on the prairies was often _____ .

   b. No one could _____ exactly how much snow would fall.

   c. Sometimes, however, the _____ proved correct.

4. respectful, to respect, respected

   a. In New York, Willa Cather was a well-known and _____ editor.

   b. Children were expected to be _____ at all times.

   c. Willa Cather soon learned _____ the European pioneers.

5. resignation, resigned, to resign

   a. Many broken Native Americans became _____ to their situation.

   b. At the height of her editorial career, Willa Cather decided _____ .

   c. She handed in her _____ .

6. to defy, defiance, defiant

   a. Alexandra was willing _____ old-fashioned customs.

   b. In spite of their _____ , the Native Americans were subdued.

   c. She was often strong-willed and _____ as a child.

B. Fill in the blanks with an appropriate word from the following list. Make any necessary changes.

hostility	*link*	*cultivate*	*adopt*	*theme*
grant	*plow*	*conventional*	*prose*	*savage*

1. Settlers on the prairies had to face Native American _____ .

2. For Willa Cather, Red Cloud was simply too _____ .

3. Her novel explored the great _____ of love and death, ambition and revenge.

4. After the new cross-country rail routes, the Pacific was _____ to the Atlantic.

5. By using the new _____ , settlers could break the hard prairie ground.

6. At last, they could _____ the richness beneath the surface.

7. She refused to _____ the appropriate, submissive behavior.

8. The _____ style of *O Pioneers!* is elegant and musical.

9. By means of generous land _____ , the government helped the railroads.

10. In despair, old Bergson looked out over the harsh and _____ landscape.

C. Match the words in column A with their antonyms in column B.

A	B
abundant	pleasant
sturdy	scarce
roam	increase
stubborn	flood
harsh	surrender
diminish	weak
stunning	flexible
subdue	crowded
drought	unimpressive
solitary	remain

D. Select the answer that is closest in meaning to the word or words in italics.

1. Hoping for a fortune, the *prospectors* went to California.
   a. missionaries   b. settlers   c. gold-seekers

2. In the summer, the plains burned under the *glare* of the sun.
   a. warmth   b. light   c. protection

3. In spite of the *forbidding* terrain, the Native Americans had prospered.
   a. frightening   b. hot   c. mountainous

4. The government helped the railroads with land grants and *subsidies*.
   a. employees   b. money   c. publicity

5. Because of the railroads, the prairies became *accessible*.
   a. crowded   b. easily reached   c. safe

6. When they moved to the West, the Cathers found a *rugged* terrain.
   a. tough   b. flat   c. rainy

7. Willa Cather loved the *grandeur* of the prairies.
   a. greatness   b. grass fields   c. freedom

8. But she was sometimes considered too *inquisitive*.
   a. conventional   b. curious   c. submissive

9. For her, the move was *unsettling*.
   a. surprising   b. exciting   c. disturbing

10. She loved to go out among the *hardy* pioneers.
    a. strong   b. happy   c. foreign

Structures

A.   In the following paragraphs, add *a(n)* or *the* where necessary.

John Bergson, _____ Swedish immigrant, is one of these settlers. For eleven years, he had fought to subdue _____ land and build _____ prosperous farm for his growing family. But in vain. Illness and misfortune have repeatedly destroyed his attempts. So in profound despair, he gives up _____ struggle, preferring death to _____ bitter life on _____ plains.

Bergson's daughter, Alexandra, is different. She is _____ fighter, _____ striver, _____ woman of extraordinary energy and common sense. She is also _____ individualist. She is willing to experiment and defy _____ forces of convention if she believes her own values and opinions are correct. Thus, as old Bergson dies, he entrusts _____ homestead to his capable daughter; he knows that Alexandra, among all his children, has _____ courage and skill to carry on.

B.   **1. Following the model, make any necessary changes.**

Model: Alexandra plans to manage the farm.
   → Alexandra will be managing the farm.

a.   The workers plan to finish the railroad line this month.
b.   Indians plan to attack the homestead tomorrow.
c.   Emil plans to return to the farm tonight.
d.   Alexandra plans to try the new machines today.
e.   Marie plans to visit the Bergson farm next weekend.

2. Following the model, combine the sentences below.

Model: "Will Alexandra be managing the farm?" the neighbors wondered.
→ The neighbors wondered whether Alexandra would be managing the farm.

a. "Will the workers be finishing the railroad line this month?" the manager asked.
b. "Will the Indians be attacking the homestead tomorrow?" the settlers wondered.
c. "Will Emil be returning to the farm tonight?" the girls inquired.
d. "Will Alexandra be trying the new machines today?" the farmers asked.
e. "Will Marie be visiting the Bergson farm next weekend?" her husband wondered.

Composition

Write a paragraph on the topic of one of the following.

A. Willa Cather's childhood was very different from Edith Wharton's. Compare these novelists' backgrounds, showing how their contrasting worlds later provided the subjects for their most famous novels. (You may wish to reread paragraphs 12–15 of the Historical Background, as well as the introduction to *The House of Mirth* on p. 11 of Unit 1.)

B. Reread paragraphs 1–11 of the Historical Background. Then in one brief paragraph, describe some of the dangers that threatened the pioneers on the prairies.

C. "Home is where the heart is." According to this proverb, what we often call home is not necessarily our birthplace or where we are currently living. Rather, it is the place to which we feel the deepest emotional attachments. Willa Cather was born in Virginia. She spent much of her adult life in New York. Yet her greatest novel describes life on the Nebraska prairies. Why?

D. Is there a particular area in your country to which you have strong emotional attachments? The seashore? The mountains? A certain city or town? Describe this place and tell why you feel close to it.

Topics for Class Discussion

Interviewing a partner or a small group of your classmates, talk about the following.

A. Is there a part of your country that is difficult to live in? Why? Is the climate unpleasant? Is the terrain forbidding? Is the area inaccessible? Is the soil poor? Please give as many details as you can.

B. The tale of Emil and his neighbor Marie is a famous love story in American literature. Does your national literature have a famous pair of lovers? Please tell their story.

C. What do you think could have been done in America to avoid the tragic disaster that awaited the Native Americans?

D. Who is the most famous novelist of your national literature? What kind of novels has he or she written? Is this novelist a modern writer? A writer of an earlier period? Tell as much as you can about the writing career of this person.

SOME INTERESTING PLACES TO VISIT

Middle Atlantic Area

Frederic Remington Art Museum
Ogdensburg, New York

Baltimore and Ohio Railroad Museum
Baltimore, Maryland

Railroad Hall
National Museum of American History
Smithsonian Institution
Washington, D.C.

Virginia Museum of Transportation
Roanoke, Virginia

Midwestern Area

Crossroads Village/Huckleberry Railroad
Flint, Michigan

Deere and Company
Moline, Illinois

Living History Farms
Des Moines, Iowa

Fort Dodge Historical Museum
Fort Dodge, Iowa

Museum of Westward Expansion
St. Louis, Missouri

National Museum of Transport
St. Louis, Missouri

Willa Cather Pioneer Memorial
Red Cloud, Nebraska

Willa Cather Historical Center
Red Cloud, Nebraska

Homestead National Monument
Nebraska

Scotts Bluff National Monument
Nebraska

Chimney Rock National Historic Site
Nebraska

Museum of the Fur Trade
Chadron, Nebraska

Union Pacific Historical Museum
Omaha, Nebraska

Rocky Mountain Area

Fort Laramie National Historic Site
Wyoming

Yellowstone National Park
Wyoming

Grand Teton National Park
Wyoming

Golden Spike National Historic Site
Brigham City, Utah

Railroad Museum
Union Station
Ogden, Utah

3

International Dimensions

Will Expansionism Triumph?

Look at the photograph below. Then, working in pairs or small groups, answer these questions.

1. One of the women in the picture is seated. Describe her dress, her jewelry, her manner. What objects, in addition to jewelry, have been used to adorn her dress? Do you think she might be a prominent member of her country's government? Its ruler? Why, or why not?

2. Turn to the photograph on p. 10. It was taken about the same time as the photograph below. How are the women in the two photographs different? How are they alike? From your observations of the clothing below, what part of the world do you think these women lived in? What state in present-day America might it be?

The regal Kapiolani and her daughter, Liliuokalani

1   In 1890, the Census[1] Bureau[2] of the United States government made a surprising official announcement: the last American frontier was vanishing. As the conquest of the nation's interior plains continued, westward expansion was coming to an end. There would soon be no more open land for ambitious pioneers. There would be no more available spaces for the settlers of the future. From the Atlantic coastline to the shores of the Pacific, the American continent, finally, would be developed.

2   Throughout the country, people were stunned by the government's news. Of course, for centuries, there had existed great Native American cultures across the interior plains. But as this Native American population was steadily subdued, pioneers from the United States had increasingly moved west to find land, more freedom, and new chances for success. Now, it seemed, after three hundred years of territorial growth, the new settlers were faced with a different situation. They had to be satisfied with limits and boundaries, as the people of Europe had long had to do.

"MANIFEST DESTINY"

3   But it was not so easy for restless Americans to accept the closing of their frontier. They had come to[3] rely on the limitless potential of their vast and bountiful[4] land. In fact, since the middle of the nineteenth century, they had even developed a philosophy of expansion, a belief in the concept of "Manifest Destiny." According to those who believed in this theory,[5] the United States was destined to develop geographically: its glory and honor lay in a steady expansion toward the ultimate boundaries of the Pacific.

4   When this expansion was over, therefore, there was an unfamiliar insecurity in the hearts of many Americans. How was their country to develop in the future? What was to replace its traditional destiny? Where would their traders find markets for commerce? And where would their dreamers escape to?

5   The answer, some people decided, was to continue to expand. There was really no reason, they insisted, why national growth had to stop with the conquest of a continent. Like the nations of Europe, America should look for new colonies to add to its power and prestige, they said.

ISOLATIONISTS VERSUS EXPANSIONISTS

6   Not everyone agreed. The opponents of expansion thought imperialism was wrong. They felt that their country should resist the strong temptation to join with Europe's powers in the escalating[6] race for land. America itself had been a colony once and had fought a bitter war to win its freedom. So it now seemed appropriate to respect the rights of others in their struggle to escape from domination.

7   Thus, in the final quarter of the nineteenth century, American opinion was sharply divided on the issue of foreign involvements. On the one hand, there were

---

1. census: population count
2. bureau: department
3. come to: become accustomed to

4. bountiful: rich in resources; abundant
5. theory: idea, belief
6. escalating: rising, growing

determined expansionists who favored a policy of imperialism. New colonies, they felt, would give Americans a chance to spread their culture and traditions overseas. They would also provide markets for America's products, while supplying the raw materials to manufacture these goods.

8   Isolationists, on the other hand, objected to these ideas. Not only was expansionism wrong, they said, but it could also jeopardize[7] America's future. It would lead to competition with the major powers of Europe; it might also invite unexpected resistance among nations that refused to be dependent.

9   In spite of these persuasive isolationist objections, expansionism became more popular toward the end of the nineteenth century. This was due to several factors. First, in 1893, Wall Street failures caused a serious depression throughout the American economy. More than ever, it seemed, new sources of trade were urgently needed. Second, since the 1880s, the United States had steadily strengthened both the size and capacity of its navy; so fears of foreign conflicts had begun to diminish. Third, in Europe and Asia, powerful nations were increasingly involved in bold imperialistic takeovers; if the United States didn't join them, the people decided, it might suddenly be left without markets, materials, and military bases. Fourth and finally, expansionists were encouraged by the energetic leaders of some of America's growing newspapers. To sell their papers, these leaders had begun to use a new and competitive sensationalism;[8] and to find continued stories for this tawdry[9] "Yellow Journalism," they needed controversy,[10] violence, and fear. So they backed the imperialists, hoping to stir up international confrontations and maybe even the drama of a war.

10   There were many reasons, therefore, for American imperialism as it intensified at the end of the nineteenth century. Some were economic, some were military, some were political, and some were philosophical. But they were often related to the sense of shock and loss that had developed as the frontier disappeared.

THE SPANISH-AMERICAN WAR

11   Unfortunately, in the 1890s, the growing insistence of expansionist supporters led to tragic confrontations overseas. One of these crises involved the Caribbean islands of Cuba and Puerto Rico. Rich in sugar and strategically located, these territories still belonged to Spain. In 1895, however, when their sugar-based economy collapsed in a depression, patriotic Cubans revolted against Spain's rule. United States President William McKinley was opposed to interference, yet the battleship *Maine* was ordered to Havana, Cuba's capital, for the protection of Americans there. Then, when a mysterious explosion sank the boat in Cuba's harbor, a war-cry spread throughout the United States. At first, McKinley was hesitant. But he finally gave in to the hysteria of the papers and the dreams for world prestige of the expansionists.

12   In April 1898, the Spanish-American War began. It was over before the year was out.[11] For Spain had neither the money nor the troops to defeat its powerful opponent.

---

7. jeopardize: endanger
8. sensationalism: emotional reporting about violence, passion, etc.
9. tawdry: cheap; inelegant
10. controversy: conflict; argument
11. before the year was out: before the year ended

So by the Treaty of Paris in 1898, the Spanish government agreed to Cuba's independence; it also ceded[12] its other possessions—Guam, Puerto Rico, and the Philippines—to the United States.* Of course, expansionists considered the settlement a victory, but anti-imperialists were unhappy. Their nation had assumed control over lands that should be free, they said; in the future it would have to make amends[13] for this mistake.

ANNEXATION OF HAWAII

13   Meanwhile, on the islands of Hawaii, another expansionist crisis had developed. It came to a head[14] when a determined native princess became queen of this remote Pacific kingdom. She was Liliuokalani—a direct descendant of Hawaii's most famous warrior chiefs. Like them, she was intensely proud of her unique Hawaiian heritage and wanted to preserve it at all costs.[15] But to do this, she decided, she had to take a strong stand[16] against increasingly powerful forces from abroad. This, unfortunately, brought an end to her brief reign.

14   Who were these foreigners and how had they gained power? Their story dates back to the European discovery of Hawaii by the famous British explorer, Captain Cook. In 1778, while crossing the ocean from New Zealand to Canada, Cook sighted land birds in the south-central Pacific. A few days later, on a distant horizon, an island suddenly appeared. It was Oahu—ancient paradise of tropical beauty protected for centuries by a vast and empty sea.

15   In Hawaii, Cook and his men were lavishly[17] welcomed by the surprised but happy natives, for their religion had promised the return of a savior and the people considered Cook to be this god. Later, however, when one of Cook's sailors became ill and died, the natives began to suspect the real truth. They started to fear both the strangers and their weapons and regretted their incautious[18] hospitality. Tensions mounted, fighting broke out, and Captain Cook was killed. But enough of the sailors had escaped with their lives to set sail once again with the captain's ship.

16   News of this discovery of Hawaii spread. And soon there were merchants from Europe and America looking for opportunity in the new Pacific land. Kamehameha, Hawaii's monarch, accepted these foreigners. He hoped that their trade would bring prosperity to his kingdom and that their knowledge would be of use to his assistants. His son and successor felt the same. So during the reign of Kamehameha II, American missionaries arrived on the islands to establish schools and churches for the people. In time, the missionaries and their descendants became prominent members of Hawaii's

---

12. cede: give up
13. make amends: pay someone in some way for a mistake
14. come to a head: reach an explosive point

15. at all costs: in spite of any difficulty
16. take a strong stand: take a firm position
17. lavishly: very generously
18. incautious: not careful

*Independence was granted to the Republic of the Philippines on July 4, 1946. Guam has remained an unincorporated American territory. In 1952, Puerto Rico achieved commonwealth status in association with the United States. For many years, there has been much debate among Puerto Ricans on the subject of their political status. Some groups favor statehood, others independence; still others have supported continuing development under improved commonwealth status.

elite.[19] They provided important leadership in the fields of education, political science, and social services. By the middle of the nineteenth century, in fact, they had persuaded the king to form a constitutional monarchy. In this new government, members of the missions often held high-ranking posts.

18   At the same time, as trade with the United States increased, American planters, businesspeople, and merchants also became more powerful in Hawaii. This was especially true after 1875, when by a special treaty, Hawaiian sugar was admitted to America duty-free. Sugar plantations then expanded on the islands, until their exports became the basis of Hawaii's economy. So by the centennial celebration of Captain Cook's arrival, foreign traders, investors, religious leaders, and educators had considerable influence in Hawaiian affairs. Independent and practical, they resented the power still held by the monarch and wanted to be free of royal interference. In 1887, therefore, they insisted upon drafting[20] a revised constitution—one which would diminish the authority of the king. Hawaii's seventh monarch, King David Kalakaua, accepted the new arrangement; but his successor, Queen Liliuokalani, refused. Repeating the slogan[21] "Hawaii for the Hawaiians," she embarked on[22] a program of changes and reforms to restore the ancient privileges of Hawaii's native people. However, this only served to enrage[23] the opposition until a successful coup d'état[24] against the queen was staged.[25] Rebels overturned the monarchy and established a new republic. Then, hoping for commercial benefits and a return to political stability, they asked for annexation by the United States government.

19   At first the Americans hesitated. Their isolationist president—Grover Cleveland—was strongly opposed to annexation. But Cleveland's successor, McKinley, was different. He was persuaded by expansionists who were seeking extra bases to maintain the growing empire of the United States. So a treaty was ratified[26] in 1898, and the Republic of Hawaii became United States land. In 1959—almost two hundred years after Captain Cook's arrival—Hawaii became the fiftieth state to enter the American union. Together with Alaska,* it was the final state to be shaped from America's push to the Pacific.

20   In this acquisition, as in the Spanish-American War, expansionists had triumphed over the nation's isolationists. Yet the debate between them did not come to an end. For in the twentieth century, as the United States was drawn toward global confrontations, a strong tradition of antiexpansionism survived. There were always Americans who defined their country's greatness in terms of a commitment to its own freedom and peace. So there were always Americans who stood ready to object whenever they felt their nation had forgotten this ideal.

---

19. elite: high society
20. draft: write
21. slogan: motto; favorite expression
22. embark on: begin
23. enrage: anger

24. coup d'état: political takeover
25. stage: organize
26. ratify: agree to the terms of a document

* In 1867, America had purchased the territory of Alaska from Russia.

The following selection is from the autobiography of Liliuokalani—the last of Hawaii's ruling monarchs. It describes her royal visit to the big island, Hawaii, and the tremendous volcanic eruptions of the island's Mauna Loa.

Liliuokalani

from
Hawaii's Story by Hawaii's Queen

by LILIUOKALANI

As though to illuminate[1] in honor of my visit, on the night preceding our ascent of the mountain a bright glow was seen on top of Mokuaweoweo. This was the portent[2] which preceded that great flow of lava which soon commenced from Mauna Loa, and took its course down the sides of that mountain toward the city of Hilo. We were thus witnesses from the very beginning of one of the most extensive and long-continued eruptions which has ever been recorded in history, for it was protracted[3] over a period of eleven months. Early on the morning following we started on horseback on our journey to the crater[4] of Kilauea, where we arrived about five o'clock the same evening. This is not, as some strangers suppose, a mountain by itself, totally distinct from the general volcanic system of Mauna Loa. That word in our language signifies the great long mountain, and the nature of the elevation well deserves the term; for in height, 13,700 feet, it is exceeded by few in the world, while in extent it includes about one-third of our largest island. The eruptions are not usually from the summit,[5] but generally through fissures[6] in its sides. One of these is the crater lake of Kilauea, a region of perpetual[7] fire, of an activity more or less pronounced,[8] yet never entirely extinct,[9] and situated some twenty miles or so east from the summit, at an elevation of about four thousand feet. It is one of the few, if not the only one, of the volcanoes in the world which can be visited at the periods of its greatest displays without the least danger to the observer; because it is always possible to watch its bubbling fires from a higher point than their source. It is not the lava from the burning lake which makes its way down the mountain, but that from other places where the concealed[10] fires of Mauna Loa burst forth....

After our refreshment, darkness quickly succeeded the setting of the sun (there being no long twilight,[11] as in more northern climates); ... The next day was spent by our party in descending the crater to the very limits of its seething[12] fires, but I remained at the hotel. They were all provided with some offerings to Pele, the ancient goddess of fire, reverenced[13] by the Hawaiian people. This custom is almost universal, even to the present day. Those born in foreign lands, tourists who scarcely know our ancient history, generally take with them to the brink[14] of the lake some coin or other trinket[15] which, for good luck, as the saying is, they cast into the lava. Our people, the native Hawaiians, have no money to throw away on such souvenirs of the past; but they carry wreaths of the pandanus flower, leis, ... which are tossed by them into the angry waves of the basin.

---

1. illuminate: light
2. portent: sign that indicates something about the future
3. protract: continue
4. crater: huge hole or pit in the ground
5. summit: top
6. fissure: hole
7. perpetual: continuous

8. pronounced: strong
9. extinct: completely finished
10. concealed: hidden
11. twilight: between sunset and nighttime
12. seething: boiling; bubbling
13. reverence: adore; respect
14. brink: edge
15. trinket: ornament of little value

EXERCISES

Reading Comprehension

A. Choose the best answer for the following:

1. In the Historical Background reading, paragraph 2
   a. gives the cause of what is presented in paragraph 1.
   b. gives the result of what is presented in paragraph 1.
   c. has no relation to paragraph 1.
2. In the nineteenth century, people who believed in America's "Manifest Destiny" felt that
   a. the United States should not expand its boundaries.
   b. the United States should remain at peace with all nations.
   c. the United States should continue to expand from coast to coast.
3. When America's continental frontier vanished, expansionists believed
   a. America should seek new territory abroad.
   b. America should be content with its continental territory.
   c. America should give back some of its land to the Native Americans.
4. When America's continental frontier vanished, isolationists believed
   a. America should seek new territory abroad.
   b. America should be content with its continental territory.
   c. America should give back some of its land to the Native Americans.
5. In paragraph 4, it is implied that America's western frontier
   a. had been a constant source of trouble with the Native Americans.
   b. had provided commercial as well as psychological advantages.
   c. had provided the basis for a national literature.
6. All of the following are reasons for the triumph of expansionism except
   a. trouble in the American economy.
   b. a stronger American navy.
   c. pressure from American isolationists.
7. "Yellow Journalism" referred to
   a. sensationalism in the newspapers.
   b. cowardice among reporters.
   c. corruption among reporters.
8. Paragraph 10
   a. offers a contrast to the preceding paragraph.
   b. presents a summary of the preceding paragraph.
   c. introduces a completely new topic.
9. As a result of the Spanish-American War, the United States acquired
   a. Pacific as well as Caribbean possessions.
   b. international prestige.
   c. new Mexican territory.
10. Why did Kamehameha, Hawaii's great king, accept the arrival of foreigners on his island?
   a. He planned to attack them secretly.
   b. He hoped that they would help in the development of his kingdom.
   c. He was afraid of them.

B. From the list below, select the word that best completes each sentence.

Maine	*Captain Cook*	*Manifest Destiny*
McKinley	*Puerto Rico*	*Oahu*
Liliuokalani	*Yellow Journalism*	*Alaska*
Kamehameha I		

1. The first Europeans to discover Hawaii were led by _____ , a British explorer.

2. When a mysterious explosion sank the battleship _____ , the Spanish-American War began.

3. To increase sales, some newspapermen used the sensationalist techniques of _____ .

4. To develop his kingdom, _____ accepted the arrival of foreigners.

5. Like her ancestors, Queen _____ was intensely proud of her Hawaiian heritage.

6. _____ was president of the United States during the Spanish-American War.

7. As a result of the Spanish-American War, the United States received Guam, the Philippines, and _____ .

8. As Captain Cook was crossing the Pacific, he came upon the lovely island of _____ .

9. Together with Hawaii, _____ became a state of the Union in 1959.

10. Some people felt that it was America's _____ to expand across the continent.

C. Study the map on p. 22. Then answer the following:

1. The U.S. Constitution was written at the Constitutional Convention of 1787. At that time, the United States was composed of thirteen Atlantic states—England's thirteen former Atlantic colonies. These states were the first to accept the nation's new Constitution; so they were the earliest states to enter the American Union as defined by that Constitution. Can you find them?

2. After settling America's Atlantic coast, pioneers began to move west across the continent. New states could be formed as soon as territories reached a population of 60,000 free settlers. Can you name some states that entered the Union soon after the first thirteen had joined?

3. Had all the land east of the Mississippi become states of the Union by the Civil War in 1860?

4. On the western border of the Mississippi River, were there any states formed before the Civil War?

5. Were there any states on the Pacific coast before the Civil War?

6. What area of the continent was the last to be settled: the coastal areas, the Mississippi valley, or the Great Plains? Why?

7. What were the last three states to be formed in the continental United States?

8. What are the two most recent American states?

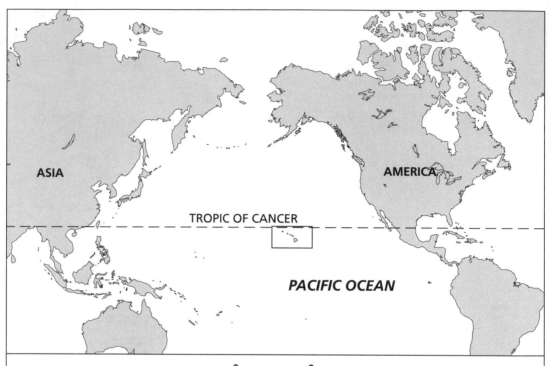

ASIA

AMERICA

TROPIC OF CANCER

PACIFIC OCEAN

※ HAWII ※

1. HILO
2. KAILUA-KONA
3. HAWAII VOLCANOES
   NATIONAL PARK
4. WAIMEA (SITE OF
   CAPTAIN COOK'S ARRIVAL)
5. PEARL HARBOR
6. HONOLULU
7. WAIKIKI
8. DIAMOND HEAD
9. KALAUPAPA PENINSULA
10. FATHER DAMIEN'S CHURCH
11. IAO VALLEY
12. LAHAINA

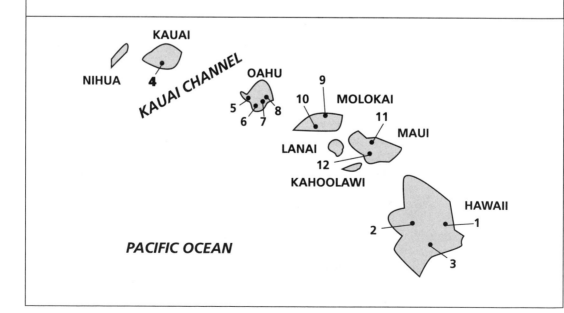

KAUAI

NIHUA

4

KAUAI CHANNEL

OAHU

9

5   8
6 7

10

MOLOKAI

11

MAUI

LANAI

12

KAHOOLAWI

HAWAII

2   1

3

PACIFIC OCEAN

D. **Study the map on p. 46. Then answer the following:**

1. Which is the largest of the Hawaiian islands? What famous natural wonders are located there?
2. Which island was first approached by Captain Cook?
3. On what island is Pearl Harbor located?
4. On what island did Father Damien—a famous missionary—build a colony for people suffering from the disease of leprosy?

Vocabulary

A. **Word Forms.** Choose the correct word form for each of the following. Make any necessary changes.

1. to rely, reliance, reliant

   a. Americans in the wilderness had to be self-_____ .

   b. People had begun _____ on America's limitless potential.

   c. They placed their trust and _____ in the nation's future.

2. replacement, to replace, irreplaceable

   a. People looked for colonies _____ their lost frontier.

   b. Isolationists, however, objected to this _____ .

   c. The ancient trees of the Pacific Northwest were _____ .

3. tempting, to tempt, temptation

   a. Isolationists said that we should not give in to the _____ of expansion.

   b. The idea was _____ , but isolationists rejected it.

   c. Great visions of glory _____ the expansionists.

4. opposition, opponent, to oppose

   a. The _____ of expansion were called isolationists.

   b. In spite of _____ , expansionists succeeded.

   c. Isolationists in the twentieth century have continued _____ expansion overseas.

5. to exceed, excessive, exceedingly

   a. Some Americans were _____ unhappy about the Spanish-American War.

   b. The height of the mountain was _____ by few in the world, said Hawaii's queen.

   c. The anti-imperialists warned that _____ ambition would only cause problems.

6. extensive, extensively, to extend

    a. The mountain chain _____ across one-third of the island.

    b. The queen made an _____ tour of the island.

    c. She discussed the issue _____ with her advisors.

7. scarce, scarcely, scarcity

    a. There is _____ any twilight in that southern area.

    b. Sugar was _____ on the mainland.

    c. There was also a _____ of tropical fruits.

8. aggression, aggressive, aggressively

    a. The patriots in Cuba were _____ .

    b. The queen did not anticipate _____ .

    c. The rebels spoke _____ when they made their demands.

B.   **Idioms and Special Expressions.**   From the following list, choose the words that best substitute for those in italics below. Make any necessary changes.

come to	come to a head
before the year was out	take a strong stand
in time	embark on
at all costs	coup d'état
elite	high-ranking posts

1. The queen *took a firm position* on the privileges of native Hawaiians.
2. She *started* a program of sweeping reforms.
3. Angry opponents then planned a *political takeover*.
4. She wanted to preserve her heritage *in spite of any difficulty*.
5. This caused the crisis to *reach an explosive point*.
6. By the end of the Civil War, Americans *had become accustomed to* relying on expansion.
7–8. *After a while,* the missionary families became prominent members of Hawaii's *high society*.
9. *Before the end of the year,* the Spanish-American War was over.
10. Members of the missions often held *high-level positions*.

C.   **Antonyms.**   Choose the italicized word that best completes the sentence.

1. Americans had come to rely on the potential of their *(poor, bountiful)* land.
2. Expansionists wanted to join Europe's *(escalating, diminishing)* race for colonies.
3. But isolationists felt that imperialism could *(protect, jeopardize)* America's future.
4. They were *(timid, outspoken)* critics.
5. They objected to the *(elegant, tawdry)* techniques of "Yellow Journalism."
6. The journalists needed *(controversy, peace)*.
7. After the Spanish-American War, Spain *(ceded, received)* several possessions.

8. Cook and his men were *(poorly, lavishly)* entertained.
9. Later, the natives regretted their *(incautious, careful)* hospitality.
10. The queen's new program only served to *(pacify, enrage)* the opposition.

Structures

A. **Match the items in column A with those in column B.**

A	B
The queen had never expected	such a tremendous explosion.
Captain Cook had never seen	such a continuous eruption.
At Mauna Loa, no one had ever witnessed	such lavish hospitality.
The sailors on the *Maine* had never heard	such effective opposition.
The explorers had never experienced	such beautiful islands.

B. **Following the model, change the sentences below.**

Model: The people placed their trust in Kamehameha.
→ Kamehameha was the person in whom the people placed their trust.

1. The advisors spoke to McKinley.
2. The sailors put their faith in Captain Cook.
3. The rebels had a meeting with Liliuokalani.
4. The isolationists got support from Grover Cleveland.
5. The natives had great respect for Kamehameha.

Composition

Write a paragraph on the topic of one of the following.

A. Throughout the nineteenth century, wilderness lands beyond the American frontier offered the chance for a new life to many pioneers. Are there undeveloped areas in your own country which offer similar opportunity? If not, are there undeveloped areas in neighboring countries? Describe this land in one brief paragraph, explaining why you would or would not like to move there.

B. Reread paragraphs 14 and 15 of the Historical Background. Then in one brief paragraph, tell the story of Captain Cook and his discovery of the Hawaiian Islands.

C. "Might makes right." According to this proverb, people will sometimes agree with an opponent not because his position is correct, but because he is powerful. From the point of view of the anti-expansionists, tell the story of the Spanish-American War to illustrate the truth of this proverb.

D. Both Hawaii and Puerto Rico are beautiful islands which many American tourists visit each year. Is there an island near your country which is a favorite with tourists? Describe this island and tell why it is so popular.

Topics for Class Discussion

Interviewing a partner or small group of your classmates, talk about the following.

A. Pretend you are an American expansionist at the end of the nineteenth century. What arguments would you use to convince your opponents of the importance of continued expansion?

B. Pretend you are an American isolationist at the end of the nineteenth century. What arguments would you use to answer those of the expansionists?

C. Does your country have, or has it ever had, colonies? Where? Were they of strategic military importance? Were they important to your nation's economy? Was your country ever a colony? Did the situation ever become a source of tragic confrontations? Please explain.

D. Are there any volcanoes in your country? Are there any other great natural wonders? ancient forests? jungles? deserts? tundra? glaciers? Please describe them with as much detail as you can.

SOME INTERESTING PLACES TO VISIT

Pacific Area

Bishop Museum; Honolulu Academy of the Arts;
    Iolani Palace; State Capitol
Honolulu, Hawaii

Waikiki Beach; Diamond Head
Honolulu, Hawaii

Queen Emma's Summer Palace; Royal
    Mausoleum; Polynesian Cultural Center
Oahu

USS *Arizona* Memorial; Pearl Harbor
Oahu

Hulihee Palace
Kailua-Kona, Hawaii

Captain Cook Monument
Kealakekua Bay, Hawaii

Volcanoes National Park; Mauna Loa;
    Mauna Kea
Hawaii

Waimea Canyon; Waipoo Falls; Wailua Falls
Kauai

Whaler's Village Museum; Brick Palace;
    Iao Valley State Park; Baldwin House
Maui

Father Damien's Church
Molokai

Glacier Bay National Park
Alaska

Denali National Park
Alaska

Klondike Gold Rush National Park
Alaska

Alaska State Museum
Juneau, Alaska

University of Alaska Museum
Fairbanks, Alaska

Anchorage Historical and Fine Arts Museum
Anchorage, Alaska

American Inventors

The New Pioneers

PREREADING

Look at the photograph below. Then, working in pairs or small groups, answer these questions.

1. Pictured in the photograph is Thomas Edison, the great American inventor. What is he holding in his right hand? Why is the object considered his most important invention? Talk about some of the ways in which this invention changed the way that Americans lived.

2. The illustration on p. 59 shows another of Edison's famous inventions. What is it? How is the couple in the illustration responding to it? Judging from the expressions on their faces, what opinion do you think they might have had of the inventor?

Edison in his laboratory at West Orange, New Jersey

1   The decades of expansion after the Civil War represent the Glorious Age of American invention. For like the eastern business leaders or the settlers of Nebraska, scientists were inspired by the spirit of progress that marked the half-century before World War I. Indeed, throughout America, conditions in the Gilded Age were ideally suited to successful scientific investigation. For one thing,[1] despite the bitter memories of civil war, there developed pride in the achievements of America's first century and a resultant confidence in future possibilities. There was also an abundant supply of manpower,[2] since highly skilled immigrants were constantly arriving at the factories and laboratories of the United States. Because of the rise of big business, moreover, there was capital available to provide support for scientific research. And in America's vast and wealthy land, there were sufficient raw materials to meet the demands of an emerging modern technology. Thus, from the Civil War to World War I, circumstances combined in the United States to encourage creative invention.

THE GLORIOUS AGE OF AMERICAN INVENTION

2   There were discoveries and improvements in the fields of communication, transportation, manufacturing, entertainment, agricultural production, energy development, and business procedures. Year after year, new methods were invented, new machinery was produced, and new laws of science were explained. Over half a million patents,[3] in fact, were issued by the United States government in the years between the Civil War and the turn of the twentieth century. By World War I, therefore, the American way of life had been completely transformed. Telephones, invented by Alexander Graham Bell in 1876, were in use throughout the nation. So, too, were sewing machines, adding machines, cameras, and typewriters— all invented or perfected just after the Civil War. On the country's roads, the motor cars of Henry Ford—first built in 1896—were already familiar sights. And in the air, even the impossible fantasy of earlier inventors had finally appeared. For on December 17, 1903, the Wright brothers had successfully tested the world's first flying machine.

3   Among all the inventors, however, no one captured America's imagination[4] like Thomas Alva Edison. Energetic, confident, and brilliantly successful, he was— like the nation itself—a fascinating[5] testament to[6] progress and prosperity. From humble beginnings he rose to the summit of wealth and prestige, yet his earthy[7] humor and unaffected[8] ways made him an enduring[9] popular hero.

---

1. for one thing: to give one reason
2. manpower: people who can work
3. patent: license that gives an inventor exclusive rights to make and sell his product
4. captured America's imagination: became extremely popular throughout America; interested everyone

5. fascinating: extremely interesting
6. testament to: example of
7. earthy: unsophisticated; hearty
8. unaffected: plain; sincere
9. enduring: lasting

EARLY YEARS OF THOMAS EDISON

4   Edison was born in Milan, Ohio, in 1847. At the time, Milan was a busy town near Lake Erie's southern shore; but in 1853, when a new railroad system bypassed[10] Milan, the fortunes of the town and its leading citizens collapsed. So the Edison family was forced to move to Michigan, where they hoped to make a fresh start on the Canadian border.

5   But in Port Huron, Michigan, the family's situation continued to decline, and little Thomas—recovering from scarlet fever[11]—was unable to go to school. He remained at home, watching his mother struggle to raise a large family despite increasing physical and financial hardships. He was the youngest Edison child. There had been seven brothers and sisters, but three had already died in the severe winter climate of the Great Lakes region. Thus, there was a fourteen-year difference between Thomas and the older Edison children—a gap which tended to make the boy a favorite with his mother.

6   Indeed, Mrs. Edison was the only one who really understood the child. For Thomas was different from other boys his age. He loved to question people, to examine things, to investigate places he had never seen. He was so curious, in fact, that he very often got himself in trouble. He was almost killed when he fell through a grain elevator; he was beaten by his father for burning down the barn; he nearly poisoned a friend with some homemade chemicals. Yet no amount of punishment could change him. He knew no fear and heeded[12] no warnings; the passion to experiment—lodged[13] deep within his soul—was just too strong to subdue.

7   When he was almost nine years old, Thomas Edison finally entered school. From the beginning, however, the experience was a disaster. School was too structured, too traditional in its memorized lessons and rigorous[14] discipline. So Edison's talent went unnoticed. He was bored, unhappy, and misunderstood; in fact, his teacher announced, he appeared to be just the hopeless dunce[15] of the classroom.

8   Edison's mother was furious. In an angry meeting, she informed the teacher that Thomas would never return to school. She would teach the boy herself, she insisted. Before her marriage, Nancy Elliott Edison had been a teacher; thus, she said, she knew well enough that the child was neither hopeless nor dumb.

9   After a mere ninety days, therefore, Thomas Edison's formal education came to an end. But true to her word,[16] for the next several years, Mrs. Edison devoted part of every day to the private instruction of her son. By her side, Edison studied English literature, European history, philosophy, and science. The favorite, always, was science. Whenever possible, he would perform at home the experiments he had read about in books. "My mother had faith in me," Edison later admitted. "If it had not been for her appreciation ... I should very likely never have become an inventor."

10   In 1859, just before the beginning of the Civil War, rail service from New England to Detroit was completed by means of a line through Port Huron. For the

---

10. bypass: go around; avoid
11. scarlet fever: childhood disease involving high temperature and skin rash
12. heed: listen to; obey

13. lodge: place firmly
14. rigorous: very strict
15. dunce: stupid person
16. true to her word: faithful to her promise

inquisitive Thomas Edison, this brought an opportunity too good to be missed. A newsboy was needed on the run to Detroit. Reluctantly,[17] his mother gave permission, and the twelve-year-old Edison began to work to earn extra money for his experiments.

11   From Port Huron, the morning train left at seven o'clock. Four hours later, it arrived in Detroit, not to leave for Port Huron again until half past five in the evening. Thus, Edison did not reach home each day until after ten at night. Yet unlike the boring routine of school, these long days were filled with adventure and excitement. So Edison's personality blossomed. He quickly became a most successful salesman—devising[18] all kinds of clever schemes for promoting his papers and candy. He also made a new circle of friends—railroad workers and telegraph operators who admired his energy, wit,[19] and imagination. Indeed, he was so quick with an argument that he persuaded a trainman to let him set up a laboratory in the back of his baggage car. There, he happily passed the hours—talking with other employees, experimenting, and dreaming, perhaps, of things to come.

12   It was at this time, however, that tragedy struck. Little by little, Edison realized that he was becoming deaf. Perhaps the cause lay in his earlier attack of scarlet fever. Perhaps—as he often wondered—his hearing had been damaged when a trainman, trying to help him, had lifted Edison by the ears onto the steps of a moving train. Whatever the cause, the result was a lifelong disability. From about the age of thirteen, Edison was severely hearing-impaired.[20] Only loud sounds, made close to him, were clearly audible.[21]

EDISON, TELEGRAPHY, AND THE NEW INDUSTRIAL RESEARCH

13   But if a near-accident on the railway line brought Edison such misfortune, another near-accident opened the door to future success. In 1862—while the Civil War raged through the East—Edison was still working on the Detroit-Port Huron train. One day, at the Mt. Clemens station stop, he suddenly noticed the stationmaster's child playing happily on the tracks. As the trains switched tracks, a car rolled toward the baby; instantly, Edison raced to the child, throwing himself and the baby out of the path of the train. Though he was too poor to give Edison a financial reward, the stationmaster offered to teach him telegraphy. So Edison gave up half of his railroad route to work every day in Mt. Clemens. In a matter of months, he had become a good telegrapher—a person whose skills were in great demand as the war effort spread across the nation.

14   Throughout the 1860s, Edison remained a telegraph operator. Restless as ever, and obsessed by[22] the desire to experiment, he worked at Western Union offices in Michigan, Canada, Indiana, Ohio, Tennessee, Kentucky, and Massachusetts. In town after town, his salary was quickly spent on books, chemicals, and scientific instruments. Often, he would anger his bosses—as he had once angered his teacher—by failing to conform to standard operating procedures. For instead of simply operating

---

17. reluctant: unwilling
18. devise: invent
19. wit: cleverness; humor

20. hearing-impaired: deaf
21. audible: capable of being heard
22. obsessed by: constantly thinking of

the telegraph, Edison was always trying to improve it; unfortunately this caused him to be fired by jealous or exasperated[23] managers.

15   Yet despite their failures and frustrations, these vagabond[24] years were of enormous importance to Edison's developing genius. They gave him the opportunity to experiment endlessly on the telegraph and related electrical devices; and this, in turn, led to further research in chemistry and mathematics. Thus, in January of 1869, Edison was ready to take a momentous[25] step. He resigned from the offices of Western Union in order to become a professional inventor.

16   Hoping to get some clients, Edison moved to New York in the spring of 1869. He was desperately poor and terribly hungry and with no immediate prospects[26] of employment. But suddenly, in one brief, dramatic encounter,[27] everything changed. An old acquaintance[28] had permitted Edison to sleep in the basement of Wall Street's Gold Indicator Company. Upstairs, some new machinery had recently been installed. When the machine broke down during a hectic trading session, hysteria swept across the exchange. No one—not even the inventor of the machine—knew what was wrong. But Edison, who had familiarized himself with the complicated mechanisms, could see that a broken spring had jammed the machine. With infinite[29] care he removed the spring, setting the intricate[30] system to work again.

17   The young inventor was a hero at last! Recognized and rewarded, he was given new problems to solve and new systems to perfect. In response, he quickly brought out[31] an improved stock ticker[32] and created an extraordinary self-correcting system for inaccurate stock quotations. For this last invention he received a handsome $40,000, and immediately, as he had always done with his telegrapher's salary, Edison invested the money in further experimentation. He set up an invention factory in Newark, New Jersey, hiring skilled artisans and scientists to work with him on his ideas. Then, within a few years, he built an expanded laboratory in Menlo Park, New Jersey. This was, in reality, the first industrial research center in America. Under Edison's direction, it soon began to turn out a steady stream of electrical equipment and related inventions. In some cases, the equipment was manufactured and marketed by Edison's own companies. In others, inventions were sold to larger companies for their own distribution or use. Both aspects of the business succeeded. While orders for machinery increased, requests for new inventions continued. And to meet these demands, Edison worked at a feverish pitch.[33] He slept very little—perhaps four hours a day. Often, he would go without sleep at all, working all night—or even several nights—on particularly difficult matters. Setbacks never disheartened him; failure never embittered. Again and again he would return to a problem—leaping with joy when solutions were found, passing out rewards when suggestions were made, encouraging, threatening, shouting, admiring. Childhood friends had found

23. exasperated: extremely annoyed; angry
24. vagabond: wandering
25. momentous: extremely important
26. prospects: possibilities; plans
27. encounter: meeting; event
28. acquaintance: friend
29. infinite: extremely great; without limits
30. intricate: very complicated
31. bring out: develop; manufacture
32. stock ticker: machine for transmission of stock prices
33. at a feverish pitch: extremely hard and with tremendous energy

him strange, but fellow scientists responded with vigor. In the intense, competitive, exciting atmosphere of Menlo Park, they put forth their very best efforts. Buoyed[34] by their leader's optimism, entertained by his humor, impressed by his stamina, and inspired by his genius, they worked with a unique combination of loyalty and efficiency.

EDISON'S GREATEST INVENTIONS

18 So as the Age of Invention got underway, Edison quickly became its acknowledged master. Year after year, he astounded the public with a series of extraordinary inventions. First he succeeded with his experiments in multiplex telegraphy, making it possible to send four messages at once over a single telegraph wire. He then devised a carbon transmitter to perfect the telephone of Alexander Graham Bell. Next came the phonograph—one of Edison's most amazing instruments. At last, sounds could be recorded, preserved, and used in limitless ways to instruct and entertain. (Edison, who had not heard anything clearly since the age of thirteen, was especially intrigued[35] with the phonograph's potential. He returned to this invention again and again, changing and perfecting it as the record business grew.)

19 Then, in 1879, came the greatest triumph. After months of research, Edison succeeded in making an efficient and practical electric light. Others before him had tried and failed, but he had refused to give up. He experimented endlessly to find a slender filament[36] that would heat to incandescence,[37] but not burn up, in an airtight[38] globe. Finally, his fragile filament of carbonized cotton thread worked. When electric current was passed through it, it steadily glowed, throwing off a clear but mellow[39] light. But the light—even when improved with a paper filament—could only last for about three hundred hours. Edison wanted something more durable. So he continued to experiment, trying over six thousand different materials to find a better filament. One day, he noticed a bamboo fan lying on one of his tables. Could bamboo fiber, perhaps, be the material he needed? After further experimentation, Edison was jubilant.[40] His filaments of carbonized bamboo could burn for about twelve hundred hours! Thus, Edison knew, he had finally found the secret of safe and durable artificial lighting.

20 Edison's work on the electric light did not end with this discovery. He would not rest, he insisted, until he had built an entire system of urban illumination. He moved into new Manhattan headquarters, therefore, and organized a massive[41] effort to bring electric lighting to a central business area of Wall Street. For this he had to lay underground cables, build a huge generating plant, and coordinate intricate wiring systems. He also needed considerable financial backing. So the inventor worked with almost super-human energy. He supervised construction, directed necessary experiments, promoted the enterprise among bankers and business leaders, and kept up a lively publicity campaign. Finally, on September 4, 1882, everything was ready. Upon Edison's order, the system was turned on, and lights appeared suddenly in the buildings

---

34. buoyed: supported; encouraged (buoy: marker that floats in the water)
35. intrigued: fascinated
36. filament: very thin substance, like a wire or thread

37. incandescence: giving off light
38. airtight: without air
39. mellow: soft
40. jubilant: very happy
41. massive: very large

Another of Edison's famous inventions

21   of the area. It was a magical moment—an instant of worldwide significance. The era of gas lamps and candlelight was over. A new age of power and energy and continuous illumination had dawned.

As Edison's inventions continued to appear, there seemed to be no limit to his physical and creative powers. In 1891, he introduced the world's first motion picture camera. Two years later, he built a movie studio—the first of its kind—on the grounds of his research center. Then, as the twentieth century dawned, Edison followed these achievements with the invention of a durable storage battery, the development of poured cement[42] construction techniques, the production of heavy mining machinery, the creation of submarine defense instruments, and the direction of biochemical experiments for the American rubber industry. His career, indeed, was long and fruitful.[43] It spanned[44] more than six productive decades, during which time Edison took out over thirteen hundred patents. In the process, he changed the world completely, bringing light and entertainment and countless labor-saving devices to millions of people.

22   When Edison died in 1931, Americans wanted to pay tribute to[45] his genius with a special, solemn[46] gesture. So for one commemorative[47] minute on the day of his funeral, they agreed to turn off nonessential lights across the nation. Thus, at 10 P.M. on October 21, there was a silent, momentary blackout. Homes were in darkness; city lights dimmed; and for a few dramatic moments, the people paused to consider what Edison had given them.

---

42. cement: mixture of water and crushed rock or clay
43. fruitful: productive; yielding good results
44. span: extend over

45. pay tribute to: honor
46. solemn: very serious and formal
47. commemorative: done in memory of something or someone

The following selection is from the autobiographical notes of Thomas Edison. It includes a description of his determination as an inventor; it also shows how his courage and creativity overcame the terrible disability of his deafness.

from
The Diary and Sundry Observations of Thomas Alva Edison

In trying to perfect a thing, I sometimes run straight up against a granite[1] wall a hundred feet high. If, after trying and trying and trying again, I can't get over it, I turn to something else. Then, someday, it may be months or it may be years later, something is discovered either by myself or someone else, or something happens in some part of the world, which I recognize may help me to scale[2] at least part of that wall.

I never allow myself to become discouraged under any circumstances. I recall that after we had conducted thousands of experiments on a certain project without solving the problem, one of my associates, after we had conducted the crowning[3] experiment and it had proved a failure, expressed discouragement and disgust over our having failed "to find out anything." I cheerily assured him that we *had* learned something. For we had learned for a certainty that the thing couldn't be done that way, and that we would have to try some other way. We sometimes learn a lot from our failures if we have put into the effort the best thought and work we are capable of....

When Bell first worked out his telephone idea I tried it and the sound which came in through the instrument was so weak I couldn't hear it. I started to develop it and kept on until the sounds were audible to me. I sold my improvement, the carbon transmitter, to the Western Union and they sold it to Bell. It made the telephone successful. If I had not been deaf it is possible and even probable that this improvement would not have been made. The telephone as we now know it might have been delayed if a deaf electrician had not undertaken the job of making it a practical thing....

Even in my courtship my deafness was a help. In the first place it excused me for getting quite a little nearer to her than I would have dared to if I hadn't had to be quite close in order to hear what she said. If something had not overcome my natural bashfulness I might have been too faint of heart to win. And after things were actually going nicely, I found hearing unnecessary.

My later courtship was carried on by telegraph. I taught the lady of my heart the Morse code, and when she could both send and receive we got along much better than we could have with spoken words by tapping our remarks to one another on our hands. Presently I asked her thus, in Morse code, if she would marry me. The word "Yes" is an easy one to send by telegraphic signals, and she sent it. If she had been obliged to

---

1. granite: kind of rock
2. scale: climb

3. crowning: most important; final

speak it she might have found it harder. Nobody knew anything about many of our conversations on a long drive in the White Mountains. If we had spoken words, others would have heard them. We could use pet names without the least embarrassment, although there were three other people in the carriage. We still use the telegraphic code at times. When we go to hear a spoken play she keeps her hand upon my knee and telegraphs the words the actors use so that I know something about the drama though I hear nothing of the dialog.

*Edison at the age of fourteen; his unhappy
days of formal schooling were over*

Reading Comprehension

A. Choose the best answer for the following:

1. "Thus, from the Civil War to World War I, circumstances combined in the United States to encourage creative invention." The reasons for this statement in paragraph 1 are given in
    a. paragraph 1.
    b. paragraph 2.
    c. paragraphs 2 and 3.

2. "Year after year, new methods were invented, new machinery was produced, and new laws of science were explained." Examples of this statement in paragraph 2 are given in
    a. paragraph 1.
    b. paragraph 2.
    c. paragraphs 2 and 3.

3. According to paragraph 3, Edison and his country may best be compared because
    a. they were both young.
    b. they were both affected by the trauma of civil war.
    c. they were both symbols of progress and prosperity.

4. As implied in paragraph 3, what is the American dream?
    a. the chance to escape from Europe
    b. the chance to rise from poverty to prosperity
    c. religious freedom

5. As a child, Edison was different from the other boys his age
    a. because he was poor.
    b. because he was unhappy.
    c. because he was obsessed by the desire to experiment.

6. Edison owed his greatest debt of gratitude to
    a. his teacher.
    b. the stationmaster at Mt. Clemens.
    c. his mother.

7. Why was Edison's work as a telegraph operator significant?
    a. It gave him a chance to travel.
    b. It gave him a chance to experiment.
    c. It taught him how to deal with people.

8. Which of the following is not true?
    a. Edison was an inspiration to his colleagues at Menlo Park.
    b. Edison was a quiet and obedient child.
    c. Edison was a man of rare energy and faith.

9. Edison invented all of the following *except*
    a. the phonograph.
    b. the movie camera.
    c. the airplane.

10. From what we are told in Edison's autobiography, we may assume that
    a. his deafness made him bitter.
    b. Edison had a positive outlook on life.
    c. Edison would have accomplished more had he not been disabled.

B. **Choose the answer that best expresses the word or words in italics.**

1. No one *captured America's imagination* like Thomas Alva Edison.
    a. fascinated Americans
    b. annoyed Americans
    c. influenced Americans
2. Edison's mother was *true to her word.*
    a. She was talkative.
    b. She did as she had promised.
    c. She told the truth.
3. He was a fascinating *testament to* progress and prosperity.
    a. contrast to
    b. example of
    c. substitute for
4. In his laboratory, Edison worked *at a feverish pitch.*
    a. until he became ill
    b. although he was ill
    c. constantly and energetically
5. Americans wanted to *pay tribute to* Edison in a special way.
    a. honor
    b. subsidize
    c. borrow from

C. **Circle the item that does not belong with the others.**

1. a. Carnegie   b. Menlo Park   c. Pittsburgh
2. a. Expansionism   b. William McKinley c. Grover Cleveland
3. a. Edison   b. Mauna Loa   c. Menlo Park
4. a. prairies   b. Pilgrims   c. *O Pioneers!*
5. a. Liliuokalani   b. Alaska   c. Kamahameha

D. **Complete the following equations.**

1. Carnegie: Scotland = Liliuokalani: _____

2. Edison: electric light = Alexander Graham Bell: _____

3. Edison: telegraphy = Henry Ford: _____

4. Honolulu: Hawaii = Havana: _____

5. expansionists: war = isolationists: _____

Vocabulary

A.   Word Forms.   Choose the correct word form for each of the following. Make all necessary changes.

1. investigation, investigative, to investigate

   a. The Gilded Age was a period of scientific _____ .

   b. Scientists everywhere began _____ new possibilities.

   c. Menlo Park was a laboratory for _____ research.

2. available, to avail, availability

   a. Manufacturers could _____ themselves of the nation's new materials.

   b. There was a continuous _____ of labor.

   c. There was also sufficient capital _____ .

3. achievement, achiever, to achieve

   a. Edison's _____ were truly remarkable.

   b. By inspiring his colleagues, he was able _____ great things.

   c. Competitive and creative, he was an _____ .

4. to appeal, appealing, appeal

   a. Because of his wit and enthusiasm, he was a man of great _____ .

   b. He _____ to many different kinds of people.

   c. Above all, he was an _____ example of the American dream.

5. scheme, schematic, to scheme

   a. As a salesman on the railroad line, he devised all kinds of _____ .

   b. He would often _____ for hours as he waited in the station.

   c. Before working on a project, the scientists would often make a _____ outline.

6. to proceed, procedure, procedural

   a. Edison was sometimes fired for refusing to follow standard _____ .

   b. Then he would _____ to another office in another town.

   c. _____ requirements were often frustrating.

7. amazement, to amaze, amazing

   a. To everyone's _____ , Mrs. Edison challenged the teacher.

   b. He _____ the neighbors with his unusual experiments.

   c. His long and fruitful career was _____ .

8. to dim, dimly, dim

    a. To pay tribute to Edison, people _____ their lights.

    b. After Edison, the age of _____ lighting was over.

    c. Bright city streets replaced _____ lit areas.

B.   **Complete each sentence with one of the words from the following list.**

                infinite   *unappealing*   *unaffected*
                 unavailable   *inaudible*

1. He found the whole idea of schoolwork _____ .

2. People were charmed by Edison's _____ manner.

3. In time, more and more sounds became _____ .

4. He replaced the broken spring with _____ care.

5. The manager of the laboratory was sometimes _____ .

C.   **Antonyms.**   **Match the words in column A with their opposite in column B.**

A	B
fascinating	unimportant
heed	simple
momentous	small
reluctant	sturdy
exasperated	sad
intricate	boring
fragile	ignore
massive	willing
solemn	pleased
jubilant	casual

D.   **From the following list, choose words that best substitute for the word or words in italics.**

    manpower   *hearing-impaired*   *rigorous*   *intrigued*
    lodge   *bypass*   *buoyed*   *fruitful*
    dunce   *vagabond*

1. From about the age of thirteen on, Edison was *deaf*.
2. He was uncomfortable in the *strict* atmosphere of the classroom.
3. His career was long and *productive*.
4. The fortunes of the town declined when the railroad *failed to pass through* it.
5. There was a plentiful supply of *people who could work*
6. The teacher thought Edison was a *stupid person*.
7. In spite of their hardships, the *wandering* years were important ones.
8. Edison's colleagues were *supported* by the master's energy.
9. They were *fascinated* by his wit and his brilliance.
10. Throughout his life, the passion to experiment was *placed firmly* in his soul.

Structures

A. Follow the model and complete the definitions below.

Model: (break up) A plow is an instrument *for breaking up* the earth.

1. *(separate)* A thresher is a machine _____ seeds.
2. *(record)* A phonograph is an instrument _____ sound.
3. *(cut)* A reaper is a machine _____ crops.
4. *(transmit)* The telephone is an instrument _____ sound.
5. *(store)* A battery is a container _____ energy.

B. Follow the model and complete the sentences below.

Model: (study) "It is necessary that he *study* harder," the teacher said.

1. *(have)* "It is urgent that we _____ a meeting at once," his mother replied.
2. *(come)* "It is imperative that my assistant _____ at once," Edison announced.
3. *(help)* "I insist that he _____ with the work," said Edison.
4. *(give)* "I demand that he _____ me his report," Edison added.
5. *(do)* "It is important that this experiment _____ again," he told them.
6. *(keep)* "It is urgent that our results _____ secret," he reminded them.

Composition

Choose one of the following.

A. Reread the first two paragraphs of the Historical Background selection. Then in your own words, complete the following summary.

"The decades of expansion after the Civil War represent the Glorious Age of American invention. Four main factors contributed to this sudden burst of creative activity.

First, _____

_____ .

Next, _____

_____ .

Third, _____

_____ .

Finally, _____

_____ .

Thus, from the Civil War to the First World War, thousands of new discoveries were made. Some of the most important inventions were _____

_____ .

There were also _____

_____ .

The greatest invention, in my opinion, was _____

because _____

_____ .

Truly, by World War I, the American way of life had been completely transformed."

B. "If at first you don't succeed, try, try again." According to this English proverb, perseverance can often make the difference between failure and success. To illustrate the truth of this proverb, tell the story of Edison's efforts to invent safe and durable artificial lighting. Use as many specific facts as possible. You may wish to refer to paragraph 19 for details.

C. The lives of Andrew Carnegie and Thomas Edison show several striking similarities. In two well-developed paragraphs, compare their rise to fame and fortune.

Topics for Class Discussion

Choose the answer that best expresses your own feelings, taste, or preference. You may substitute your own answer for any of the choices given. Please explain your answers, sharing your responses with a partner, a small group, or with all of your classmates.

1. In your opinion, who made the greatest contribution to twentieth-century American life? Why?
   a. Andrew Carnegie
   b. Willa Cather
   c. Thomas Edison

2. How would you most enjoy spending an evening?
   a. getting business tips from Carnegie
   b. discussing literature with Willa Cather
   c. working in a laboratory with Edison

3. Which of Edison's inventions do you consider the most useful?
   a. the light bulb
   b. the movie camera
   c. the phonograph

4. Which invention do you think most changed America?
   a. the automobile
   b. the telephone
   c. the light bulb

5. How would you most like to spend your next vacation?
   a. at an elegant resort on the beach in Hawaii
   b. on a camping expedition in Alaska
   c. at a horse ranch in the Rocky Mountains

6. What do you think of Mrs. Edison's decision to teach young Thomas?
   a. It was foolish. The child should have learned to discipline himself at an early age.
   b. It was appropriate. More than anyone, she understood what her child really needed.
   c. It was risky. She could have caused him to become dependent and antisocial.

7. If someone were to give you a gift today, what would you most enjoy receiving?
   a. a sound movie camera
   b. a car
   c. an antique chandelier

8. Whom do you most admire and why?
   a. Andrew Carnegie
   b. Liliuokalani
   c. Thomas Edison

New England Area

Museum of Science
Boston, Massachusetts

Middle Atlantic Area

International Museum of Photography at
    George Eastman House
Rochester, New York

Locust Grove (former home of Samuel F. B.
    Morse)
Poughkeepsie, New York

Museum of Broadcasting
New York, New York

Edison National Historic Site
West Orange, New Jersey

National Museum of American History
Smithsonian Institution
Washington, D.C.

Southeast Area

Wright Brothers National Memorial
Kitty Hawk (Outer Banks)
North Carolina

Midwestern Area

Greenfield Village and Henry Ford Museum
Dearborn, Michigan

Fair Lane Mansion
Dearborn, Michigan

Seven Acres Antique Village and Museum
Union, Illinois

Museum of Science and Industry
Chicago, Illinois

Rocky Mountain Area

Pioneer Auto Show and Antique Town
Murdo, South Dakota

5

A Vision of Justice

Progressive Reformers

PREREADING

Look at the photograph below. Then, working in pairs or small groups, answer these questions.

1. Pictured in the photograph are crowds of newly arrived immigrants on Hester Street, New York, 1899. Describe the busy street scene. From what you can see of the buildings, what do you think the living conditions were like in these apartments? Do you think the people in this neighborhood could all speak English? If not, what other languages might they have spoken? Was their lack of English a serious problem for them? Why, or why not? What jobs do you think they found?

2. Turn to the photograph on p. 78. Pictured is Jane Addams, the great American reformer. Describe her clothing, her manner, the chair she is seated on. Does she seem to be one of the newly arrived immigrants on crowded Hester Street? Why, or why not?

Hester Street, Manhattan, at the turn of the twentieth century

1   Toward the end of the nineteenth century, as industrial expansion transformed the United States, many people began to worry about the harmful effects of rapid modernization. In the past, they said, Americans had been more secure, more self-sufficient.[1] On their own farms, they had produced the food they needed. In local shops, they had made the goods they used. And countless opportunities for commerce and trade had encouraged the hopeful pioneers.

EFFECTS OF INDUSTRIAL EXPANSION

2   All that was changing, insisted these observers. Expanding cities were replacing the nation's farms, enormous factories were taking over shops, and in every major industry, gigantic corporations were merging[2] to prevent free competition. People were losing control, it seemed, over their social and economic destinies.

3   Indeed, as these Americans realized, industrialization, urbanization, and the rise of monopolies had reduced many people to a helpless new dependence. Consumers, for example, were often at the mercy of[3] dishonest manufacturers; with little legal protection, they had to accept defective products, impure drugs, or contaminated[4] foods. On the farms out west, rural workers faced additional injustice: they often paid the railroads exorbitant[5] rates in order to ship their products. Of course, among small business owners, there was increasing insecurity, since larger companies could either buy up competitors or force them out of business. And throughout the nation's industries, workers were also at a growing disadvantage, for rising immigration had begun to create an unending supply of labor. This meant that people could easily be replaced, so workers had to endure appalling[6] exploitation.[7] In dangerous factories or unhealthful mines, they labored ten or even eleven hours a day. Sometimes, their little children labored with them. They, too, faced the dreaded possibility of accidents, sickness, or even death on the job.[8] Yet for many of these families, neither wages nor benefits were ever sufficient to assure a decent and healthful standard of living.

4   Clearly, by the turn of the twentieth century, many consumers, farmers, workers, and small business owners had become victims of economic expansion. As a result, there was a real possibility that anger and resentment[9] would turn into revolt. For the sake of the country and all of its people, therefore, there was a critical need for widespread[10] reform.

DEVELOPMENT OF LABOR UNIONS

5   One important response to this need was the growth of labor unions in the United States. Local unions had occasionally been formed in the decades before the Civil War;

---

1. self-sufficient: self-reliant; able to take care of oneself
2. merge: join together
3. at the mercy of: with no protection from
4. contaminated: impure
5. exorbitant: extremely high
6. appalling: horrible
7. exploitation: taking advantage of people
8. on the job: while working
9. resentment: unexpressed anger
10. widespread: extensive

but in 1866, a year after the Civil War ended, workers organized the National Labor Union—the first American workers' federation to be organized on a nationwide basis. Unfortunately, it was able to last only a few years. For in 1873, following the collapse of a prestigious Wall Street bank, there was a severe depression. Workers abandoned their union efforts in the hopes of finding employment, and the National Labor Union, like the banks, collapsed.

6   But meanwhile, another nationwide group had been formed: the Noble Order of the Knights of Labor. Founded in 1869, the Knights of Labor included skilled workers from different crafts. It was well organized and well directed, and thus it survived the panic of 1873. By the 1880s, in fact, it had begun to coordinate effective strikes against management injustice.

7   One of its strikes, however, ended in tragedy. In Chicago, at the McCormick Harvester Company, union members had been denied their request for an eight-hour work day. As angry workers gathered at Haymarket Square, an anarchist's bomb killed some policemen. Many people blamed the union for this outbreak of violence. In the resulting panic that swept across the nation, the Knights of Labor rapidly declined.

8   Yet as it declined, the Knights of Labor were followed by still another effort at union organization. In 1886—the year of the Haymarket Riot—the American Federation of Labor was formed under the efficient leadership of Samuel Gompers. Born in London of Dutch-Jewish parents, Gompers had come to the United States during the American Civil War. Like Carnegie, he was only thirteen when he reached America. Also like Carnegie, he found early employment in the factories of a newly industrialized nation. But Gompers' determination, unlike Carnegie's, did not take him to corporate management. Rather, it led to the organization of workers in a courageous attempt to secure their rights. Denouncing[11] violent confrontations, he preferred to combine collective bargaining[12] with the judicious[13] use of well-timed walkouts.[14] So little by little, Gompers and the AFL became powerful and respected. Higher wages, shorter work days, and greater benefits were won as more and more workers joined the successful organization. This did not mean, of course, that there were no more tragic confrontations like the Haymarket Riot or the Homestead Strike. On the contrary, under the pressures or rapid industrialization toward the turn of the twentieth century, strikes too often led to panic and disorder. In 1894, for example, railroad workers at Chicago's Pullman plant struck in response to a wage cut. When federal troops arrived to guard the railroad's mail service, violence raged for days around the plant. Similar outbreaks in the mining industry were among the most violent in labor's history.

9   Nevertheless, in spite of their setbacks, workers continued to make progress through organization. By World War I, more than two million workers belonged to the growing AFL. Samuel Gompers was still its president—a position he maintained until his death in 1924. In the 1930s, after bitter disputes, some industrial unions separated from the craft-dominated AFL to form the Congress of Industrial

---

11. denounce: reject; criticize strongly
12. collective bargaining: discussions between employers and employees' representatives

13. judicious: careful; well-planned
14. walkout: strike

Organizations (CIO). But in 1955, both organizations finally merged to become modern America's great federation of craft and industrial unions.*

THE PROGRESSIVE MOVEMENT

10   In addition to the rise of labor unions, there was another response to the need for reform at the end of the nineteenth century. This was the Progressive movement, a crusade[15] for change that started during the 1890s and reached its peak before the First World War. Its supporters, as the name implies, were deeply committed to progress—

An immigrant family in one of New York's tenements, 1910

---

15. crusade: dedicated campaign

* Craft union: skilled workers; industrial union: unskilled workers

not to the technological breakthroughs of science, but to immediate and lasting improvements in the living and working conditions of the American people.

11   Though Progressive reformers were concerned with the rights of all Americans, they were initially drawn to the teeming[16] slums[17] of the nation's growing cities. There, they felt, their work was most urgently needed. For at the dawn of the twentieth century, immigration to the United States had begun to soar to unprecedented[18] levels. Between 1900 and 1920, in fact, almost fifteen million people reached the ports of America. They came from Italy, Greece, eastern Europe, Russia, and Asia, following the German, Irish, and Scandinavian immigrants who had arrived in the middle of the nineteenth century. With little knowledge of English, they had to take the lowest-paying unskilled jobs available. With no experience in American customs, they were excluded from the security of a shared national tradition. And with totally inadequate legal protection, they were frequently cheated by unscrupulous[19] landlords who could charge high rents for substandard housing. Thus, in every way, these twentieth-century immigrants were continually exposed to the worst effects of rapid industrialization. It was for this reason that the Progressive movement started in the nation's urban centers.

12   Before long, however, Progressive reformers expanded their activities. From community action, they turned to state and national politics, for in matters of housing, employment, consumer protection, and public health, they realized that the people's rights could only be secured through legislation. So by World War I—as a direct result of Progressive reforms—workers, farmers, consumers, and small business owners could begin to count on the protection of the law.

13   Two reformers were especially responsible for the success of the American Progressive movement. They were Jane Addams—Chicago's pioneering social worker—and Jacob Riis—New York's determined journalist.

FOCUS ON JANE ADDAMS

14   Jane Addams was born in Cedarville, Illinois—not far from the growing industrial city of Chicago. Her father was a prosperous businessman, and Jane was given all the advantages his wealth and position could provide. In 1881, she received her B.A. degree from Rockford College, having graduated with highest honors and a record of outstanding achievements as a scholar, editor of the college paper, public debater, and dedicated advocate[20] of women's rights. Only a few decades earlier, reformers like Susan B. Anthony and Elizabeth Cady Stanton had fought for the right of American women to receive a college education. Thus, Jane Addams was proudly aware that she was among the first generation of American women to reach the cherished academic goal. This privilege, she felt, placed enormous responsibilities upon her and her fellow graduates: somehow, they had to make a real contribution to the improvement of America's changing society.

---

16. teeming: very crowded
17. slum: very poor urban district
18. unprecedented: said of something that has never happened before
19. unscrupulous: dishonest
20. advocate: energetic supporter

15   Despite her longing to be of service, Jane Addams did not discover an immediate outlet[21] for her talents. After seven years of travel and further study, however, she found her inspiration in the work of England's new reformers. Helping the poor, these reformers had decided, could best be accomplished by living among them. Thus, as needs arose, they could directly provide essential services, skills training, counseling,[22] and recreation. And their guidance would be effective because of its basis in the shared experience of a common environment.

16   To bring about this unique interaction, the British reformers had built a settlement, or community house, in the poorest slums of London. It was the first experiment of its kind, and its remarkable achievements had a profound effect on the career of Jane Addams. In 1889, she arrived in Chicago to form her own settlement among the city's tenements. There, she decided, she could provide an opportunity for women to put their education to practical use.[23]

17   Hull House—America's new settlement—began operations in the fall of 1889. Soon, it offered a day-care center, health services, counseling programs, social clubs, and facilities for adult education. It also had a growing staff of dedicated reformers— men and women who wanted careers in the new profession of social work. Led by Jane Addams, they fought for years to improve the housing and working conditions of the residents of Chicago. They also supported national campaigns for labor reform, public health improvements, women's suffrage, and the rights of children. So by the turn of the twentieth century, Hull House was more than a community experiment. It had become an international center for research and training, a primary model for additional settlements, and a continuous source of Progressive reform throughout the United States. For her extraordinary achievements, Jane Addams was awarded the Nobel Peace Prize in 1931.

FOCUS ON JACOB RIIS

18   Meanwhile, in New York City, the Progressive movement had found another leader in the person of Jacob Riis. Unlike Jane Addams, Riis was not born in America. He arrived in the United States in 1870—a poor but ambitious immigrant. In his native country, Denmark, his father had been a respected schoolteacher of modest means. But young Jacob had grown tired of studying carpentry and had decided to come to America to seek his fortune. Perhaps, he thought, if he could make a good living, he might win the hand of[24] his beloved childhood sweetheart.

19   For the romantic and idealistic Danish boy, however, New York was a terrible shock. Week after week, he wandered through its miserable[25] slums, hoping to find a few odd jobs[26] to pay for his food and lodging. Sometimes, in utter dejection,[27] he would venture[28] beyond Manhattan to the brickyards of New Jersey or to Pennsylvania's

---

21. outlet: means of expression
22. counsel: give advice
23. put ... to practical use: use ... in a meaningful way
24. win the hand of: marry
25. miserable: terrible; very poor

26. odd jobs: temporary chores
27. dejection: depression
28. venture: dare to go

mines. But everywhere, it seemed, only violence, discrimination, and exhausting labor awaited America's newcomers.

20   Yet for seven years Riis persevered, accepting any employment that promised better wages and the chance to rise above immigrant despair. Finally, in 1888, an opportunity appeared. Riis was offered a job as police reporter for a major New York newspaper. He accepted immediately and found his life's work as a journalist in the tenement district of the Lower East Side. He reported its crime, its brutality, and the anguish[29] of its people. But his articles and famous books were more than eyewitness accounts; they went beyond the surface of things to uncover hidden social causes. Thus, there were chilling[30] illustrations of child labor abuses, absentee landlord[31] greed, and wretched[32] working conditions; there were also investigations of corrupt city politics, illegal drug and alcohol traffic, fire hazards,[33] health hazards, and totally inadequate schools. Occasionally, graphic[34] photographs would accompany his descriptions, for Riis was one of America's earliest camera journalists. He was also an extremely thorough researcher, adding careful statistics and scientific facts whenever they were needed to support his conclusions.

21   In time, through the work of Jacob Riis, New York began a program of Progressive reform. Laws were passed to begin urban renewal; parks and recreation facilities were established; public health services were expanded; and schools were improved. Encouraged by these gains, Riis then started to tour the country to promote additional Progressive reforms.

PRESIDENT THEODORE ROOSEVELT

22   In their nationwide campaigns, Jacob Riis, Jane Addams, and Samuel Gompers had a powerful ally. This was Theodore Roosevelt, who became America's president after the assassination of William McKinley in 1901. Roosevelt had formerly been the Police Commissioner of New York City. He had sometimes accompanied Jacob Riis on his investigations of the slums and had therefore acquired firsthand knowledge of the needs of many Americans. So in his two terms as president, he was determined to bring about sweeping changes.

23   In 1903, for example, he established the Department of Commerce and Labor—a government agency with specific new powers to limit the formation of monopolies. The president then turned his attention to major reforms in the railroad industry. At the same time, with a new Pure Food and Drug Act, he increased the government's authority in matters of consumer protection. Finally, to America's workers, Roosevelt also offered support. Thus, in matters of corporate growth, transportation services, consumer protection, and labor relations, he showed that the government had begun to take charge of protecting Americans from the dangers of development. Here indeed was a long-awaited triumph for both labor leaders and the Progressive reformers. It was also a new and vigorous direction in the history of American politics—one which was to continue and expand throughout the emerging twentieth century.

---

29. anguish: extreme suffering
30. chilling: terrifying; very disturbing
31. absentee landlord: landlord who does not live in the building he rents

32. wretched: miserable
33. hazard: danger
34. graphic: vivid; realistic

To further[1] the cause of Progressive reform, Jane Addams wrote essays, gave speeches, and published several well-known books. Among these was her autobiography, *Twenty Years at Hull-House*. It was a sensitive, well-written account of the reformer's early life, her efforts to establish Hull House, and the continuing struggle for social justice at the turn of the twentieth century.

In the following passage, Jane Addams discusses the origins of America's settlement movement. It was a response, she tells us, to the immediate needs of the nation's poor and to the longing for fulfillment among more fortunate Americans.

Jane Addams

from
Twenty Years at Hull-House

by JANE ADDAMS

We have in America a fast-growing number of cultivated young people who have no recognized outlet for their active faculties. They hear constantly of the great social maladjustment, but no way is provided for them to change it, and their uselessness hangs about them heavily.... These young people have had advantages of college, of European travel, and of economic study, but they are sustaining this shock of inaction. They have pet phrases, and they tell you that the things that make us all alike are stronger than the things that make us different. They say that all men are united by needs and sympathies far more permanent and radical than anything that temporarily divides them and sets them in opposition to each other.... They tell their elders with all the bitterness of youth that if they expect success from them in business or politics or in whatever lines their ambition for them has run, they must let them consult all of humanity; that they must let them find out what the people want and how they want it. It is only the stronger young people, however, who formulate this. Many of them dissipate[2] their energies in so-called enjoyment.[3] Others, not content with that, go on studying and go back to college for their second degrees; not that they are especially fond of study, but because they want something definite to do, and their powers have been trained in the direction of mental accumulation. Many are buried beneath this mental accumulation with lowered vitality and discontent[4]....

This young life, so sincere in its emotion and good phrases and yet so undirected, seems to me as pitiful as the other great mass of destitute[5] lives. One is supplementary to the other, and some method of communication can surely be devised. Mr. Barnett, who urged the first Settlement,—Toynbee Hall, in East London,—recognized this need of outlet for the young men of Oxford and Cambridge, and hoped that the Settlement would supply the communication. It is easy to see why the Settlement movement originated in England, where the years of education are more constrained[6] and definite than they are here, where class distinctions[7] are more rigid. The necessity of it was greater there, but we are fast feeling the pressure of the need and meeting the necessity for Settlements in America....

---

1. to further: to promote, encourage
2. dissipate: waste; use foolishly
3. so-called enjoyment: something that is not really enjoyment
4. discontent: unhappiness
5. destitute: very poor
6. constrained: restricted
7. distinctions: differences

✖ EXERCISES

Reading Comprehension

A.   Choose the best answer for the following:

1. In the Historical Background reading, paragraph 2
   a. presents a contrast to paragraph 1.
   b. presents a continuation of paragraph 1.
   c. has no relation to paragraph 1.

2. What is the main topic of paragraph 3?
   a. the causes of industrialization in the United States
   b. the effects of industrialization in the United States
   c. the rise of labor unions in America

3. Paragraph 4 presents
   a. a summary of what has just been said.
   b. a contrast to what has just been said.
   c. a completely new topic.

4. Labor unions and the Progressive movement are both examples of
   a. the evils of urbanization.
   b. violent protest against rapid modernization.
   c. responses to the need for reform in America.

5. Samuel Gompers favored all of the following except
   a. collective bargaining.
   b. violent confrontations.
   c. well-timed strikes.

6. What is the main topic of paragraph 11?
   a. the problems of immigrants at the turn of the twentieth century
   b. reasons for immigration to America
   c. successful immigrants of the twentieth century

7. In paragraph 13, Jane Addams and Jacob Riis are introduced as examples of
   a. struggling immigrants.
   b. Progressive reformers.
   c. American educators.

8. Why did Jane Addams want to make a contribution to American society?
   a. She had known poverty and suffering as a child.
   b. She wanted to put her education to practical use.
   c. She wanted to prove to her father that she could succeed.

9. Settlements were
   a. low-income housing projects.
   b. middle-income suburbs.
   c. community houses in tenement districts.

10. Like Carnegie, Jacob Riis
    a. experienced a traumatic arrival in America.
    b. rose to great heights of wealth and prestige.
    c. made a great contribution to American industry.

B. Answer *true* or *false* to the following.

1. Industrial expansion brought insecurity to many Americans.
2. Because of continuous immigration, people had to accept poor working conditions.
3. Railroads always charged fair prices for freight transportation.
4. As monopolies developed, there was more opportunity for small businessmen.
5. At the end of the nineteenth century, consumers had inadequate legal protection.
6. Higher wages and shorter work days were priority goals of the early unions.
7. In general, emigration from northern Europe preceded emigration from southern and eastern Europe.
8. Immigrants often found the opportunity they had dreamed about.
9. Like Jacob Riis and Jane Addams, Theodore Roosevelt was a Progressive reformer.
10. Liberal politicians in the twentieth century expanded the Progressive ideal.

C. Complete the sentences below with adjectives from the following list. Use as many adjectives as possible for each person.

brave	*creative*	*well organized*	*aggressive*
determined	*ambitious*	*patriotic*	*insecure*
successful	*clever*	*impatient*	*observant*
foolish	*patient*	*heroic*	*understanding*
idealistic	*sensitive*	*unlucky*	*wise*

1. Carnegie was ...

2. Willa Cather was ...

3. Queen Liliuokalani was ...

4. King Kamehameha was ...

5. Mrs. Edison was ...

6. Thomas Edison was ...

7. Jane Addams was ...

8. Samuel Gompers was ...

9. Jacob Riis was ...

10. Theodore Roosevelt was ...

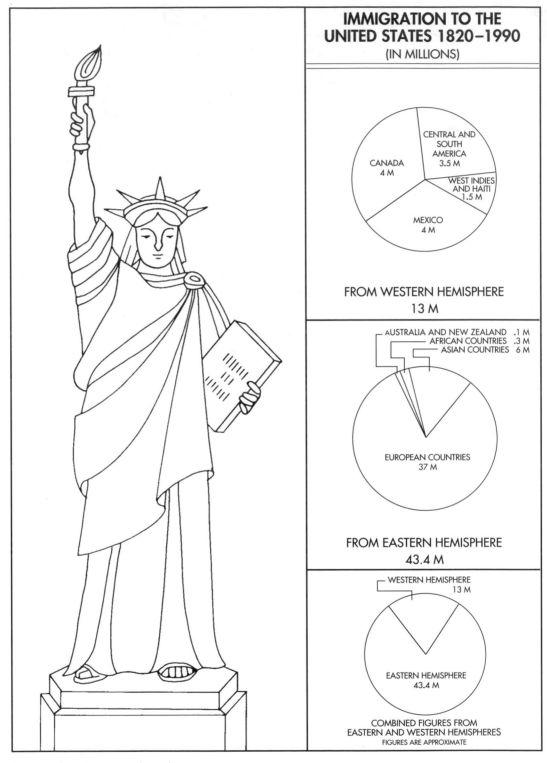

IMMIGRATION TO THE UNITED STATES 1820–1990
(IN MILLIONS)

CENTRAL AND SOUTH AMERICA
3.5 M

CANADA
4 M

WEST INDIES AND HAITI
1.5 M

MEXICO
4 M

FROM WESTERN HEMISPHERE
13 M

AUSTRALIA AND NEW ZEALAND .1 M
AFRICAN COUNTRIES .3 M
ASIAN COUNTRIES 6 M

EUROPEAN COUNTRIES
37 M

FROM EASTERN HEMISPHERE
43.4 M

WESTERN HEMISPHERE
13 M

EASTERN HEMISPHERE
43.4 M

COMBINED FIGURES FROM EASTERN AND WESTERN HEMISPHERES
FIGURES ARE APPROXIMATE

Source: United States Immigration and Naturalization Services

D.   **Study the immigration statistics on p. 82. Then answer the following.**

1. Between 1820 and 1990, about how many people came to the United States from Europe?
2. About how many came from Australia and New Zealand? Why do you think the figure from Europe is so much greater? Give as many reasons as you can.
3. About how many people emigrated from Canada between 1820 and 1990? From Asian countries? From Haiti and the West Indies?
4. To the left of the illustration's immigration statistics, the artist has drawn the Statue of Liberty. Why? For the millions who came to America what did this figure represent? Make as many suggestions as possible.
5. Approximately how many people, in total, immigrated to America between 1820 and 1990? Do you think some of them found what they were looking for? Do you think many of them did?

Vocabulary

A.   **Word Forms.   Choose the correct word form for each of the following. Make all necessary changes.**

1. defect, defective, defectively
   a. Consumers often had to accept _____ merchandise.
   b. The goods were assembled _____ .
   c. There could even be _____ in essential items.

2. exclusive, exclusively, to exclude
   a. Immigrants felt _____ from the American way of life.
   b. They could never live in _____ urban areas.
   c. Many jobs, they realized, were given to native-born Americans _____ .

3. legislator, legislation, legislative
   a. Congress is the _____ body in the United States.
   b. Progressive reformers hoped to influence powerful _____ .
   c. Because of their efforts, new _____ was passed.

4. fulfillment, fulfilling, to fulfill
   a. Jane Addams found _____ at Hull House.
   b. It was a _____ career.
   c. She was able _____ her dreams of service.

5. consultation, consultant, to consult
   a. The workers often _____ with Gompers.
   b. In some settlements, patients could have a _____ with their doctor.
   c. Social workers sometimes become _____ to urban agencies.

B.   Circle the word that does not belong with the others.

1. a. gigantic   b. huge   c. expensive
2. a. urban   b. metropolitan   c. rustic
3. a. rustic   b. crowded   c. rural
4. a. monopoly   b. opportunity   c. combination
5. a. first   b. initial   c. last
6. a. silence   b. argument   c. debate
7. a. vitality   b. energy   c. patience
8. a. deny   b. formulate   c. express

C.   Substitute a verb phrase from the following list for the italicized word or words in the sentences below. Be sure to use the correct form of the verb.

count on	bring out	give up	carry on
set up	look ahead	take up	manage to

1. After the Civil War, settlers decided to *accept* the challenge of the prairies.
2. In order to *continue* the struggle, there were economic and political developments during the Civil War.
3. Carnegie *succeeded in* keeping his prices competitive.
4. At the nation's Centennial, people *anticipated the future* with mixed emotions.
5. Eventually, John Bergson *abandoned* the struggle to conquer the prairies.
6. Edison was allowed to *establish* his laboratory in the railroad baggage car.
7. In response to the demand on Wall Street, he *developed* a new stock ticker.
8. Because of the Progressive reformers, people could start *relying on* the protection of the law.

D.   Match the words in column A with those in column B.

A	B
merge	dishonest
contaminated	crowded
appalling	self-reliant
self-sufficient	impure
widespread	extensive
unscrupulous	danger
teeming	horrible
judicious	combine
advocate	supporter
hazard	careful

Structures

A. Following the model, fill in the blanks below by supplying the gerund form of the italicized verb.

Model: *(help)* She enjoyed *helping* Chicago's immigrant poor.

1. *(travel)* When she finished _____ in Europe, Jane Addams decided to establish a settlement.

2. *(leave)* Riis regretted _____ his childhood sweetheart abroad.

3. *(try)* Despite many setbacks, he kept _____ to find a good job.

4. *(argue)* Roosevelt disliked _____ about the urgent need for reform.

5. *(sell)* The company admitted _____ defective merchandise.

6. *(raise)* At a meeting with management, Gompers discussed _____ all salaries.

7. *(refuse)* He resented their _____ to agree to his plan.

8. *(copy)* Jane Addams suggested _____ the British model.

9. *(work)* She didn't mind _____ hard to help Chicago's immigrants.

10. *(build)* Riis proposed _____ a park for the children of his district.

B. Following the model, fill in the blanks below by supplying the gerund form of the italicized verb.

Model: *(establish)* After much hard work, she succeeded in *establishing* the settlement.

1. *(win)* Jane Addams looked forward to _____ the vote.

2. *(work)* She was used to _____ on difficult projects.

3. *(organize)* Instead of _____ violent confrontations, Gompers preferred to use peaceful techniques.

4. *(call)* He would put off _____ a strike until all negotiations had failed.

5. *(cheat)* The company was suspected of _____ its customers.

6. *(sell)* It was accused of _____ contaminated products.

7. *(lose)* They were suddenly afraid of _____ all their customers.

8. *(win)* They were also worried about _____ back the public's confidence.

9. *(send)* Roosevelt took care of _____ a telegram to his supporters.

10. *(be)* Riis took advantage of _____ a reporter to expose the dishonesty of the landlords.

Composition

Choose one of the following.

A. Turn to the photograph on p. 19. In a few brief paragraphs, compare the sod house in that photo with the tenements on Hester Street. Do you think the pioneers faced the same challenges as the immigrants in the large cities? In what ways were their lives similar? In what ways were they different? In your opinion, which offered more opportunities: the great plains or the big cities? Why?

B. According to an English proverb, "Man does not live by bread alone." This means that we need more than material things in order to lead a fully satisfied life. Do you think Jane Addams would agree? Tell the story of her decision to open Hull House in order to support your argument.

C. Pretend that you are a European at the turn of the twentieth century. You live on a poor farm with your parents, your spouse, and four growing children. After several bad harvests, you are finding it increasingly difficult to support this large family. The children are always hungry. Your parents become ill. You try to look for a better farm with more fertile land, but the few good parcels are extremely expensive. To look for work, you travel to every town in the area; you find, however, that many other farmers are also desperate, and that there are simply no jobs for so many people.

    One day, you get a letter from a cousin in America. He lives with his family in a New York City tenement. His wages are low, his housing is poor, and he must face tremendous discrimination. Yet he and his wife, as well as his two oldest sons, have all found employment. They hope to be able to save a little money in order to move to a better apartment. His two youngest children are in school. One is a very good student. She hopes to be able to finish high school and maybe even become a teacher. She has learned English quickly. "If you come over," your cousin concludes, "I can get you a job where I work. But I cannot promise you that life will be easy."

    Write an answer to this letter from America. In accepting or rejecting your cousin's offer, give as many specific details about your future plans as possible.

Topics for Class Discussion

Interviewing a partner or small group of your classmates, talk about the following.

A. Jacob Riis and Andrew Carnegie had a similar traumatic experience. What was this experience? How was it traumatic for each of them? How did each of them cope with it? Was their later success related in a meaningful way to this experience? Why?

B. Enormous numbers of immigrants have come to America. Have many people immigrated to your country? Why did they choose to go to your country? Did they settle in any specific areas of your country? Please give as many details as you can.

C. Jane Addams was a well-known American reformer. In your country's history, is there anyone who fought for social justice and/or political reform? Please describe this person.

D. Chicago and New York are two of America's largest cities. Describe two of your nation's largest cities. Are they near each other or far away? Are they known for different industries? different attractions? What would you recommend to your classmates if they were planning to visit both of them?

 # SOME INTERESTING PLACES TO VISIT

Middle Atlantic Area

Museum of the City of New York
New York, New York

Ellis Island Immigration Museum
Statue of Liberty National Monument
New York

Theodore Roosevelt Birthplace National
    Historical Site
New York, New York

Sagamore Hill National Historic Site
    (Theodore Roosevelt family home)
Oyster Bay, Long Island, New York

Midwestern Area

Jane Addams' Hull House
University of Illinois Campus
Chicago, Illinois

Chicago Historical Society
Chicago, Illinois

Rocky Mountain Area

Theodore Roosevelt National Memorial Park
North Dakota

Mount Rushmore National Memorial
    (great mountain sculptures of Washington,
    Jefferson, Lincoln, and Theodore Roosevelt)
South Dakota

6

An Old Order Passes

World War I

Look at the illustration below. Then, working in pairs or small groups, answer these questions.

1. What is the purpose of this World War I poster? Why has the artist chosen eagles as symbols for the pilots? What kind of person would most likely respond to the poster? Judging from the aircraft in the background, and from what you may know of military history, when do you think this poster was printed?

2. Turn to the photograph on p. 95. Crowded into an old French church are rows of sick and wounded American troops. Has there been heavy fighting around the church? How do you know? Do you think adequate medical care is available to these soldiers? Do they look comfortable? Safe? If they were at this point to see the recruiting poster below, what would they think? Would they agree with its emphasis on the glory of warfare? Why, or why not?

Poster for recruiting American pilots during World War I

JOIN THE
ARMY AIR SERVICE
BE AN AMERICAN EAGLE!
CONSULT YOUR LOCAL DRAFT BOARD. READ THE ILLUSTRATED
BOOKLET AT ANY RECRUITING OFFICE, OR WRITE TO THE CHIEF

HISTORICAL BACKGROUND

1 June 1914. In the capitals of Europe, as the warm and gentle summer days continued, the traditional elegance of an old-world order seemed destined to live on forever. For the carefree members of a privileged aristocracy, for the fashionable families of long-established leisure, and for the prominent representatives of an expanding middle class, life was easy, gracious, and secure. Decades of prosperity had brought peace and plenty. And wealth, in turn, had brought assurance. So in the stately[1] manors, dignified townhouses, and imperial gardens of Europe's elite, there was an optimistic faith in the continent's future. No one could imagine the fateful[2] events that would start a world war in a matter of weeks. Thus, no one could know that those final days in June were but the fading twilight moments of an opulent[3] age. Not until August 1914, did the terrifying truth begin to take shape. Then, as the massive weapons of modern technology exploded across the fields of France, the serenity[4] and confidence of an older culture vanished. "The lamps are going out all over Europe," said British Foreign Secretary, Sir Edward Grey. "We shall not see them lit again in our lifetime."

2 Indeed, Lord Grey was right. From one single event on the 28th of June, there developed over four long years of devastating warfare. Thirty nations, eventually, were drawn into the conflict; among their citizens, more than sixty million soldiers were sent to do battle.[5] There was no peace, no end to the destruction, until November 1918. By then, about ten million men had died in the fighting; another thirty million, approximately, had either been wounded, or captured, or were listed as missing.

3 In the process, around the war-torn sections of Europe, Russia, and the Middle East, civilians had experienced continuous upheaval.[6] While starvation and disease had spread from nation to nation, terrible new weapons had sent death from the skies or from invisible depths of international waters. Cities, towns, and vast country fields lay demolished[7] beyond recognition. Internal revolutions had toppled[8] old governments; imperial dynasties had forever disappeared; and the customs of centuries had crumbled to nothing in the face of such prolonged[9] and indescribable destruction.

4 Thus, when the shattering conflict was finally over, the entire political, economic, and social framework of the twentieth century had changed. Everywhere, for both soldiers and civilians, the long years of violence had swept away the past. And as a new world order began to take shape, no one—whether soldier, president, peasant, or king—could ever return to the life that had vanished with the coming of the world's first modern war.

1. stately: very formal and elegant
2. fateful: bringing about a change in one's destiny
3. opulent: wealthy; luxurious
4. serenity: peace
5. do battle: fight
6. upheaval: great confusion
7. demolish: destroy
8. topple: fall or cause something else to fall
9. prolonged: long and continuous

CAUSES OF WORLD WAR I

5   It all began on the streets of Sarajevo, a town in the Balkan area of Bosnia. Today, the region is part of Bosnia and Herzegovina, but in 1908, Bosnia had been taken over by its powerful neighbor, Austria-Hungary. Angered by this annexation, militants in Bosnia had begun to plot against the Austro-Hungarians. They were assisted in their efforts by fanatical[10] revolutionaries from another neighboring nation: Serbia. Though significantly smaller than Austria-Hungary, Serbia was fiercely nationalistic. Its people were proud of their ancient Slavic heritage and wanted to preserve it at all costs. So some of its radical leaders supported Bosnian subversion,[11] since many of the inhabitants of Bosnia were Serbs. They secretly helped the Sarajevo terrorists to organize a bold assassination plan.

6   On the morning of June 28, this plan was ready to go into effect.[12] Francis Ferdinand, heir to Austria-Hungary's throne, was touring Sarajevo with his beloved wife. Suddenly, shots rang out from the crowded streets and the royal couple slumped[13] down in their seats. Within a short time, both husband and wife were dead. And within a few days, there was an international crisis.

7   Austria-Hungary demanded immediate reparations[14] from its Serbian neighbor. To most of these conditions, Serbia quickly agreed, though it refused to let agents from Austria-Hungary investigate its government. Meanwhile, Austria-Hungary had se-cured a German promise of support. So it rejected Serbia's apologetic responses and began to mobilize its army.[15] Serbia too, had begun mobilization.

8   Because of a complicated network of national alliances, hopes for world peace soon disappeared. Russia rapidly mobilized its army to come to the aid of fellow Slavs in Serbia. Fearing this enormous buildup, Germany answered by declaring war on Russia. France, too, then mobilized its army, for it had promised to support its Russian ally. This, in turn, brought a German declaration of war against the French. Finally, after Germany threatened to invade neutral Belgium, Britain honored its Belgian alliance and entered the war against Germany.

9   Thus, by the beginning of August, the major world powers were rushing to arm for a tremendous and unprecedented confrontation. Little by little, more nations joined the buildup. Bulgaria and the Ottoman Empire (present-day Turkey and some surrounding regions) sided with the Central Powers (Germany and its allies). Italy, Portugal, Greece, Montenegro, and Romania however, declared war against them and sided with the Allies (England and its partners). With the exception of Scandinavia, the Netherlands, Switzerland, and Spain, therefore, the continent of Europe became a massive battle zone.*

10   Across this battlefield, there were two major fronts. Armies of the eastern theater fought in Russia, central Europe, and the Ottoman Empire. The western front referred to the war as it developed across Belgium and France.

---

10. fanatical: violently dedicated
11. subversion: plotting against authority
12. to go into effect: begin
13. slump: slide slowly

14. reparations: amends; attempts to repay an injury
15. mobilize an army: get troops ready for battle

* Deep into Africa and far off in Asia, the fighting also spread quickly. Japan joined the Allies, while colonial territories were often brought into the conflicts of the embattled countries that had colonized them.

TRENCH WARFARE ALONG THE WESTERN FRONT

11   Initially, the Central Powers were successful in the west, for they quickly pushed into the territory of France. But the Allies soon rallied to[16] a stubborn defense, and the battle lines of the western front were rapidly established. From the North Sea down to Switzerland—a distance of about four hundred miles—opposing armies dug into their trenches[17] and waited for the chance to overrun their enemies. It never came. After three long years of indescribable suffering, no army was able to break through this trench line for a decisive[18] victory against its foe. There were, of course, enormous battles—terrible calamities[19] that took the precious lives of millions upon millions of people.* But the long-hoped-for triumph eluded[20] all the troops.

12   So from the end of 1914 until the beginning of 1918, the armies of the western front were deadlocked.[21] Gone were the cavalry charges and great pitched battles[22] of previous generations. Instead, as young men were sent against enemy trenches, they were mowed[23] down by the machine guns of modern technology. Yet because of other new "advances"—because of long-range artillery,[24] aerial bombardment,[25] gas attacks, and tank maneuvers[26]—the men could not find safety in their own inadequate trenches. They had no alternative but to "go over the top" toward the rapid-fire bullets of automatic guns. Here indeed was a new kind of conflict—more savage and extensive than any the world had ever known. It was a war of attrition,[27] a fight to the final casualty. So as the months became years, the death toll[28] soared. But except for a few small desperate gains, the fortified trench line remained unchanged. In fact, by 1918, it hadn't moved in either direction for more than several miles.

EASTERN FRONT CONFLICTS AND THE RUSSIAN REVOLUTION

13   No such deadlock immobilized[29] the eastern front. Despite initial losses to Germany, Russia made significant gains against the Austrian army. This caused Germany to launch a new offensive. Underfed and poorly equipped, the Russians fought back fiercely; but the troops of the Czar suffered staggering losses during their long and bitter campaigns. So in 1917, tensions within the Russian Empire exploded. The Romanov Czar was finally forced to abdicate,[30] and a series of revolutions brought

---

16. rally to: recover energy for
17. trench: long, narrow hole in the ground
18. decisive: significant; very important
19. calamity: tragedy
20. elude: escape from
21. deadlocked: unable to move
22. pitched battle: battle organized in an open field
23. mow: cut
24. artillery: guns
25. aerial bombardment: attacks from the air
26. maneuver: movements
27. attrition: loss of people
28. death toll: total number lost
29. immobilize: keep from moving
30. abdicate: give up royal power

* For example, after their first drive toward Paris, the Central Powers were finally stopped in the three-day battle of the Marne. The casualties numbered well over half a million, but there was no final victory for either side. Later, in 1916, the Germans again launched a powerful campaign into the territory of France around Verdun. The battle raged for months. Before it was over at the end of the year, France and Germany had each lost about a half a million men. Still more appalling were the statistics at the Somme—a counter-offensive launched by the Allies while the battle of Verdun was in its fury. From Britain, France, and Germany combined, there were 1,250,000 casualties.

the Bolsheviks* to power. Then, under the leadership of Nikolai Lenin, Russia decided on a truce[31] with the Central Powers. Though the conditions of peace were extremely harsh, the Russians accepted them. There was no other way, their leaders felt, for Russia to reorganize after the long years of chaos.

14   Peace with Russia meant that the Central Powers could concentrate their forces on the western front. But the Allies also had an extra advantage. For in April 1917, after almost three years of neutrality, the United States had entered the war on the side of the Allied powers.

15   America's president, Woodrow Wilson, had wanted to stay out of Europe's conflict. Indeed, when elected to the presidency in 1912, he had intended to concentrate on Progressive legislation and other domestic reforms. But the outbreak of war in 1914 had changed everything, and international tensions had increasingly become the focus of Wilson's administration. In 1916, in spite of these tensions, he had still stressed neutrality and had successfully run for re-election. Yet in the first year of his second term of office, he had reversed his position and had joined the Allied cause.

AMERICAN INVOLVEMENT

16   What brought America into the First World War? The main issue centered upon submarine attacks in the Atlantic. To keep supplies from reaching the enemy, Britain had imposed a blockade[32] on Germany's ports. So for Germany, gaining control of the seas became critical. Not only was it necessary to cut off British commerce, but it was also important to break the embargo[33] that was causing such a shortage of food and equipment. In 1915, therefore, Germany intensified a submarine offensive against ships in the vicinity[34] of the British Isles. This meant that passenger boats and merchant vessels, as well as military ships, were in grave[35] and immediate danger.

17   Americans were angered by this tough naval campaign. They felt that American passengers, as neutrals, had a right to safe passage across the Atlantic. But in spite of protests from President Wilson, the submarine attacks continued. In May 1915, when the British liner *Lusitania* was sunk, almost two thousand civilian lives were lost. The number included over one hundred Americans. So Wilson then made stronger demands for an end to the offensive against unarmed ships.

18   At first, Germany complied with[36] Wilson's request, as the Central Powers were unwilling to risk war with another powerful nation. But in 1917, when it became clear that the decisive months of fighting were at hand,[37] Germany resumed the submarine campaign. Its people, both at home and on the front, were starving. Military supplies were running low, and there was such a need for soldiers that boys were being drafted ahead of time. To their leaders it was clear, after over three years of increasing exertion,[38] that the nation could not hold on[39] forever. The British blockade and the western front both had to be broken quickly.

---

31. truce: end to the fighting
32. impose a blockade: keep enemy ships within their harbor
33. embargo: trade barrier
34. vicinity: area

35. grave: serious
36. comply with: agree to
37. at hand: near
38. exertion: effort
39. hold on: continue to struggle

* Bolsheviks: This group became the Communist party.

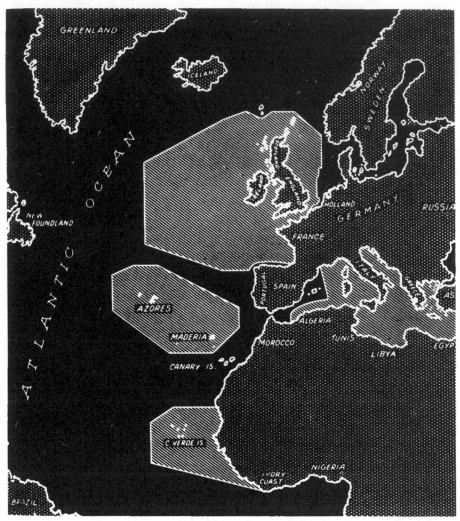

No ship was safe in shaded areas—unrestricted submarine war of 1917.

19   This ambitious attempt proved disastrous. The renewal of unrestricted submarine warfare caused America to enter the war. And America's entry into the war made victory for the Central Powers impossible. For the appearance of two million Yankee soldiers brought life to the exhausted men of the Allied campaign. And though American casualties totaled almost a hundred thousand, the American Expeditionary Force (AEF) and its extensive supplies gave critical support to the last Allied campaigns. In France, the AEF's soldiers contributed to important victories at Château-Thierry, Belleau Wood, St.-Mihiel, and the Meuse-Argonne campaign. Ultimately, against these campaigns, the drained and weary remnants[40] of the Central Powers

---

40. remnants: small remaining number

* Map by Charles G. Lancelot. Caption by Milton Lancelot. From *Clear for Action* by Foster Hailey and Milton Lancelot (New York: Bonanza Books, a division of Crown Publishers, Inc., by arrangement with Meredith Press, 1964), p. 115.

crumbled. There were internal revolts in Austria-Hungary; Bulgaria and the Ottoman Empire surrendered; then Germany and the Allies began to negotiate for peace.

20   On November 11, 1918, an armistice went into effect. Guns were silenced across miles of crowded trenches, and the terrible explosions were heard no more. But for the survivors, broken in body and wounded in spirit, nothing would ever be the same. They little remembered the streets of Sarajevo, and the pistol that had somehow started it all. They only knew that their own worlds had been shattered by the unspeakable horrors of the world's first total war.

Europe, 1918

No battle statistics or military summaries can give an accurate picture of the First World War's impact.[1] No history textbook can ever fully describe how the war changed the lives of those who lived it. But among those who experienced the interminable[2] suffering, some immortal[3] accounts of the bitter years remain. All the physical pain, the yearning[4] for lost innocence, the loneliness, and the terror can be found in the works of some writers who survived. In their profound and haunting[5] novels, the massive campaigns of the war are recreated; we see desperate civilians and terrified troops fighting in vain against the mounting confusion; we enter their world of bravery and passion; and as we follow their journeys from hope to despair, we weep for the trauma that so shook the world.

One American writer—Ernest Hemingway—is especially remembered for his timeless account of the First World War. At age 18, Hemingway was sent to the Italian campaign against Austria-Hungary. He had volunteered for ambulance duty and had been shipped to the Italian front by the American Red Cross. Seriously wounded during a machine-gun attack, he was hospitalized in Milan for several months.

After the war, Hemingway went back to his home in Illinois, but his experiences, like those of many soldiers, had left him restless. So he moved to Toronto, where he worked as a reporter—a profession he had begun before the war. From Toronto, he traveled to Chicago; then he returned to Europe in 1921. In 1926, he completed *The Sun Also Rises*—a novel about postwar disillusionment.[6] It was his first great critical success. Three years later, still filled with the themes of the war and its effect, he published *A Farewell to Arms*. It has remained one of America's great literary classics.

Essentially, the book is a love story, a deeply moving[7] tale of passion set against the backdrop of World War I. Frederick Henry, an American volunteer with the ambulance corps, is wounded during a fierce attack on the Italian front. As he recuperates, he falls in love with Catherine Barkely, an English nurse on duty in Milan. Slowly, in the barbaric[8] confusion that closes in on them, the lovers find a fragile peace together. But their destiny is a tragic one; ultimately, they must share in the doom[9] of a condemned generation.

In the following selection, Frederick Henry has returned to duty after his long recuperation.[10] He hears a terrible account of the fighting that has gone on in his absence. There are rumors of a new Austrian offensive, yet in spite of increasing despair, some of Henry's colleagues still hope that their sacrifices will not have been in vain. In response, Henry keeps a diplomatic silence, for he has seen too much pain to have kept any ideals. As he considers the futility[11] of heroic dreams, a bombardment escalates in the countryside around him.

---

1. impact: effect
2. interminable: without end
3. immortal: everlasting
4. yearning: longing, deep desire
5. haunting: never to be forgotten
6. disillusionment: loss of ideals

7. moving: emotionally affecting
8. barbaric: uncivilized
9. doom: tragic destiny
10. recuperation: recovery from illness or accident
11. futility: uselessness

from
A Farewell to Arms

by ERNEST HEMINGWAY

I did not say anything. I was always embarrassed by the words sacred, glorious, and sacrifice and the expression in vain. We had heard them, sometimes standing in the rain almost out of earshot,[12] so that only the shouted words came through, and had read them, on proclamations[13] that were slapped up by billposters over other proclamations, now for a long time, and I had seen nothing sacred, and the things that were glorious had no glory and the sacrifices were like the stockyards[14] at Chicago if nothing was done with the meat except to bury it. There were many words that you could not stand to hear and finally only the names of places had dignity. Certain numbers were the same way and certain dates and these with the names of the places were all you could say and have them mean anything. Abstract words such as glory, honor, courage, or hallow[15] were obscene beside the concrete names of villages, the numbers of roads, the names of rivers, the numbers of regiments and the dates. Gino was a patriot, so he said things that separated us sometimes, but he was also a fine boy and I understood his being a patriot. He was born one. He left with Peduzzi in the car to go back to Gorizia....

The wind rose in the night and at three o'clock in the morning with the rain coming in sheets there was a bombardment and the Croatians came over across the mountain meadows and through patches of woods and into the front line. They fought in the dark in the rain and a counterattack of scared men from the second line drove them back. There was much shelling and many rockets in the rain and machine-gun and rifle fire all along the line. They did not come again and it was quieter and between the gusts[16] of wind and rain we could hear the sound of a great bombardment far to the north.

The wounded were coming into the post, some were carried on stretchers, some walking and some were brought on the backs of men that came across the field. They were wet to the skin and all were scared. We filled two cars with stretcher cases as they came up from the cellar of the post and as I shut the door of the second car and fastened it I felt the rain on my face turn to snow. The flakes were coming heavy and fast in the rain....

---

12. out of earshot: too far away to be heard
13. proclamation: official announcement
14. stockyard: place where animals are killed

15. hallow: consecrate; make holy
16. gust: sudden wind

✖ EXERCISES

Reading Comprehension

A. Choose the best answer for the following:

1. According to information in paragraph 1,
   a. Europe's aristocrats had long been afraid of war.
   b. Europe's aristocrats were hoping for a war.
   c. Europe's aristocrats never imagined the terrible destruction that lay ahead.

2. Paragraph 2
   a. continues what has previously been discussed.
   b. contrasts with what has previously been discussed.
   c. has no relation to what has previously been discussed.

3. The main topic of paragraph 3 is
   a. the causes of World War I.
   b. the effects of World War I.
   c. the major campaigns of World War I.

4. Paragraph 4
   a. presents a summary of paragraphs 1, 2, and 3.
   b. presents a contrast to paragraphs 1, 2, and 3.
   c. introduces an entirely new topic.

5. What is the topic of paragraphs 5 and 6?
   a. the causes of World War I.
   b. the effects of World War I.
   c. the major campaigns of World War I.

6. From the assassination in Sarajevo, an international crisis developed because
   a. Europe's aristocrats were angry over the death of Francis Ferdinand.
   b. Europe's nations were linked together in a complicated system of alliances.
   c. people were hoping to end the Russian Revolution.

7. As it developed in World War I, trench warfare was
   a. efficient but destructive.
   b. useless and destructive.
   c. safe and efficient.

8. The major effect of World War I in Russia was
   a. friendship with Germany.
   b. friendship with America.
   c. the rise of Lenin and the Communist party.

9. What was the issue that brought America into World War I?
   a. rivalry with Communist Russia
   b. submarine warfare in the Atlantic
   c. hatred of Francis Ferdinand

10. From what is said in the final paragraphs, we may assume that
    a. many of the soldiers were proud to die for a worthy cause.
    b. some of the soldiers did not even know what they were fighting for.
    c. the soldiers who survived escaped all suffering.

B. **Fill in the blanks below with an appropriate word from the following list.**

Central Powers	*Allies*	*Czar*	*United States*
eastern theater	*Sarajevo*	*Germany*	*Russia*
Francis Ferdinand	*Lenin*	*armistice*	*western front*

After the assassination of _____ in _____ , hopes for world peace quickly died. For by the beginning of August 1914, the major world powers were rushing toward a confrontation. Germany and its allies were called the _____ . England and its partners were the _____ . The struggle between them would take millions of lives and totally alter the modern world.

There were two major battlefronts on the continent of Europe. Armies of the _____ fought in Russia, Central Europe, and the Ottoman Empire. The _____ referred to the war in Belgium and France. This endless trench line was deadlocked for almost four years.

But there was no such deadlock in eastern Europe. There, in long and bitter campaigns, the armies of _____ suffered staggering losses. Finally, there was a revolution. The _____ was forced to abdicate and _____ came to power. His country then agreed upon a truce.

Meanwhile, after almost three years of neutrality, the _____ had entered the war on the side of the Allies. It had taken this step because of _____ 's policy of unrestricted submarine warfare. Fresh and energetic, American soldiers brought life to the Allied campaign. So within a year, the exhausted remnants of the Central Powers crumbled. On November 11, 1918, an _____ was agreed upon, and the terrible ordeal of World War I was over at last.

C. **Put the following statements in the correct order.**

1. a. Austria-Hungary annexed Bosnia.
   b. Francis Ferdinand was assassinated.
   c. With Serbian assistance, Bosnian terrorists planned a secret attack.
2. a. Francis Ferdinand was assassinated.
   b. The continent of Europe became a massive battle zone.
   c. The world's major powers declared war on one another.
3. a. Lenin came to power.
   b. Russia's troops suffered staggering losses.
   c. The Russian Czar was forced to abdicate.

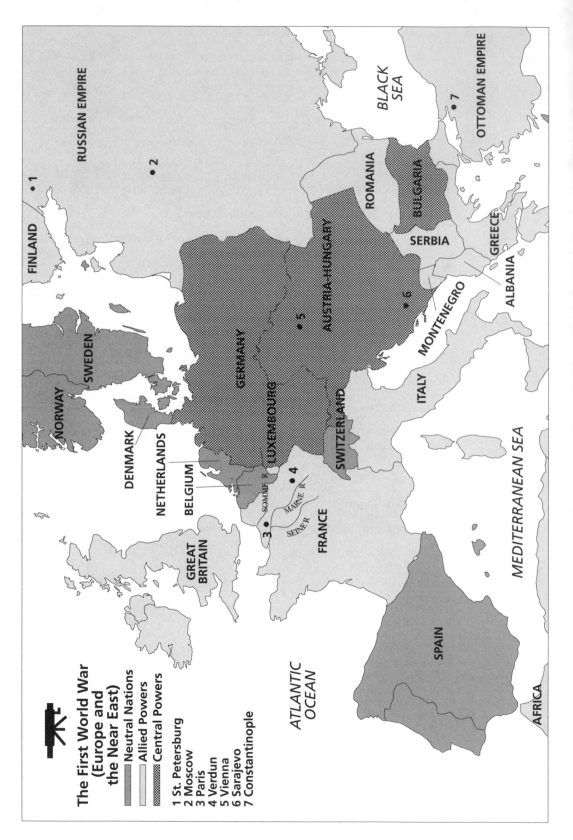

The First World War
(Europe and
the Near East)

Neutral Nations
Allied Powers
Central Powers

1 St. Petersburg
2 Moscow
3 Paris
4 Verdun
5 Vienna
6 Sarajevo
7 Constantinople

FINLAND

RUSSIAN EMPIRE

•1

•2

NORWAY

SWEDEN

DENMARK

NETHERLANDS

BELGIUM

LUXEMBOURG

GERMANY

AUSTRIA-HUNGARY

ROMANIA

BULGARIA

SERBIA

GREECE

ALBANIA

MONTENEGRO

BLACK
SEA

•7

OTTOMAN EMPIRE

SWITZERLAND

ITALY

SOMME R.

MARNE R.

SEINE R.

3•

•4

•5

•6

FRANCE

GREAT
BRITAIN

ATLANTIC
OCEAN

SPAIN

AFRICA

MEDITERRANEAN SEA

4. a. Britain imposed a blockade on Germany's ports.
   b. The United States entered World War I.
   c. The *Lusitania* sank.
5. a. American soldiers joined the Allies in Europe.
   b. An armistice was agreed upon to end the First World War.
   c. Governments and armies among the Central Powers collapsed.

D. **Study the map on p. 100. Then answer the following:**

1. The war began with a pistol shot in Sarajevo. What nation was Sarajevo a part of at that time? Why was this a source of tension?
2. To the south of Austria-Hungary was a small but fiercely nationalistic country. Some of its radicals helped the terrorists of Sarajevo. What nation was this?
3. Name four major nations on the side of the Central Powers.
4. Name six nations that remained neutral during the war.
5. Name ten nations on the side of the Allied powers.
6. The Battle of Verdun was one of the most horrible confrontations of the war. Before it was over, France and Germany had each lost about half a million men. In what country did this take place?
7. During the war, which nation experienced a socialist revolution—one that would profoundly change the course of twentieth-century history?

E. **Match the definitions in column B with the items in column A.**

A	B
Bosnia	war zone in Russia, Central Europe, and the Ottoman Empire
Sarajevo	
Serbia	trench line from Belgium through France to the Alps
Francis Ferdinand	leader of revolution in Russia
Central Powers	Austria-Hungary, Germany, and their allies
Allied Powers	agreement to end the fighting
Western front	England, France, and their partners
Eastern theater	Balkan region annexed by Austria-Hungary
Czar Nicholas II	town in Bosnia where World War I began
Lenin	British ship sunk by German submarine
Lusitania	heir to Austro-Hungarian throne
Armistice	last ruler of Russia's Romanov dynasty
	Slavic nation to the south of Austria-Hungary

Vocabulary

A. From the following list, choose the words that best substitute for the italicized words in the sentences below. Make all necessary changes.

gracious *network* *sacred* *imperial*
assurance *alternative* *cellar* *in vain*
framework *protest*

1. For the aristocrats of Europe, life before the war was *elegant* and secure.
2. The soldiers had no *choice* but to go over the top of the trenches.
3. The war changed the entire *basis* of twentieth century society.
4. In the gardens *of the emperor,* there was an optimistic faith in the continent's future.
5. In Hemingway's story, the wounded are brought up from the *basement* of the military post.
6. Hemingway's hero is embarrassed by words like *holy.*
7. He knows that many of their sacrifices have been *meaningless.*
8. For the aristocrats before the war, wealth had brought *confidence.*
9. There was a complex *interlocking system* of alliances.
10. Despite Wilson's *complaints,* the submarine attacks continued.

B. Choose the words that are closest in meaning to the italicized words in the following sentences.

1. In the *stately* manors of Europe's elite, there was confidence in the future.
   a. stone b. ancient c. elegant
2. No one knew that those final days in June were the twilight moments of an *opulent* age.
   a. traditional b. wealthy c. privileged
3. As massive weapons exploded across Europe, the *serenity* of an older culture vanished.
   a. peace b. wealth c. privileges
4. Throughout the war, civilians experienced continuous *upheaval.*
   a. attacks b. confusion c. terror
5. Never had people known such *prolonged* and appalling destruction.
   a. vicious b. modern c. long-lasting
6. There was no *decisive* battle for the soldiers in the trenches.
   a. easy b. significant c. short
7. There were, however, many *calamities.*
   a. tragedies b. cease-fires c. bombardments
8. Millions upon millions of men were *mowed down.*
   a. imprisoned b. cut down c. promoted
9. There was submarine warfare in the *vicinity* of the British Isles.
   a. waters b. ports c. area
10. Passenger ships, as well as military vessels, were in *grave* danger.
    a. serious b. unexpected c. moderate

C.   Match the words in column A with those in column B.

A	B
demolish	cease-fire
topple	everlasting
slump	guns
elude	movement
artillery	escape from
maneuver	uncivilized
truce	destroy
impact	fall
immortal	effect
barbaric	slide

Structures

A.   In each pair below, fill in the correct form of the participle.

1. terrifying, terrified
   a. Soldiers in the trenches were _____ of gas attacks.
   b. For those who lived it, the war was a _____ experience.

2. devastating, devastated
   a. Civilians were _____ by the constant upheavals.
   b. The tank maneuvers and aerial attacks were _____ .

3. appalling, appalled
   a. Around the world, people were _____ by the war's destruction.
   b. The death toll for both sides was _____ .

4. shattering, shattered
   a. When the _____ conflict was over, the entire framework of the modern world had changed.
   b. Civilians as well as soldiers were _____ by the war.

5. exhausting, exhausted
   a. American soldiers brought life to the _____ Allied troops.
   b. It was _____ to live in the dangerous, dirty trenches.

B.   Following the model, change the sentences below.

Model: Intelligent diplomats could have avoided war.
   → War could have been avoided by intelligent diplomats.

1. The plot must have horrified many of the Serbians.
2. Lord Grey may have received secret information.
3. Enemy submarines should have warned the ship's passengers.
4. Submarine warfare might have broken the British embargo.
5. Lenin could have continued the war.

Composition

Choose one of the following.

A.   Reread paragraphs 16–20 in the Historical Background. Then in your own words, tell how the United States was finally drawn into the First World War.

B.   Complete the following introductory sentences in one well-developed paragraph. (You may wish to refer to paragraphs 1–4 in the Historical Background reading.)

"As World War I began, Lord Grey sadly observed, 'The lamps are going out all over Europe. We shall not see them lit again in our lifetime.' Indeed, he was right. After four long years of devastating warfare, nothing in the world was ever the same. For example, …"

C.   There is an English proverb which says, "Let sleeping dogs lie." It means that it can sometimes be disastrous to disturb a powerful and potentially dangerous opponent. Retell the story of the events that led to World War I, showing how a terrorist attack on a great nation's representative led to immense and tragic consequences.

D.   Like Willa Cather and Edith Wharton, Hemingway found the subject of his greatest novel in the experiences of his own youth. Reread the original selection and its introduction on pp. 96–97. Then write two brief paragraphs. In the first, describe Hemingway's involvement in World War I; in the second, tell the story of *A Farewell to Arms,* showing any similarities between the story and the life of the novelist.

Topics for Class Discussion

Interviewing a partner or small group of your classmates, talk about the following.

A.   Aerial bombardment, tanks, and automatic weapons were technological advances that brought great harm to all people. Can you think of other scientific breakthroughs which have caused ill, as well as good, in the modern world?

B.   Reread the first four paragraphs of the Historical Background reading. What do you think Sir Edward Grey meant when he said, "The lamps are going out all over Europe. We shall not see them lit again in our lifetime"?

C.   How would you describe Hemingway's style as it appears in the brief selection from *A Farewell to Arms?* Is it very fancy or rather plain? Are there many difficult words or is the vocabulary, on the whole, rather easy and direct? Is there a lot of repetition? Do you think that this style of writing is appropriate for the subject? Why?

D.   Notice that Hemingway makes specific mention of the weather in his description of the escalating bombardment. What kind of weather is it? Throughout the book, there are similar references to the same kind of weather. What do you think it symbolizes?

SOME INTERESTING PLACES TO VISIT

Middle Atlantic Area

United States Military Academy
West Point, New York

United States Naval Academy
Annapolis, Maryland

The Tomb of the Unknown Soldiers
Arlington National Cemetery
Arlington, Virginia

National Air and Space Museum
Smithsonian Institution
Washington, D.C.

Southeastern Area

Ernest Hemingway Home and Museum
Key West, Florida

7

The Roaring Twenties

Explosive Reaction

PREREADING

Look at the illustration below. Then, working in pairs or small groups, answer these questions.

1. Describe the couple in the picture. What are they doing? How are they dressed? How would you describe their manner?

2. Turn to the photograph of Edith Wharton on p. 10. It was taken only about twenty years before the picture below. Did fashions change greatly in America during that brief period? Do you think this change represented a corresponding difference in life styles and attitudes? What do you think might have caused such a change?

Life magazine, February 1926; a Jazz Age flapper dances the Charleston in this famous cover drawing by John Held, Jr.

1   After the armistice that ended World War I, a conference for peace was organized in France. So in December 1918, President Wilson sailed for Europe to take part in the negotiations. It was indeed a historic voyage, for Wilson was the first American president to travel to Europe while in office. He had decided to cross the ocean to promote cooperation among the leaders of the troubled, war-torn countries. His mission, he had insisted, was to bring about the Fourteen Points—a program for justice and international harmony that Wilson had proposed toward the end of the war.

FOURTEEN POINTS AND THE LEAGUE OF NATIONS

2   Central to the Fourteen Points was Wilson's call for a "peace without victory." Like Abraham Lincoln, he wanted the end of war to be an end to bitterness and mistrust. Thus, among other things, he proposed a withdrawal[1] from conquered territory, an end to secret treaties, freedom of the seas, unrestricted[2] trade, arms reduction, and the right of self-determination[3] for subject peoples.[4] Most significant was his final request for a global association, a League of Nations, which would settle disputes among its members and thus guarantee a new world security.

3   Unfortunately, events soon made a mockery[5] of Wilson's ideals. For across the devastated lands of Europe, thousands of people were starving and homeless. Their leaders were exhausted by war and shocked by its terrible aftermath.[6] Afraid to trust their former enemies, they were suspicious of Wilson's generous proposals. So as the bargaining at Versailles* continued, the concept of a "peace without victory" was forgotten. Harsh demands and bitter penalties were placed upon the Central Powers. But to Wilson's satisfaction, the League of Nations was not eliminated[7] from the terms of the final treaty. This league, he believed, would undo all the harm that had been done by the ministers at Versailles.

4   However, events again mocked Wilson's plans. When he returned to America, the president found that he had lost much support. People objected to the Treaty of Versailles as it was finally presented to Congress. They thought it would involve the country too deeply in Europe's affairs. They also feared it would jeopardize the nation's future independence. But Wilson—proud and unyielding[8]—would not agree to modifications. He wanted Americans to show a total acceptance of his efforts at Versailles. Only then, he felt, would the ideals that he cherished have a chance to transform a lost and ravaged[9] world. Thus, in the end, Wilson the moralist defeated Wilson the politician. Twice his treaty was put to a vote, and twice it was rejected by a divided Senate. Finally, the United States made a separate peace with Germany, and hopes for American participation in the League of Nations died.

---

1. withdrawal: removal
2. unrestricted: without rules or barriers
3. right of self-determination: right to choose one's own political future
4. subject peoples: people under the authority of another nation

5. mockery: joke
6. aftermath: results of violence
7. eliminate: remove
8. unyielding: stubborn
9. ravage: destroy

* Versailles—French palace where peace conference was held.

THE ROARING TWENTIES

5 Meanwhile, in the presidential elections of 1920, a warm and easygoing Warren G. Harding took the place of Woodrow Wilson. Clearly—with the terrible warfare over at last—Americans were looking for a new direction. Many were hoping to put the past and its illusions behind them. Many were determined to turn squarely toward the present to enjoy whatever pleasures it might offer. Thus, from 1920 to 1929, the Jazz Age exploded across America. It was a time for celebration, a time for forgetting— a giddy[10] decade of mounting prosperity and radical social change.

6 For example, there was a significant shift in the financial habits of many Americans. Under pressures from the war, the nation's economy had rapidly developed. So new consumer items—costly but exciting—were beginning to appear from coast to coast. There were washing machines, refrigerators, cosmetics, cars, and clothing. And since there was also a lot of cheap credit,[11] Americans began to buy. They went on a shopping spree that lasted almost ten years. Older habits of payments in cash were abandoned. Savings accounts just as quickly disappeared. For few could resist the temptation to buy luxuries that had never been dreamed of in a pioneer past.

7 In addition to these economic developments, there was also a change in women's status in the twenties. Women had contributed greatly to the war effort both at home and abroad. They had won their voting rights, finally, after almost a century of struggle.* Now, having joined with enthusiasm in the postwar celebrations, many women refused to return to a subservient[12] domestic role. They were determined to assert themselves,[13] to find a long-denied freedom. So in their fashions as in their manners, they rebelled. Skirts climbed up from ankle length to an inch above the knee. Hair that had been tied back tightly was cut off straight and short. Instead of stately waltzes, these flappers[14] danced the Charleston. They smoked and drank and raced their convertibles around elegant suburbs and through crowded city streets. More than anyone else, they were the liberated leaders of a national upheaval.

PROHIBITION

8 Not everyone, of course, joined in the Jazz Age revolution. In fact, throughout the twenties, there was a continuous current[15] of conservative reaction to the dynamic tendencies of the times. For instance, there was Prohibition. During World War I, an amendment forbidding the "manufacture, sale, or transportation of intoxicating liquors within ... the United States" was proposed. Drinking lowered the army's efficiency, it was argued. Its production also used up the grain that was needed for a wartime food supply. So in 1920, after patriotic Americans had passed this

---

10. giddy: dizzy; changeable
11. cheap credit: money that can be easily borrowed
12. subservient: inferior; under another's authority
13. assert oneself: insist on one's rights

14. flappers: liberated ladies of the Jazz Age (They occasionally wore open boots which made a flapping noise as they walked.)
15. current: direction of flowing water; trend

* Adopted in 1920, the Nineteenth Amendment to the United States Constitution provided, finally, for universal female suffrage. (See *America: Past and Present*, Vol. II, Unit 9, for an analysis of the great struggle leading to the Nineteenth Amendment.)

amendment, Prohibition went into effect. And until the law's repeal[16] more than thirteen years later, the United States was, officially, "dry." No one could legally buy, sell, make, or ship intoxicating beverages. This did not mean, of course, that no one drank. On the contrary. For the prosperous new business leaders, for the flappers and their boyfriends, for the trendy[17] consumers and Jazz Age high society, alcohol—as a forbidden pleasure—became all the more desirable. Secret bars, or speak-easies, appeared across the nation. Rumrunning, or smuggling, spread out along the borders. And bootleggers—illegal distributors—began to earn their fabulous[18] profits. Unfortunately, as Prohibition continued, organized crime also grew rapidly. For rival gangs[19] controlled key cities where there was money to be made on the public's thirst. Al Capone's mob ruled Chicago; others ran New York, Philadelphia, Kansas City, and Detroit. Gangland killings were commonplace,[20] and mobsters[21] terrorized uncooperative agents who threatened to interfere with their operation.

9   Thus, in the end, the conservative endeavor[22] to dry up America backfired.[23] The country was determined to have its fun. And in this determination, people had the limitless support of three new and powerful allies. These were radio, movies, and the car.

10   Though the radio was invented before World War I, commercial broadcasting in America did not develop before 1920. After that date, living rooms rocked with the rhythms of jazz as Americans danced to the exciting new music of Louis Armstrong's trumpet or Duke Ellington's band.

11   At the same time, movie screens were constantly projecting irresistible images of the new good life. First came the superstars of silent pictures—stars like Charlie Chaplin, Rudolf Valentino, and Gloria Swanson. Then, after 1927, heroes of the talkies began to thrill fans with daring scenes of love and adventure. Even getting to the theater was an exhilarating[24] experience, for as the prices of Ford's cars came down, the freedom provided by new automobiles spread. Unchaperoned,[25] and unconcerned, young people could at last escape from the watchful eyes of their elders. Like the bootleggers and movie queens, they could turn away from the conventions[26] of the past and join up with the generation in revolt.

12   Needless to say, there was a price to be paid for all the merrymaking[27] and the debt. As the decade wore on, America's financial situation worsened. Also, the carefree crowds could rarely find a lasting satisfaction. All-night parties and shocking fashions were less and less exciting. Fancy motorcars became a bore. Yet World War I had forever buried the comfort and security of the past. As its finest writer noted, Jazz Age society was increasingly troubled by bittersweet longings for a

---

16. repeal: remove a law that had previously been passed
17. trendy: fashionable
18. fabulous: great
19. gang: rough, disorderly group
20. commonplace: customary, usual
21. mobsters: gangsters, criminals

22. endeavor: attempt
23. backfire: fail
24. exhilarating: very exciting
25. unchaperoned: unsupervised
26. conventions: traditions
27. merrymaking: celebrating

simpler era. It had "grown up to find all Gods dead, all wars fought, all faiths in man shaken...."*

13 Because of such profound disillusion, Americans in the Roaring Twenties were fanatical hero-worshipers.[28] They wanted new gods to replace those that had died. So they wildly adored[29] their screen stars, athletes, millionaires, and musicians. Among all the many celebrities, one name, especially, stood out. One figure became a legend in his time by capturing the imagination of young and old alike. This was Charles A. Lindbergh, an American pilot who made the first successful solo flight across the Atlantic Ocean.

FOCUS ON CHARLES LINDBERGH

14 Born in Detroit in 1902, Lindbergh was raised on the family farm in Minnesota. His grandfather, a sturdy pioneer, had come from Sweden to America in 1860. His father was a respected attorney and a U.S. Congressman from his Minnesota district. But although he admired his energetic father, Lindbergh had no great interest in either politics or the law. Like his grandfather, he was drawn to the challenge of unconquered frontiers. In fact, as he grew older, one desire increasingly took hold of him. He was determined to become a pilot in the dawning age of flight.

15 To learn to fly, Lindbergh left the University of Wisconsin in 1922. Two years later, he was an air cadet in the United States Army. After graduating with highest honors in 1925, Lindbergh became an airmail pilot on the route from St. Louis to Chicago. One day, while flying the mail, he began to shape an ambitious plan. A Frenchman had offered $25,000 to anyone who could fly the Atlantic nonstop. Lindbergh decided to compete for the prize.

16 With financial backing[30] from some business leaders in St. Louis, he quickly designed a special plane for the attempt. Then, in the early morning of May 20, 1927, Lindbergh took off from a muddy runway near Manhattan. Flying north, he passed over Cape Cod, Nova Scotia, and the tip of Newfoundland. At this point, in his fragile, single-engined craft, he headed out to sea. With no radio for communication (the plane was already overloaded with fuel), and with only a simple compass and a map for guidance, Lindbergh was determined to cross the north Atlantic.

17 In the event of a crash, he knew, there would be little chance of survival, for the *Spirit of St. Louis* was far from the ship lanes of the middle Atlantic. Still, in spite of the risks, Lindbergh had chosen this lonely northern path—the most dangerous and yet the shortest route to Europe. He was a gifted[31] navigator, a superb pilot, and a man of rare courage and strength. Yet others, just as brave, had attempted to cross this sea, and no one had completed the nonstop flight before.** In fact, just days before Lindbergh's departure, two French aviators en route to the United States had suddenly disappeared. Others had crashed in test flights or on takeoffs. So Lindbergh allowed

---

28. worship: love, display total devotion
29. adore: worship

30. financial backing: financial assistance
31. gifted: very talented

* F. Scott Fitzgerald, *This Side of Paradise.*
** In 1919, two British pilots had flown from Newfoundland to Ireland. No one had yet made a nonstop flight from the United States to continental Europe.

himself to have no false hopes. It would take both skill and good fortune, he knew, to finish the 3,600-mile flight.

18   Daylight, like the American continent, vanished beyond Newfoundland. Then often, during the long dark hours of his first night aloft,[32] Lindbergh was surrounded

Enduring symbol of the American dream, Charles A. Lindbergh became a national hero during the wild and irresponsible Roaring Twenties.

32. aloft: in the air

by fog or tossed[33] by the winds of fierce local storms. He had to climb over the clouds for a glimpse[34] of the stars or drop down toward the sea to gauge[35] the wind's direction. Near the water, there was danger from the icebergs below; at higher altitudes, the air was bitter cold. Yet Lindbergh managed to stay on course. He continued to head eastward in the darkness.

19   Light returned with the dawn on his second day aloft. Lindbergh's ordeal,[36] however, continued. For a desperate urge to get some sleep increased with the warm rays of the sun. Hour after hour, in the intensifying glare, he fought this deadly exhaustion. Finally, as if in a dream, Lindbergh saw a beautiful sight. Land birds! A little further on, there were fishing boats tossing in the rough waves of the sea. And then, like a mirage,[37] the green fields of Ireland came into view. Smiling joyously at the upturned faces, he swooped[38] over the coast in a magnificent salute before turning his little plane toward England. Another sunset colored the skies as he reached the coast of France. And as he headed toward Paris, darkness had once again enveloped the earth.

20   But at Le Bourget field, the crowds had already gathered. They had had reports of his steady approach from observers in Britain and France. So they had flooded the field with the lights of their cars and were waiting for the impossible—for a tiny silver plane to arrive from America. At 10:20 P.M. it happened. The *Spirit of St. Louis* appeared in the sky and then landed, gracefully, in Europe. Its pilot received a tumultuous[39] greeting that lasted for days in the French capital. Then, in other European cities, the enthusiastic welcome was repeated. But as great as these celebrations were, nothing equaled the spectacular[40] reception that Lindbergh received in the United States. He returned with his plane on the American ship *Memphis* to find his fellow Americans wild with delight. There were speeches, parties, tours, and parades. And unlike many a superstar's fame, the excitement Lindbergh generated[41] refused to die down. Somehow, he was special, and the public couldn't get enough of him.

21   What was the secret of Lindbergh's appeal? What was the source of his tremendous popularity? He was young, to be sure, and very handsome, with a boyish charm and a flashing smile that people found enchanting. But it was more than personal charisma. Lindbergh was a symbol, an image of the noble pioneer that had long since vanished from America. Sturdy, confident, and self-controlled, he was also a modest man of integrity. Thus, in the corrupt, confusing twenties, he was a living reminder of the frontier values that were central to America's past. He also represented the future, for his achievement led to the limitless possibilities of modern aviation. So when they cheered for Charles Lindbergh, the crowds were applauding the American dream—renewed and reshaped to fit the twentieth century.

---

33. toss: throw up and down
34. glimpse: very brief view
35. gauge: judge
36. ordeal: very difficult experience
37. mirage: illusion that appears, sometimes, in the desert

38. swoop: descend swiftly
39. tumultuous: wild
40. spectacular: fabulous
41. generate: create

Like Lindbergh, F. Scott Fitzgerald was an American symbol. But instead of representing the American dream, he was an image of the Jazz Age revolution. Born in Minnesota in 1896, Fitzgerald was pampered[1] by an adoring mother who wanted only the best for her son. In 1911, he was sent to prep school[2] in New Jersey; then, just before the war broke out, he entered Princeton University, where his extraordinary writing talent soon attracted attention. Instead of completing his studies, however, Fitzgerald left the university and entered the army. While he was stationed in Kansas, the war came to an end. But by then he had started his first novel—a story about his wild and irreverent[3] days at Princeton. He had also met Zelda Sayre—the unconventional[4] beauty who was soon to become his wife.

In March 1920, Fitzgerald's first novel was published. And immediately, *This Side of Paradise* was an immense success. Its descriptions of the Lost Generation* were masterful; its scenes of gaiety and despair were superb. In 1922, his second great novel, *The Beautiful and the Damned* appeared. It was followed, three years later by *The Great Gatsby*—perhaps Fitzgerald's finest work. By then he and his wife were international celebrities. In Europe as well as America, they were living the life described in his books—one of wild rebellion, hysterical merriment, drinking, and self-deception. In 1930, as the Roaring Twenties ended, Zelda had the first of several breakdowns. Depressed and disillusioned, Fitzgerald carried on. In 1934, *Tender Is the Night* appeared—a beautifully written story of the emotional wasteland at the heart of high society. Six years later, fighting alcoholism and mounting debts, F. Scott Fitzgerald died. He was working on *The Last Tycoon,* which had the makings of a masterpiece.

The following selection is from *The Great Gatsby*. Gatsby, a mysterious millionaire, is giving an extravagant party. As yet no one knows of his passion for Daisy—his first real love and now a neighbor's wife. His past as a bootlegger is also unclear. But his fantastic parties, where forbidden liquor flows, are famous.

---

1. pamper: spoil; give a person everything he or she wants
2. prep school: private school that prepares students for college
3. irreverent: without respect
4. unconventional: unusual

* After the First World War, confused and disillusioned young people were often referred to as the Lost Generation.

from
The Great Gatsby

by F. SCOTT FITZGERALD

There was music from my neighbor's house through the summer nights. In his blue gardens men and girls came and went like moths among the whisperings and the champagne and the stars. At high tide in the afternoon I watched his guests diving from the tower of his raft,[5] or taking the sun on the hot sand of his beach while his two motor boats slit[6] the waters of the Sound, drawing aquaplanes[7] over cataracts of foam. On week-ends his Rolls-Royce became an omnibus, bearing parties to and from the city between nine in the morning and long past midnight, while his station wagon scampered[8] like a brisk yellow bug to meet all trains. And on Mondays eight servants, including an extra gardener, toiled[9] all day with mops and scrubbing-brushes and hammers and garden-shears, repairing the ravages of the night before....

At least once a fortnight a corps[10] of caterers[11] came down with several hundred feet of canvas and enough colored lights to make a Christmas tree of Gatsby's enormous garden. On buffet tables, garnished[12] with glistening[13] hors-d'oeuvre, spiced baked hams crowded against salads of harlequin[14] designs and pastry pigs and turkeys bewitched[15] to a dark gold. In the main hall a bar with a real brass rail was set up, and stocked with gins and liquors and with cordials so long forgotten that most of his female guests were too young to know one from another....

I believe that on the first night I went to Gatsby's house I was one of the few guests who had actually been invited. People were not invited—they went there. They got into automobiles which bore them out to Long Island, and somehow they ended up at Gatsby's door. Once there they were introduced by somebody who knew Gatsby, and after that they conducted themselves according to the rules of behavior associated with amusement parks. Sometimes they came and went without having met Gatsby at all, came for the party with a simplicity of heart that was its own ticket of admission....

---

5. raft: floating platform
6. slit: cut a narrow opening
7. aquaplane: flat board for water skiing
8. scamper: run back and forth
9. toil: work
10. corps: well-organized group
11. caterers: people who supply food, etc. for a party
12. garnish: decorate
13. glistening: shining
14. harlequin: multi-colored, as in traditional clown's costume
15. bewitched: put under a magical spell

EXERCISES

Reading Comprehension

A. **Choose the best answer for the following:**

1. Paragraph 2 of the Historical Background reading gives
   a. the results of World War I.
   b. an analysis of Wilson's Fourteen Points.
   c. the causes of World War I.
2. Wilson's program was rejected at Versailles because
   a. Europe's ministers did not like America's president.
   b. throughout postwar Europe, there was still great hatred and mistrust.
   c. the Fourteen Points were too harsh and bitter.
3. Put the following statements in the correct order.
   a. World War I came to an end.
   b. Wilson's idealism was rejected in America.
   c. Wilson's idealism was rejected in Europe.
4. Paragraphs 6 and 7 present
   a. a contrast to paragraph 5.
   b. a summary of paragraph 5.
   c. examples of what was said in paragraph 5.
5. Prohibition was
   a. a thirteen-year period when liquor was outlawed in America.
   b. one of Woodrow Wilson's post-war proposals.
   c. the name of Lindbergh's aircraft.
6. During the years of Prohibition in America,
   a. everybody drank intoxicating liquors.
   b. no one drank intoxicating liquors.
   c. some people drank intoxicating liquors.
7. During the Jazz Age revolution, people were encouraged by all of the following *except*
   a. television.
   b. radio.
   c. movies.
8. What is the subject of paragraph 12?
   a. how people enjoyed themselves in the twenties
   b. how people became slowly disillusioned in the twenties
   c. the growth of organized crime in the twenties
9. From what we are told in paragraphs 14 and 15, we may assume that Lindbergh entered the trans-Atlantic competition
   a. because he was poor.
   b. because he disliked his rivals.
   c. because he loved flying.

10. In the novels of F. Scott Fitzgerald, readers can find
    a. immortal descriptions of the Jazz Age in America.
    b. accurate portrayals of the dawning age of flight.
    c. a summary of the lives of America's frontier heroes.

B. **Idioms and Special Expressions.** **Choose the answer that is closest in meaning to the words in italics.**

1. *They went on a shopping spree.*
   a. They went window shopping.
   b. They spent a lot of money buying whatever they wanted.
   c. They toured the shopping district.

2. *The United States was officially dry* during Prohibition.
   a. According to the records, no rain fell
   b. Statistics showed that there was no humidity
   c. The manufacture, sale, or transportation of liquor was illegal

3. *Needless to say,* there was a price to be paid for all the merrymaking and the debt.
   a. Of course,
   b. As explained above,
   c. However,

4. Needless to say, *there was a price to be paid for* all the merrymaking and the debt.
   a. there were enormous expenses involved in
   b. there were serious consequences because of
   c. there were extensions of credit because of

5. *Still,* in spite of the risks, Lindbergh had chosen the lonely, northern route.
   a. Nevertheless,
   b. Moreover,
   c. Therefore,

C. **Write *true* or *false* next to the following statements.**

1. Wilson went to Europe with optimistic plans for the continent's future.
2. In Europe, hostility and resentment ended soon after World War I.
3. During the twenties, Americans wanted to forget the trauma of war.
4. During Prohibition, Americans drank secretly.
5. There was a significant decrease in organized crime throughout the twenties in America.
6. During the Jazz Age, Americans saved most of their earnings.
7. Dancing and drinking brought great satisfaction to Jazz Age high society.
8. People adored the superstars of the twenties because they wanted something to believe in.
9. Lindbergh's receptions were greater in Europe than in America.
10. Lindbergh was a symbol of America's frontier heritage.

D. Who Am I?   Below is a list of names. Place the appropriate person next to each identifying statement.

Jacob Riis	Thomas Edison
Captain Cook	Ernest Hemingway
Andrew Carnegie	F. Scott Fitzgerald
Charles Lindbergh	Jane Addams
Willa Cather	Queen Liliuokalani

1. Though my teacher insisted I had no ability, I changed the world with my inventions.
2. While sailing eastward across the Pacific, I came upon the lovely Hawaiian Islands.
3. My novel about the First World War has become an American classic.
4. When I came to America, I was a poor boy; but I retired from business a multimillionaire.
5. I, too, was one of America's poor immigrants; later, as a journalist and photographer, I never forgot the pain of that experience.
6. I was the last reigning monarch of the Kingdom of Hawaii.
7. Raised on America's prairies, I returned to Nebraska for the subject of my first great novels.
8. Though raised in wealth and comfort, I devoted my life to the poor in Chicago.
9. Living the life described in my novels, my wife and I were international celebrities.
10. "Lucky Lindy," they called me. But it took more than good fortune to make my trans-Atlantic flight.

Vocabulary

A. Word Forms.   Choose the correct word form for each of the following. Make all necessary changes.

1. harmony, to harmonize, harmonious

   a. The Fourteen Points was a program for international justice and

      _____ .

   b. But the ministers were not interested in a _____ settlement.

   c. It becomes impossible _____ without close cooperation.

2. significance, significant, significantly

   a. The most _____ aspect of the Fourteen Points was Wilson's proposal for a League of Nations.

   b. It was a suggestion of great _____ for the future of the world.

   c. After World War I, Americans were _____ less idealistic.

3. to rebel, rebellion, rebellious, rebel

    a. The Roaring Twenties was a time of great _____ in America.

    b. _____ women refused to accept the traditional rules of proper behavior.

    c. These flappers were perhaps the decade's greatest _____ .

    d. They _____ in their fashions as well as their manners.

4. to deceive, deception, deceptive

    a. The theme of self- _____ is central to Fitzgerald's novels.

    b. His heroes and heroines often _____ one another.

    c. They find the pleasures of parties and alcohol _____ .

5. immense, immensely, immensity

    a. Fitzgerald's first novel was _____ successful.

    b. The _____ of the vast Atlantic did not keep pilots from competing for the prize.

    c. There was an _____ reception for Lindbergh in Paris.

B. **Complete each sentence with a word from the following list.**

    irreverent   *unconventional*   *unchaperoned*
    unconcerned   *irresistible*

1. Before the war was over, Fitzgerald had met the lovely, _____ Zelda Sayre.

2. His books describe the _____ merrymaking of the Jazz Age.

3. In their new automobiles, young people could at last go out _____ .

4. They became more casual and _____ .

5. For consumers in the Jazz Age, luxuries were often _____ .

C. **In your own words, define the italicized words below.**

1. There was a revolution in women's *status* during the Jazz Age.
2. There was also a current of conservative reaction to the *dynamic* tendencies of the time.
3. The Fourteen Points was a program for justice that Wilson had *proposed* toward the end of the war.
4. In spite of the program, harsh demands and bitter *penalties* were placed upon the Central Powers.
5. Wilson hoped that the League of Nations would settle all *disputes* among its member nations.
6. Twice his treaty was put to a vote, and twice it was *rejected* by a divided Senate.

7. But even to save the treaty, he would not make any *modifications*.
8. The Roaring Twenties was a time for forgetting, an age of postwar *celebration*.
9. Wilson wanted his idealistic vision to *transform* a lost and ravaged world.
10. The new League of Nations, he hoped, would *guarantee* a new world security.

D.   **Synonyms.** **Circle the word that does not belong with the others.**

1. a. withdrawal	b. removal	c. invasion
2. a. mockery	b. example	c. joke
3. a. cause	b. result	c. aftermath
4. a. eliminate	b. add	c. remove
5. a. unyielding	b. stubborn	c. unconcerned
6. a. restored	b. devastated	c. ravaged
7. a. subservient	b. inferior	c. supportive
8. a. repeal	b. removal	c. renewal
9. a. endeavor	b. fail	c. attempt
10. a. succeed	b. fail	c. backfire

E.   **Below in column A is a list of words that refer to certain aspects of life in the twenties. Match them with their definitions in column B.**

A	B
flapper	secret bar
Charleston	illegal manufacturer or distributor of liquor
speak-easy	liberated woman
bootlegger	a wild and exuberant dance
rumrunning	smuggling intoxicating beverages into America

Structures

A.   **In the paragraphs below, fill in the blanks with an appropriate infinitive or infinitive phrase from the list below.**

to approach	*to enter*	*to take off*	*to stay*
to keep	*to convince*	*to give in*	*to provide*
to try	*to get*		

Without financial backing, Lindbergh could not afford _____ the competition. So he did not hesitate _____ potential supporters among the business leaders of St. Louis. He managed _____ them of his ability as a pilot. Before long, therefore, they consented _____ the money for the *Spirit of St. Louis*. They felt that Lindbergh deserved a chance _____ to win the prize.

As he prepared _____ , Lindbergh hoped that the weather would be clear over the Atlantic. Then, in the air, he remembered _____ a careful record of his flying time and gas consumption. Though he wanted desperately _____ some sleep, he refused _____ to this dangerous desire. He struggled _____ awake until the epic journey was over.

B. **Following the model, change the sentences below.**

Model: "This engine needs repairing," Lindbergh announced.
→ "This engine needs to be repaired," Lindbergh announced.

1. "This dress needs shortening," the woman insisted.
2. "This car needs polishing," the student decided.
3. "Does this story need rewriting?" Fitzgerald asked.
4. "I think the characters need developing," his editor answered.
5. "Postwar Europe needs rebuilding," said President Wilson.

Composition

Choose one of the following.

A. In the selection from *The Great Gatsby,* Fitzgerald describes the magnificent parties given on Gatsby's estate. Have you ever been to a memorable party or great feast? Was it a wedding, anniversary, or birthday celebration? In one brief paragraph, describe this occasion, giving as many specific details as you can remember.

B. Reread paragraphs 1–5 in the Historical Background. Then in two brief paragraphs, discuss Woodrow Wilson's failure to bring about a new age of peace after World War I. In your first paragraph, talk about Wilson's Fourteen Points; in your second paragraph, show how first Europe and then the United States rejected Wilson's ideals.

C. "Gather ye rosebuds while ye may." This is a famous line from an English poem by Robert Herrick. It means that people should enjoy themselves while they have the chance, for time and youth and the pleasures of the present will all pass quickly. With reference to this proverb, describe the Jazz Age revolution in America.

D. Charles A. Lindbergh and F. Scott Fitzgerald both achieved fame during the twenties in America. Yet although they became international symbols, they each represented opposing aspects of the American experience in the Jazz Age. In two well-developed paragraphs, show how these Americans were a study in contrasts.

Topics for Class Discussion

Choose the answer that best expresses your own feelings, taste, or preferences. You may substitute your own answer for any of the choices given. Explain your answers, sharing your responses with a partner, a small group, or with all of your classmates.

1. What do you think of Wilson's plans for Europe's reconstruction?
   a. They were noble. If the ministers had followed him, he would have brought about a new and better world.
   b. They were too idealistic. He would have achieved more if he had been more realistic.
   c. They were uninformed. As an American, Wilson could not possibly have understood the needs and problems of Europe.

2. What is your opinion of America's refusal to join the League of Nations?
   a. It was a good decision. As the outbreak of World War I had shown, international alliances were dangerous.
   b. It was unfortunate. America should have done all in its power to bring about a new global harmony.
   c. It was an appropriate response to Europe's rejection of their president's Fourteen Points.

3. If you could enter a time capsule that would bring you back into the twenties, how would you choose to spend an evening?
   a. discussing literature with F. Scott Fitzgerald
   b. flying with Lindbergh in the *Spirit of St. Louis*
   c. dancing the Charleston in a New York speak-easy

4. What historical moment would you like most to have witnessed? Why?
   a. Cook's arrival in Hawaii
   b. the completion of the first transcontinental railroad in Utah
   c. Edison's invention of the light bulb
   d. Lindbergh's landing in Paris
   e. Armistice Day in the trenches of World War I

5. Whom do you most admire and why?
   a. Wilson
   b. Lindbergh
   c. Fitzgerald

6. What do you think is the saddest thing about the Roaring Twenties in America?
   a. rejection of Wilson's League of Nations
   b. the rise of organized crime
   c. the sense of lost innocence among America's youth

7. From what you have read of America's novelists so far, whose work appeals to you the most? Why?
   a. Willa Cather's
   b. Ernest Hemingway's
   c. F. Scott Fitzgerald's

8. Prohibition was an attempt to regulate drinking in the United States. Does your country have rules concerning the manufacture, sale, or consumption of alcohol? Is drinking forbidden? Is there a legal age for drinking? Are there laws against driving under the influence of alcohol? Do you feel these laws are adequate? Are they too strict? Not strict enough?

SOME INTERESTING PLACES TO VISIT

Middle Atlantic Area

The Museum of Broadcasting
New York, New York

Woodrow Wilson School of Public
    and International Affairs
Princeton, New Jersey

Woodrow Wilson House
Washington, D.C.

Washington National Cathedral
    (tomb of Woodrow Wilson)
Washington, D.C.

National Air and Space Museum
Washington, D.C.

Southeastern Area

Woodrow Wilson Birthplace
Staunton, Virginia

Oscar Getz Museum of Whiskey History
Bardstown, Kentucky

Midwestern Area

President Harding's Home and Museum
Harding Memorial
Marion, Ohio

Charles A. Lindbergh Historic Site
Little Falls, Minnesota

Financial Collapse

The Depression

PREREADING

Look at the photograph below. Then, working in pairs or small groups, answer these questions.

1. Why is there a long line of people on the street? What do you think has happened to these people? Can you see any women standing in the line? Why might they be absent? During what season of the year was this photograph taken? Why would it have been an especially difficult time for the people waiting in line? How much will each meal at the restaurant cost? With a one-dollar donation, how could somebody make a difference to the people standing in line?

2. Turn to the photograph on p. 133. Heading toward California in the hopes of finding employment during the Great Depression, these Oklahoma farmers were photographed in February, 1937. What hardships do you think they faced on their journey? How were these hardships similar to those faced by the city dwellers shown below? How were they different?

Sixth Avenue and 42nd Street, New York, 1932

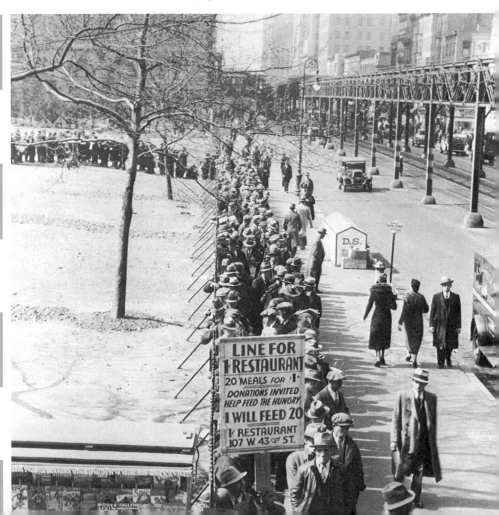

1   With a dramatic and sudden shock, the Roaring Twenties ended on October 24, 1929. On that memorable date—forever known as Black Thursday—the American stock market fell with a crash, bringing the country's entire economy down with it.* Fortunes collapsed, banks failed, and desperate investors lost all of their savings. Then, as the disaster spread, businesses, shops, and factories closed. Millions of people were thrown out of work, which further curtailed[1] consumer spending. So the number of bankruptcies[2] continued to multiply. As the new decade dawned, therefore, more and more people defaulted[3] on loans, mortgages, or installment accounts. There was no way, it seemed, to stop the vicious[4] downward spiral of the economy. By 1933, about a quarter of America's work force—a total of thirteen million people—was unemployed. Eighty-five thousand businesses had failed; five thousand banks had closed; and nine million savings accounts had quickly disappeared. Everywhere, the confidence of the Jazz Age had vanished like a dream. In its place had appeared the terrible realities of America's Great Depression.

2   Until 1940, Americans struggled to cope with the staggering[5] consequences of this depression. Thus, the history of the United States between the two world wars can be roughly[6] divided into two very different decades: first came the wild and irresponsible[7] twenties; then came the grim[8] collapse. Yet although the thirties were vastly different from the Jazz Age that preceded them, their financial troubles were directly related to conditions in the twenties.

CAUSES AND RESULTS OF THE CRASH

3   What were these factors that led to a crash? For one thing, as we have seen, Americans in the twenties had gone on a spending spree. They had rushed to buy the merchandise that was suddenly being produced. Toward the end of the decade, however, this buying tapered off.[9] All the automobiles, refrigerators, and luxury items had already been bought by those who could afford them. So demand began to fall short of supply. To remedy this situation, of course, manufacturers needed new markets both at home and abroad. But in the United States, there was a very unequal distribution of income. Many farmers, miners, and laborers were struggling to survive. They could barely afford the necessities of life, let alone its luxuries. So even with the extension of credit, there was a large segment[10] of the population that was just too poor to participate in the spending. Abroad, in the aftermath of World War I, there was a similar situation. Europeans were experiencing a severe economic crisis. To make matters worse, high American tariffs were keeping many countries from trading in the

---

1. curtail: reduce
2. bankruptcy: financial failure
3. default: fail to pay; fail to fulfill an obligation
4. vicious: fierce; terrible
5. staggering: astonishing, overwhelming

6. roughly: approximately
7. irresponsible: without a sense of responsibility
8. grim: horrible
9. taper off: diminish; slow down
10. segment: section

* The market had been falling and rising unsteadily throughout September and October; but it was the losses on Black Thursday which brought on the final, disastrous panic.

United States. There was simply no way for devastated Europe to become the new market America needed.

4   As the Roaring Twenties came to an end, therefore, the business boom[11] of the Jazz Age also began to recede.[12] Sales fell off, inventories[13] swelled, and production slowed down. Then, when this decline was reflected on Wall Street, investors panicked. For at that time, stocks could be bought with as little as ten percent down;[14] the remainder was often borrowed from brokers, who in turn would take out loans from the banks. In a rising market, of course, these credit arrangements worked. But as more and more stocks began to fall, the system became a deathtrap. Brokers demanded more money from their customers to cover the diminishing value of their stocks. Many investors simply couldn't raise the money; so they lost all their stocks and the savings that had bought them. This, unfortunately, left the brokers in the middle. As their customers defaulted, they were unable to make payments on their own loans from the banks. So, one after another, the nation's banks collapsed. Disaster also struck their depositors, for when they rushed to withdraw their savings, they found that the money had already been lost. Thus, with a terrific explosion, the credit bubble that had grown throughout the twenties burst at last.

5   In the White House at the time of the crash was President Herbert Hoover. Like Coolidge and Harding before him, he supported big business and minimal interference in the nation's economy. When the American system collapsed, therefore, Hoover— like everyone else— was at a loss for[15] a solution.

6   Initially, he believed that conditions would correct themselves after a brief, recessionary[16] period. But as the economy worsened, he was faced with a crisis of tremendous proportions. The jobless rate soared, hunger was spreading, and homeless vagabonds were beginning to gather in both urban and rural areas. Yet despite his sincere desire to be of service, Hoover was unable to alleviate[17] the nation's sufferings. He refused to plunge[18] the government into debt in order to fund emergency measures. The best approach, he insisted, was for private institutions and local government to come up with whatever was necessary.

7   But hunger, as one advisor later argued, is not debatable. There were food riots and labor disturbances in the cities; on farms, there was violent resistance to foreclosures[19] on property and equipment. Somehow, the people had to eat, to survive, to find work, to recover their pride. In the land of plenty, over a quarter of the population was helpless, desperate, and increasingly angry.

FRANKLIN D. ROOSEVELT AND THE NEW DEAL

8   So in the presidential elections of 1932, as the depression neared its lowest point, Hoover and the Republicans were swept out of office. They were replaced by the Democrats under the vigorous leadership of Franklin Delano Roosevelt. Confident

---

11. boom: great prosperity
12. recede: move back; decrease
13. inventory: unsold merchandise
14. down: offered as an initial cash payment
15. at a loss for: unable to think of

16. recession: economic slowdown
17. alleviate: soften
18. plunge: force downward
19. foreclosure: taking back property after nonpayment of mortgage

and charismatic, Roosevelt had promised energetic action—a New Deal of reform and relief. And as soon as he took office in 1933, a time of great activity—the famous First Hundred Days—began.

9   First, the president closed America's banks for a period of four days. Then, in a radio message—the first of his many "fireside chats"[20]— he assured the public that only unsound[21] institutions would be forbidden to reopen. Roosevelt next asked Congress to pass important emergency measures. One was the creation of the Civilian Conservation Corps, a program designed to provide thousands of jobs for America's desperate youth. Over two million people between the ages of eighteen and twenty-five were given jobs planting forests, improving farmland, building dams, and restoring historic sites. They received a dollar a day plus room and board in specially created work camps. At the President's request, Congress also created the Public Works Administration, an agency empowered to spend millions of dollars on construction projects across the nation. Still more jobs became available with Roosevelt's Tennessee Valley Authority. This was an ambitious plan to create hydroelectricity and promote conservation around the Tennessee River Valley.

10   But in spite of these efforts, Roosevelt knew, many Americans had remained jobless and destitute.[22] So for them he created the Federal Emergency Relief Administration—a department that was authorized to spend millions of dollars on state and local relief. And to prevent another disaster caused by Wall Street speculation,[23] Congress acted on the president's proposal for a Federal Securities Act. After 1933, investment procedures were placed under more stringent[24] government control.

11   Thus, by the end of his first three months in office, Roosevelt had managed to stem[25] the tide of economic collapse. People were even beginning to hope that conditions would quickly improve. Yet although the worst seemed over, economic recovery was painfully slow. What was needed, Roosevelt decided, were some fundamental changes in the American system. In 1935, therefore, the president launched[26] a new period of activity: the Second Hundred Days. He signed into law the National Labor Relations Act, giving workers a guaranteed right to organize and bargain collectively. With the Wealth Tax Act, he increased the tax burden on Americans in high-income brackets.[27] Other laws placed tough restrictions on banks as well as utility companies. And a system of Social Security was established to give Americans retirement pensions.

12   Clearly, with these pieces of legislation, the president had moved beyond his earlier programs of emergency relief, for he had expanded the permanent role of government in American society. To equalize income, protect the elderly, safeguard investors, support workers, and encourage farmers, he had established a system of modern social welfare within the traditional capitalism of the United States. His presidency, therefore, was a significant chapter in the history of the Progressive movement in America. And although the depression did not come to an end until

---

20. fireside chat: informal address to the nation by President Roosevelt
21. unsound: in poor condition
22. destitute: extremely poor
23. speculation: unsound investment

24. stringent: very tight
25. stem: hold back
26. launch: begin; introduce
27. bracket: category

America's involvement in the Second World War, Roosevelt's programs enabled[28] many people to weather its storm.[29]

13   The president, of course, was never alone in his demands for social improvement. In Congress, on the Supreme Court, and at state and local levels of government, there were liberal leaders in the Progressive tradition who firmly supported Roosevelt's New Deal.

FOCUS ON FIORELLO LA GUARDIA

14   Most famous, perhaps, among these supporters was the Mayor of New York— Fiorello La Guardia. Lively, unconventional, and deeply committed to the welfare of the people, La Guardia was a trusted and beloved figure throughout the terrible ordeal of the depression. Though born in New York City in 1882, he was raised in the Southwest, far from the dirt and poverty of Manhattan's slums. His father, an accomplished[30] Italian musician, was leader of the 11th U.S. Army Infantry Band. His mother was Jewish—a native of Trieste on the Austro-Italian border. Fiorello's childhood, then, was a multicultural one—filled with music and the animated[31] sounds of the several languages that both parents spoke with ease. It was also a time when the inquisitive[32] child developed an abiding[33] hatred of injustice. Why, he wondered, did clever politicians take advantages of the Native Americans who lived nearby? Why did the railroad companies refuse to help laborers who were injured on the job? And why, especially, did other children laugh at him because his father spoke Italian? With increasing determination, Fiorello decided that he would someday fight against such prejudice and corruption.

15   At the turn of the century, because of his father's ill health, Fiorello went to Europe with his family. Friends recommended him to the American consulate in Budapest, where he served as a clerk for three years. Then he was transferred for three more years to a consular post near Trieste. It was during these diplomatic terms that La Guardia acquired his extraordinary proficiency[34] in foreign languages. He mastered Italian, German, Yiddish, French, and Hungarian. He also studied history and political science—both of which proved useful in later political life. But most important, it was at this time that La Guardia developed his own inimitable[35] style. Short, stocky,[36] and enormously energetic, he was known for his quick wit, hot temper, and passionate dedication to justice. "La Guardia is a small package," a reporter once remarked, "but so is a bomb." Nothing frightened him. No one could threaten him. Everyone who needed consular assistance found him ready to be of service.

16   In 1906, Fiorello returned to New York. By day he worked as an interpreter on Ellis Island, helping the thousands of immigrants who arrived each week in America. At night, he studied law. Finally, in 1914, he decided to try to fulfill the dream he had long before fashioned.[37] He became a candidate for election to the United States Congress. As a Republican, he was told, he didn't have a chance. For years, the

---

28. enable: make possible
29. weather a storm: survive
30. accomplished: talented
31. animated: lively
32. inquisitive: curious

33. abiding: deep and permanent
34. proficiency: skill
35. inimitable: cannot be copied
36. stocky: strong and heavy
37. fashion: create

Democratic machine[38] had used every means—both fair and foul[39]—to guarantee victory in his district. Besides, people added, an Italian-American had never been elected to the House of Representatives before. His candidacy was a joke, they insisted.

17   But Fiorello surprised everyone, including the professional politicians. Though defeated in 1914, he ran a remarkably close race. Then in 1916, when he tried again, he won. People everywhere had responded to the unforgettable presence of La Guardia. He had addressed them often in their own languages. He had used his warm and winning wit. He had delivered dramatic speeches and had shared in exciting debates. But most of all, he had convinced the voters that he would remain an honest and caring representative. And as his colleagues in Washington soon discovered, La Guardia was true to his word. Rejecting the humble role often adopted by new members of Congress, he spoke out with zest[40] against abuses and corruption that conflicted with the rights of all free citizens. Then, when the First World War broke out, he was one of several representatives who offered to volunteer for active duty. So in 1918, La Guardia was back in Italy. But in addition to fulfilling diplomatic duties, he was flying bombing raids across the Italian front.

18   Back in the United States during the Roaring Twenties, Fiorello was reelected several times to Congress. He was unseated,[41] finally, in the Democratic sweep[42] that brought Roosevelt to office in the depression. But this defeat served to open the door that led to La Guardia's greatest triumph. In 1933, he was elected Mayor of New York City—an office he held, through successive reelections, until 1945. Thus, he presided over[43] America's largest city during the dismal[44] days of economic chaos.

19   Like Roosevelt, La Guardia was ideally suited to the task. Without wasting a moment, he reorganized the city's government in order to cut expenses and avoid bankruptcy. Then he appointed able assistants to direct relief, construction projects, and key municipal services. Under the mayor's dynamic supervision, no dishonesty, no inefficiency, was tolerated. La Guardia also made certain that New Yorkers received their full fair share of New Deal funds. In the end, therefore, the enormous metropolis survived and recovered.

20   Yet it was something more than brilliant city management that made Fiorello a legend. He seemed to be everywhere, to have an interest in everything, to have an inexhaustible[45] supply of the sheer joy of living.[46] Nothing could keep him from racing with the engines to help extinguish[47] city fires. At public concerts, he personally conducted symphony orchestras. On Sundays, to give local news and shopping tips, he had a regular radio show. And once, when the newspapers struck throughout the city, he even read the comics in a broadcast to New York's children. "Fiorello," a rival candidate once asked in wonder, "what are you in politics for, for love?" When their mayor retired in 1945, many New Yorkers would have answered enthusiastically. It had indeed been love. Love of a challenge. Love of people. Love of long-cherished visions of justice.

---

38. machine: political organization
39. fair and foul: just and unjust
40. zest: enthusiastic energy
41. unseated: removed from office in an election
42. sweep: huge victory

43. preside over: rule
44. dismal: very depressing
45. inexhaustible: without end
46. the sheer joy of living: the joy of living itself
47. extinguish: put out

In addition to suffering from the financial crash, farmers in the thirties were also the victims of terrible natural disasters. There was an extended drought across the Great Plains in the early years of the decade. Then, in the fall of 1933, rising winds brought savage dust storms. Thousands of families lost their crops, their livestock, and even their homes. Desperate for work, they abandoned the land and headed out west, hoping to find employment in the rich agricultural territory of California.

But on the West Coast, there was further trouble. Wages dropped as the supply of migrant workers soared.[1] Floods made living conditions unbearable.[2] And everywhere, the Okies* found violent prejudice, for no one wanted them camping in the countryside or competing for jobs as the harvest drew near.

John Steinbeck's *The Grapes of Wrath*—one of America's greatest novels— tells of the hardships, the heroism, the broken dreams, and the determination of these migrant workers in the depression. Steinbeck was born and raised in California. As a journalist in the thirties, he had become thoroughly familiar with the land and people of California. He had witnessed the influx[3] of its hungry migrants, and had often reported on their struggles for survival. In 1939, while the depression still lingered, his monumental[4] tribute, *The Grapes of Wrath*, appeared. Praised for both its artistry and its powerful social comment, the book was an immediate and lasting success. In 1962—six years before his death— Steinbeck received the Nobel Prize for literature.

In the following selection, Steinbeck describes the great migration of farmers to California. He begins by condemning the development of large-scale farming—a system that separated landowners from the laborers. Then he describes the angry desperation of the Okies.

from
The Grapes of Wrath

by JOHN STEINBECK

And it came about[5] that owners no longer worked on their farms. They farmed on paper; and they forgot the land, the smell, the feel of it, and remembered only that they owned it, remembered only what they gained and lost by it. And some of the farms grew so large that one man could not even conceive of[6] them any more, so large that it took batteries[7] of bookkeepers to keep track of[8] interest and gain and loss; chemists

---

1. soar: rise dramatically
2. unbearable: cannot be endured
3. influx: arrival of large numbers of people
4. monumental: great; immense

5. come about: happen
6. conceive of: imagine; comprehend
7. batteries: large groups
8. keep track of: remember; keep control of

* Because many had come from Oklahoma, the migrants were often called *Okies*.

to test the soil, to replenish;[9] straw bosses[10] to see that the stooping[11] men were moving along the rows as swiftly as the material of their bodies could stand. Then such a farmer really became a storekeeper, and kept a store. He paid the men, sold them food, and took the money back. And after awhile he did not pay the men at all, and saved bookkeeping. These farms gave food on credit. A man might work and feed himself and when the work was done, might find that he owed money to the company. And the owners not only did not work the farms any more, many of them had never seen the farms they owned.

And then the dispossessed[12] were drawn west—from Kansas, Oklahoma, Texas, New Mexico; from Nevada and Arkansas families, tribes, dusted out,[13] tractored out.[14] Carloads, caravans, homeless and hungry; twenty thousand and fifty thousand and a hundred thousand and two hundred thousand. They streamed over the mountains, hungry and restless—restless as ants, scurrying[15] to find work to do—to lift, to push, to pull, to pick, to cut—anything, any burden to bear, for food. The kids are hungry. We got no place to live. Like ants scurrying for work, for food and most of all for land.

We ain't foreign. Seven generations back Americans, and beyond that Irish, Scotch, English, German. One of our folks in the Revolution, an' they was lots of our folks in the Civil War—both sides. Americans.

They were hungry, and they were fierce. And they had hoped to find a home, and they found only hatred. Okies—the owners hated them because the owners knew they were soft and Okies strong, that they were fed and the Okies hungry; and perhaps the owners heard from their grandfathers how easy it is to steal land from a soft man if you are fierce and hungry and armed. The owners hated them. And in the towns, the storekeepers hated them because they had no money to spend. There is no shorter path to a storekeeper's contempt,[16] and all his admirations are exactly opposite. The town men, little bankers, hated Okies because there was nothing to gain from them. They had nothing. And the laboring people hated Okies because a hungry man must work, and if he must work, if he has to work, the wage payer automatically gives him less for his work; and then no one can get more.

And the dispossessed, the migrants, flowed into California, two hundred and fifty thousand, and three hundred thousand. Behind them new tractors were going on the land and the tenants were being forced off. And new waves were on the way, new waves of the dispossessed and the homeless, hardened, intent, and dangerous....

---

9. replenish: renew
10. straw bosses: not the real owners
11. stoop: bend
12. dispossessed: those who have lost their homes
13. dusted out: ruined because of the dust storms

14. tractored out: ruined because tractors could do the job of people
15. scurry: run back and forth
16. contempt: hatred

February, 1937. Weary but undefeated, these Oklahoma farmers are crossing the desert en route to California and the hope of employment.

✖ EXERCISES

Reading Comprehension

A.   Choose the best answer for the following:

1. In the Historical Background reading, the main topic of paragraph 1 is
    a. the causes of the depression in America.
    b. the results of the depression in America.
    c. the factors that led to economic recovery.

2. The causes of America's Great Depression are discussed in
    a. paragraph 1.
    b. paragraph 2.
    c. paragraphs 3 and 4.

3. All of the following are reasons for the crash in America except
    a. unequal distribution of income.
    b. economic recovery in Europe.
    c. overproduction of consumer goods.

4. Put the following in the correct order.
    a. Investors were ruined.
    b. Stocks fell.
    c. Brokers and banks were ruined.

5. From what we are told in paragraph 5, we may assume that
    a. Herbert Hoover favored only the rich.
    b. Hoover was cautious.
    c. Hoover was lazy.

6. What is the subject of paragraphs 9 and 10?
    a. a description of Roosevelt's presidential campaign
    b. a comparison between Roosevelt and Hoover
    c. a description of Roosevelt's First Hundred Days

7. In paragraph 12, the author
    a. gives a summary of paragraph 11.
    b. offers a contrast to paragraph 11.
    c. introduces a completely new topic.

8. In paragraph 14, Fiorello La Guardia is introduced as an example of
    a. Roosevelt's supporters.
    b. Roosevelt's opponents.
    c. Roosevelt's rivals.

9. When La Guardia entered politics, which of the following was not a disadvantage?
    a. He was a Republican.
    b. He could speak many languages.
    c. He was Italian.

10. La Guardia and Roosevelt may best be compared because
    a. they were both Republicans.
    b. they were both efficient administrators during America's Great Depression.
    c. they were both Democrats.

B. In the paragraph below, fill in the blanks with any appropriate word from the following list.

production	*sales*	*inventories*	*depositors*
brokers	*down*	*customers*	*loans*
Wall Street	*banks*	*stocks*	*savings*

As the Roaring Twenties came to an end, therefore, the business boom of the Jazz Age also began to recede. _____ fell off, _____ swelled, and _____ slowed down. Then, when this decline was reflected on _____ , investors panicked. For at that time, stocks could be bought with as little as ten percent _____ ; the remainder was often borrowed from _____ , who in turn would take out _____ from the banks. In a rising market, of course, these credit arrangements worked. But when a lot of stocks began to fall, the system became a deathtrap. Brokers demanded more money from their _____ . Many investors simply couldn't raise the money, so they lost all their _____ and the savings that had bought them. This left the brokers in the middle. As their customers defaulted, they were unable to make payments on their own loans to the _____ . One after another, then, the nation's banks collapsed. Disaster also struck their _____ : rushing to withdraw their _____ , they found that the money had already been lost. So with a terrific explosion, the credit bubble that had grown throughout the twenties burst at last.

C. Idioms and Special Expressions.   From the list below, choose the word or words that best substitute for the italicized words in the following sentences. Make all necessary changes.

at a loss for	*stem the tide of*	*weather the storm*
let alone	*fair and foul*	*open the door to*

1. With the programs of his First Hundred Days, Roosevelt was able to *prevent further* economic collapse.
2. Hoover, on the contrary, had been *unable to think of* a solution.
3. The Democrats used every means—both *good and bad*—to win New York's elections.
4. Roosevelt's leadership enabled many Americans to *survive*.
5. During the twenties, many Americans could barely afford life's necessities; *they certainly could not afford* its luxuries.
6. Losing New York's Congressional election *provided the opportunity for* La Guardia's greatest triumph.

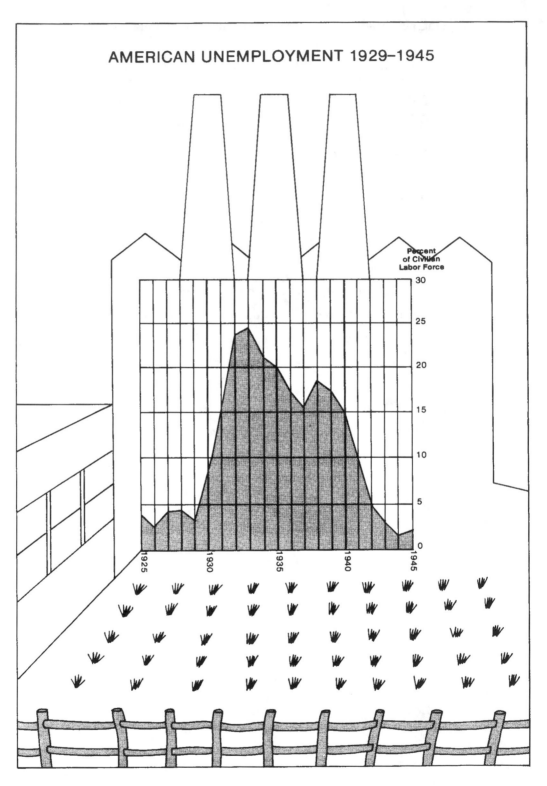

AMERICAN UNEMPLOYMENT 1929–1945

Percent
of Civilian
Labor Force

30

25

20

15

10

5

0

1925   1930   1935   1940   1945

Sources: *Historical Statistics of the United States*
United States History Atlas

D. Study the graph on p. 136. Then answer the following:

1. In the middle of the Roaring Twenties, what percentage of the nation's workers was unemployed?
2. Toward the end of the Roaring Twenties—just before the crash—was the figure very different?
3. How would you describe the rise in unemployment from 1929 to Roosevelt's election in 1932? A steep climb? A slow rise? A very insignificant change?
4. At the time of Roosevelt's election, what percentage of the nation's workers was unemployed?
5. After Roosevelt's election, did unemployment continue to rise?
6. What happened in 1938?
7. Judging from your answer to question 6, do you think everything Roosevelt tried was successful?
8. The United States entered the Second World War in 1941. Did this have any effect on unemployment? Is this usual in wartime? Why?
9. In 1945, at the end of World War II, was unemployment higher or lower than in 1925? How would you describe the two decades in between: very eventful? not very eventful? especially quiet and peaceful?
10. In the design around her map, the artist has included factory chimneys, the wall of an office building, and a country fence. Why?

Vocabulary

A. Substitute a verb phrase from the following list for the italicized word or words in the sentences below. Be sure to use the correct form of the verb.

comply with	cope with	bring about
hold on	taper off	take part in
wear on	preside over	can't stand to
stand out		

1. Among all the heroes of the Roaring Twenties, one name *was especially famous.*
2. La Guardia *ruled* New York during the dark days of economic chaos.
3. As the Jazz Age *continued,* America's financial condition worsened.
4. During World War I, Germany first *agreed to* Wilson's requests.
5. Toward the end of the war, as supplies diminished, the Central Powers could no longer *endure.*
6. Throughout the thirties, Americans had to *manage in spite of* economic chaos.
7. Sales had *decreased slowly* toward the end of the twenties.
8. In 1918, as he sailed for Europe, Wilson was determined to *establish* a new world order.
9. In *A Farewell to Arms,* the hero *hated to* talk about honor and patriotism.
10. He refused to *participate in* idealistic discussions.

B. From the list below, choose a word that best substitutes for the italicized words in the following sentences.

spiral	*minimal*	*pension*	*tolerate*
remedy	*fundamental*	*supervision*	*condemn*
severe	*retire*		

1. What was needed, Roosevelt decided, were some *very basic* changes in the American system.
2. La Guardia would not *allow* corruption in his government.
3. Under his *careful administration*, New York City survived and prospered.
4. In the thirties, Americans experienced *very serious* economic difficulties.
5. Though he wanted to help, Hoover was unable to find a *cure*.
6. There was no way, it seemed, to stop the downward *curve* of the economy.
7. In *The Grapes of Wrath*, Steinbeck *severely criticized* the impersonal relationships of modern farming.
8. Hoover insisted on *the least possible* federal interference in the nation's economy.

9-10. After the Social Security Act, people who had *stopped working* could still receive a *regular money payment*.

C. Match the words in column A with their synonyms in column B.

A	B
curtail	talented
vicious	categories
staggering	fierce
roughly	soften
accomplished	reduce
alleviate	poor
destitute	approximately
stringent	enormous
brackets	tight

Structures

A. Following the model, change the sentences below.

Model: When the stocks began *to fall,* investors panicked.
 → When the stocks began falling, investors panicked.

1. As the market continued *to drop,* even the brokers were ruined.
2. Though the banks hated *to close,* they had no other choice.
3. Soon, the factories had ceased *to produce* new merchandise.
4. People in California began *to resent* the arrival of more workers.
5. So they started *to cause* a lot of trouble for the migrants.
6. Yet the migrants preferred *to stay* on the West Coast.
7. Steinbeck loved *to write* about their courage and determination.
8. He also liked *to describe* the landscape of America.

B.　Following the model, supply the future perfect continuous form of the italicized verbs.

Model: *(travel)* "By tomorrow night, we *will have been traveling* for three days straight," the migrant worker said.

1. *(fly)* "By tonight," I _____ for two full days," Lindbergh thought.

2. *(stand)* "By three o'clock, we _____ in this line for five hours," the customer complained.

3. *(speak)* "By noontime, I _____ for over an hour," La Guardia realized.

4. *(work)* "By sunset, we _____ for twelve straight hours," the farmer announced.

5. *(living)* "By Sunday, they _____ in that trench for a week," the general argued.

Composition

Write a paragraph on the topic of one of the following.

A. Basing your facts on information given in the first paragraph of the Historical Background, describe the terrible economic results that followed the stock market crash of 1929.

B. Reread the first two paragraphs (p. 131) of the introduction to the selection from Steinbeck's *The Grapes of Wrath*. Then turn to the photograph on p. 133. In one brief paragraph, describe the family in the picture, telling why you think they have left their Oklahoma farm and what they are hoping to find in California.

C. There is an English saying which insists that "A bird in the hand is worth two in the bush." It means that it is sometimes better to be content with what one has instead of risking everything in the hopes of getting more. To illustrate the truth of this proverb, show how speculation on Wall Street led to America's Great Depression.

D. Though vastly different in temperament, background, and political loyalties, Franklin D. Roosevelt and Fiorello La Guardia admired and respected one another. What do you think they shared in common? In shaping your comparison, give as many specific details as possible.

Topics for Class Discussion

Choose the answer that best expresses your own feelings, taste, or preference. You may substitute your own answer for any of the choices given. Please explain your answers, sharing your responses with a partner, a small group, or with all of your classmates.

A. If you had the opportunity, whom would you most like to interview? Why?
   1. Franklin D. Roosevelt
   2. Fiorello La Guardia
   3. John Steinbeck

B. Make up five questions that you would like to ask the person of your choice.

C. Has your country ever experienced a severe economic crisis? When? How long did it last? Did you personally experience this crisis? If not, did your parents or grandparents go through it? What were conditions like throughout your country at that time? Share as many details as you can with your classmates.

D. For Fiorello La Guardia, proficiency in foreign languages was very helpful. What foreign languages are you presently studying? How do you think this effort will be of help to you? Be as specific as possible.

SOME INTERESTING PLACES TO VISIT

Northeastern Area

Roosevelt-Campobello International Park
Maine, United States, and
New Brunswick, Canada

Home of Franklin D. Roosevelt National
Historic Site
Franklin D. Roosevelt Library and Museum
Hyde Park, New York

Trinity Church and New York Stock Exchange
Wall Street District
New York, New York

Museum of the City of New York
New York, New York

Rockefeller Center
New York, New York

La Guardia and Wagner Archives
La Guardia Community College
Long Island City, New York

Midwestern Area

Chicago Board of Trade and
Chicago Mercantile Exchange
Chicago, Illinois

Herbert Hoover Presidential Library
Herbert Hoover National Historic Site
West Branch, Iowa

Pacific Area

Hoover Institution
Stanford University
Palo Alto, California

9

Toward the Unthinkable

A Second World War

PREREADING

Look at the photograph below. Then, working in pairs or small groups, answer these questions.

1. Pictured in the photograph are American soldiers crossing the English Channel en route to the Normandy coastline and the invasion of Nazi-occupied Europe. How old do you think these soldiers are? Describe their uniforms, their equipment. Judging from the expressions on their faces, what do you think they are thinking?

2. Turn to the photo on p. 148. Pictured are Allied prisoners of war liberated by American forces toward the end of World War II. How would you describe these people? Judging from the expressions on their faces, what do you think they are thinking?

Crossing the English Channel toward occupied France, June, 1944

1   When Americans joined the fighting of World War I, President Wilson made a solemn prediction. Their efforts, he promised, would "make the world safe for democracy." Their struggle would bring an end to oppression and to the terrible conflicts it had created. Indeed, throughout Europe and America, many observers shared a similar hope. It was "the war to end all wars," they said. That violent upheaval—unlike any the world had ever known—would never be repeated. For after what they had seen of modern warfare, people thought it would be easy to build a permanent peace—a security based upon freedom, the control of aggression, and international cooperation.

2   No generation was ever more tragically deceived. World War I ended with the armistice of November 1918. In September 1939, the Second World War began. Not even a quarter century separated these two global catastrophes.[1] In fact, for many people, memories of the first ordeal had not yet faded when the second conflict started. Yet in spite of these memories, in spite of the unforgettable suffering that was World War I, no one in the 1930s could ever have imagined the horror that lay ahead. Even today, half a century later, it is difficult to summarize, to comprehend, such devastation. With over twenty nations drawn into the struggle, and with the widespread use of technology's latest weapons, World War II left a staggering seventy-eight million casualties. Among these were over forty million soldiers—more than twenty-five million wounded and almost fifteen million killed in action. The remaining casualties—almost another forty million—were civilian. Thousands upon thousands perished of starvation, disease, air attacks, ground attacks, and the unspeakable cruelties of systematic genocide.[2] They died in the countryside, in cities, or at the hands of their captors in concentration camps. From such total and relentless[3] warfare, escape was impossible. It was like nothing the world had ever experienced—six years of destruction that threatened the earth with complete annihilation.[4]

CAUSES OF WORLD WAR II

3   In those two fateful decades between the world wars, what was it that went wrong? How did such a second disaster develop from the ruins of the first? Several factors—all closely related—combined to light the dreaded fuse. One, in fact, was clear to some observers from the moment that the First World War was over. In his autobiography, for example, Fiorello La Guardia made the following statement about Americans after 1918: "The people themselves were sick of the war, tired of hearing about it, and in no mood to face their responsibilities for post-war reconstruction of the devastated countries and their disputed economies. Not enough Americans realized the great significance of those problems. The public wanted to forget Europe, forget war and ignore the problem of preventing future wars. The result was that Europe was to become once more a fertile breeding ground for world war."

---

1. catastrophe: tragedy
2. genocide: mass murder of a whole race or nation

3. relentless: constant; without pause or pity
4. annihilation: destruction

4   With his customary insight,[5] La Guardia focused clearly on a major source of trouble. Americans in the Roaring Twenties turned inward. They refused to join the League of Nations and pushed up their tariffs to protect their own economy. To be sure, such isolationist feelings had always played an important role in American politics. They were part of America's tradition since the earliest days of the Republic. In 1918, however, they no longer related in any meaningful way to global affairs. Wealthy and productive, the United States had become one of the world's strongest powers. Its economic and political influence was extensive. By retreating from international involvements, therefore, it lost the opportunity to use this prestige for greater world cooperation.

5   Another cause for tension in Europe was the agreement that had ended World War I. The Treaty of Versailles was harsh and unrealistic. According to its oppressive terms, Germany had to sign a hated "war guilt clause"—a statement of responsibility for the First World War. It also had to surrender valuable land while agreeing to make huge payments to the victors. In time, among some of its people, a smouldering[6] resentment developed. They remembered Wilson's promise of a "peace without victory" and blamed his stubborn allies for rejecting it.

6   Meanwhile, around the globe, economic difficulties were steadily intensifying. This was due mainly to Wall Street's collapse, which had created a severe worldwide depression. Conditions were particularly bad in countries that had been ravaged by World War I. Would there ever be prosperity again, despairing people wondered. Would the suffering and hunger ever end?

7   Many of these victims of financial collapse were also faced with political instability. For in the aftermath of World War I, as governments toppled and dynasties fell, enormous power gaps had appeared. So throughout Europe and Asia, rival groups had begun to vie[7] for power. Violence developed and terrorism spread. Anarchy,[8] it seemed, was descending upon two continents.

8   Indeed, World War I had not "made the world safe for democracy." It had created instead a bitter, insecure, and mistrustful world—a place where totalitarian governments[9] could easily come to power. And that is exactly what happened in the years between both wars. In Italy, Benito Mussolini seized dictatorial control. In Russia, Joseph Stalin consolidated[10] his totalitarian regime.[11] Militant leaders gained prominence[12] in Japan, while democracy faltered[13] throughout eastern Europe, Portugal, Spain, Albania, Turkey, and Greece. In China, there was political turmoil.[14] There was also trouble in the Middle East. And where World War I had left the deepest wounds, Adolf Hitler began his rise to power. To the broken Germans, he promised a new era of greatness, a chance to restore both pride and prosperity. Instead of defeat, there would be conquests; instead of weakness, strength. Yet as his enemies realized, these visions of glory masked an evil

---

5. insight: understanding
6. smouldering: slowly burning
7. vie: compete
8. anarchy: total confusion; lack of political order
9. totalitarian government: dictatorship

10. consolidate: unite; make stronger
11. regime: rule
12. prominence: social or political importance
13. falter: become weak
14. turmoil: great confusion

ideology[15] of racism, brutality, and the suppression[16] of human rights. It was the Jews, Hitler insisted, who had contributed to Germany's downfall; so as part of his Nazi program, Hitler swore to get revenge. No sooner had he gained control than the ruthless[17] persecution of Germany's Jews began. Terror tactics[18] silenced all opposition. The machinery of representative government crumbled. And by 1934, under Hitler's iron rule, rearmament had started for Nazi expansion.

9   To summarize, then, we may mention five key factors that contributed to the failure of peace after World War I. These were American isolationism, Allied humiliation[19] of the defeated Central Powers, economic crises, political instability, and the spread of militant dictatorial regimes. A weary pacifism, especially among some European nations, may also be mentioned. In France, for example, and also in England, memories of the hideous[20] war years lingered. "Never again," said many survivors, "will we rush to such carnage[21] and destruction. Our children, at least, will be spared what we have seen."

10   Thus it was that aggression went unchecked[22] throughout the 1930s. First, in direct defiance of the Treaty of Versailles, Hitler remilitarized[23] the Rhineland—territory that lay on the Franco-German border. Then he annexed Austria. Next, he invaded Czechoslovakia; and finally, in 1939, his armies entered Poland. It was only at this point that France and Britain—the allies of Poland—declared war. But it was too late. By the summer of 1940, Norway, Denmark, Luxembourg, Belgium, Holland, and France had fallen to the Germans. Hitler's ally Mussolini had conquered Albania and Ethiopia. And in Asia, Japanese armies had won a series of victories toward establishing control in eastern Asia. So as new alliances were established and power blocs formed, Europe's conflict became a world war. England and its supporters were called the Allies. Germany and its principal allies—Italy and Japan—were referred to as the Axis coalition.[24] The titanic[25] struggle between them both would leave much of the world in ruins.

END OF AMERICAN NEUTRALITY

11   Separated by two vast oceans from the belligerent[26] nations, Americans at first remained neutral. "It is not our war," the isolationists insisted. "Its outcome[27] will in no real way affect us." But when France collapsed and England stood alone, neutrality sentiment in the United States diminished. This was especially true after Churchill sent an urgent plea to Roosevelt. Without American aid, he had warned, the future of both England and America would be endangered. So in 1941, at Roosevelt's request, Congress passed the Lend-Lease Act. This emergency legislation gave enormous powers to the president. It authorized him to lend or lease equipment to nations whose security was essential to America. Thus, billions of dollars worth of supplies were soon being made and shipped abroad.

---

15. ideology: set of ideas
16. suppress: keep down
17. ruthless: without mercy
18. tactics: methods
19. humiliate: embarrass or dishonor
20. hideous: horrible
21. carnage: killing and wounding

22. unchecked: unstopped
23. remilitarize: fortify
24. coalition: alliance; association
25. titanic: gigantic
26. belligerent: hostile; at war
27. outcome: result

12   Meanwhile, Congress had also passed the Selective Training and Service Act, a law that created America's first peacetime draft.[28] In opposition to Japanese expansion, it also declared a widening embargo on strategic[29] materials to Japan. By 1941, therefore, in spite of its official neutrality, the United States was increasingly committed to the Allied cause. Yet it was not until the end of that year that America actually entered the war. What brought on this final step? America's embargo had angered the Japanese, for they had begun to depend on American metals and oil. So to secure new supplies, Japan had stepped up[30] expansion in southeast Asia. Then, under pressure from militant leaders, Japanese forces had attacked Pearl Harbor, Hawaii, on December 7, 1941. Within four days, the United States was at war with the Axis coalition. It was the end of American isolationism, for ahead lay four long years of combat.

13   At home, these years would bring about extensive changes. America's economy, for example, soared as a result of a massive wartime effort. Shipyards produced over seventy-five thousand vessels; aircraft plants built almost three hundred thousand planes; expanding factories made millions of trucks and guns. Of course, with over fifteen million Americans in the armed services, new workers were needed to sustain this effort. So patterns of employment shifted dramatically throughout the country. Household workers left domestic jobs to fill openings on the assembly lines; in addition, over six million women went to work; so also did older men who had already retired. These and other changing patterns created problems and adjustments. For example, in the absence of their soldier-husbands, women had to manage the households as well as hold down new jobs. Families had to relocate as industries developed in different areas. There were also new taxes, new wage and price regulations, and rationing[31] restrictions on essential items such as gasoline, meat, textiles, and automobiles. Yet despite all the demands that were placed upon Americans, attitudes on the home front remained confident and aggressive; for unlike many other nations, America's mainland was spared the devastation of battle.

MAJOR TURNING POINTS IN THE WAR

14   Abroad, in both Europe and the Pacific, the story was different. The war in Europe ended on May 7, 1945. On that day, as the Allied armies swarmed[32] around Berlin, Hitler's devastated troops surrendered. It had taken many years and millions of casualties to stop the Nazi advance. For half of the war, in fact, the Allies had known mainly defeat. But there had come a turning point in 1942. In Egypt, after a British victory at El Alamein, Allied forces had begun a campaign to push Axis armies out of Africa. Meanwhile, at Stalingrad, the Russians had resisted a massive Nazi attack. So within a year, because of these gains, the stubborn reconquest of Europe had begun. The Allies in Africa had turned northward into Italy, while Soviet forces had continued to march to the west. Then in 1944 had come the final struggle. With the largest water-borne[33] force in military history, the Allies had landed in Normandy on the western

---

28. draft: call to service in the army
29. strategic: essential
30. step up: increase
31. ration: limit the amount of items per consumer
32. swarm: crowd around
33. water-borne: carried over water

Allied prisoners of war, liberated by the U.S. Seventh Army, 1945

coast of France. Slowly but surely, they had pushed on toward Berlin, where the Nazis had at last been trapped by advancing Soviet troops.

15   No military summaries, however, can give a true record of this conflict in Europe. Only the statistics—the chilling accounts of human loss—can in some way recreate the horror of those years. While the fighting raged, over ten million people—more than half of them Jews—died in Nazi concentration camps. Over half a million civilians perished of starvation during the bitter seige[34] of Leningrad. Of Russia's military force, the war took over thirteen million lives. Germany's casualties—both civilian and military, totaled almost seven million. For Poland, the number was over six million; for Italy, almost five hundred thousand; and for nation after nation, across the battle-scarred[35] continent, it was the same grim story. Never in their histories had they ever experienced such sustained and savage destruction.

16   As in Europe, the war in the Pacific also had a turning point during 1942. That was the year that Allied forces began to push successfully toward Japan. From bases

---

34. siege: attack on a city

35. scar: mark on the skin from a cut or wound

in Australia, American troops moved northward to the Solomon Islands, winning key land and sea battles at Guadalcanal (August 1942 to February 1943). Allied forces also gained control of New Guinea after the epic naval Battle of the Coral Sea (May 1942). Meanwhile, not far from Hawaii, American forces at Midway Island won another major naval battle in June. Thus, from fortified positions in both the South Pacific and the Central Pacific, Allied troops could begin to curtail the Japanese offensive. Under the direction of General Douglas MacArthur, Admiral Chester Nimitz, and Admiral William Halsey, they could organize a double counterattack—one that reached the Philippines in 1944 and then, in 1945, the islands of Iwo Jima and Okinawa near Japan. The price to be paid for this success was high, however, for Japanese troops defended every island with formidable[36] courage. So in the fierce campaigns from Midway to Okinawa, there were extensive American casualties. Combined with the casualties that were suffered in Europe, United States losses reached over a million in this second world war.

17   But Japanese losses were also enormous as the island-hopping Americans advanced. By the spring of 1945, therefore—after the Axis powers had surrendered in Europe—Japan was faced with the increasing possibility of an Allied invasion on the mainland.

18   Such an assault was never attempted. For on August 6, 1945, Americans dropped the world's first atomic bomb on Hiroshima. Three days later, a second was exploded over Nagasaki. More than one hundred thousand civilians died in the searing[37] heat of these radioactive blasts. Both cities were destroyed. Within several days, a traumatized Japan surrendered.

19   World War II was finally over, and an uneasy quiet settled upon the earth. But unlike 1918, there were now no illusions about postwar imperatives.[38] From the scientific advances made in two great conflicts had come the ultimate weapon. There would be no survivors, everyone realized, in a nuclear World War III.

20   Thus, the legacy[39] left by the Second World War was an awesome[40] and most sacred obligation. Never again could political tensions lead to worldwide confrontation. Never again could the mounting hostilities of 1918–1939 be repeated. Somehow, to the world's eternal[41] rivalries, nonmilitary solutions would have to be found. But would this mandate for the future be respected? To many who could remember the first half of this century, the chances for tomorrow seemed slim indeed.

---

36. formidable: impressively strong
37. sear: burn severely
38. imperatives: necessities

39. legacy: something that is left for future generations
40. awesome: inspiring fear or wonder
41. eternal: without end

In 1933, as a result of rising Nazi persecution, a Jewish physicist was forced to leave Germany, his native land. Like other Jews in those increasingly tense years, both he and his family decided to seek refuge in America. Thus it was that Albert Einstein came to live in the United States.

Einstein was born in southern Germany in 1879. Within a year, his parents moved to Munich, where young Albert entered school at the age of six. For the sensitive, artistic, and fiercely independent boy, the rigorous discipline of academic routine was difficult. He hated the insistence on repetitive drills, memorized facts, and total conformity to regulations. So in both grammar school and high school, Einstein was often restless and disturbed. His brilliant mind was unable to find an outlet for its enormous creative energy.

In 1898, after his parents had moved away from Munich, Einstein entered the Federal Polytechnic School of Zurich. Among the talented students of the famous Swiss academy, he found himself in a more congenial[1] setting. He studied with determined enthusiasm as his delight in mathematics and theoretical physics deepened. But when he graduated, despite his brilliant record, Einstein was unable to find a teaching position. So to support himself, he began working in 1902 at the patent office in Berne. Part of his job was to simplify the descriptions of proposed new inventions. As Einstein later admitted, the years in Berne were invaluable, for they provided him with the free time he needed to think about physics. And they gave him the chance to discuss his conclusions with a group of interested colleagues.

Einstein's genius blossomed. By 1909, in fact, he had become well known, for his revolutionary theories had begun to appear in a series of papers prepared in 1905. Central to these theories was the celebrated equation $E = mc^2$. Mass and energy were equivalent, Einstein insisted. "The velocity[2] of light (c) is a very large number, and with this squared the formula states that a small quantity of mass can transform into a very large amount of energy."*

In the 1930s, as Europe moved closer to a second world war, an important series of scientific breakthroughs confirmed Einstein's ideas. It was discovered that the heavy nuclei of uranium atoms could be bombarded[3] and split by neutrons.[4] As a result of this fission,[5] tremendous quantities of energy could be released. Additional neutrons would also appear, so that a chain reaction of atomic fission could be set in motion. Thus, it might be possible to create a gigantic bomb—an enormous explosion of staggering proportions.

Many of the scientists involved in this research escaped from Europe when the war broke out. Some of them, like Einstein, found sanctuary[6] in America. But as news of the Axis triumphs followed, they became worried. Would Hitler and his allies be the first to develop the ultimate bomb? Somehow, the Allies had to prevent this. Somehow, their governments had to win the weapons race.

---

1. congenial: pleasantly suitable
2. velocity: speed
3. bombard: attack continuously
4. neutron: uncharged atomic particles
5. fission: splitting an atom
6. sanctuary: place of safety

*Aylesa Forsee, *Albert Einstein: Theoretical Physicist* (NY: Macmillan, 1963), p. 32.

In order to encourage such nuclear research, Einstein was asked by his fellow scientists to write to President Roosevelt. He agreed. The ultimate result was America's Manhattan Project—an intensive government effort to develop the atom bomb.

For Einstein, making this bomb under the pressures of war had seemed necessary. But its devastating effects on the people of Japan tormented him. So after the war, he turned his attention to the promotion of peace in a nuclear age. The following selection, taken from an address prepared for the World Congress of Intellectuals (1948), gives a summary of his postwar position.

from
Message for the World Congress of Intellectuals
by ALBERT EINSTEIN

We meet today, as intellectuals and scholars of many nationalities, with a deep and historic responsibility placed upon us....

By painful experience we have learned that rational thinking does not suffice[7] to solve the problems of our social life. Penetrating[8] research and keen scientific work have often had tragic implications for mankind. On the one hand, they produced inventions which liberated man from exhausting physical labor, making his life easier and richer, but on the other hand, they introduced a grave restlessness into his life, making him a slave to his technological environment, and—most catastrophic of all— creating the means for his own mass destruction. This is indeed a tragedy of overwhelming poignancy![9]

However poignant the tragedy is, it is perhaps even more tragic that, while mankind has produced many scholars so extremely successful in the field of science and technology, we have been so inefficient in finding adequate[10] solutions to the many political conflicts and economic tensions which beset[11] us. No doubt, the antagonism[12] of economic interests within and among nations is largely responsible for the dangerous and threatening situation in the world today. Man has not succeeded in developing political and economic forms of organizations which would guarantee the peaceful coexistence of the nations of the world. He has not succeeded in building the kind of system which would eliminate the possibility of war and banish[13] forever the murderous instruments of mass destruction.

We scientists, whose tragic destiny it has been to help make the methods of annihilation ever more gruesome[14] and more effective, must consider it our solemn and transcendent[15] duty to do all in our power in preventing these weapons from being used for the brutal purpose for which they were invented. What task could possibly be more important to us? What social aim could be closer to our hearts? That is why this congress has such a vital mission. We are gathered here to take counsel with each other. We must build spiritual and scientific bridges linking the nations of the world. We must overcome the horrible obstacles of national frontiers....

---

7. does not suffice: is not enough
8. penetrating: beyond the surface
9. poignancy: sadness
10. adequate: sufficient
11. beset: surround and confuse
12. antagonism: hostility; rivalry
13. banish: send away
14. gruesome: horrible
15. transcendent: of highest importance

Reading Comprehension

A. Choose the best answer for the following:

1. "No generation was ever more tragically deceived." This statement in paragraph 2
   a. introduces a contrast to paragraph 1.
   b. presents a conclusion to paragraph 1.
   c. continues the topic of paragraph 1.

2. The causes for World War II are discussed in
   a. paragraph 1.
   b. paragraph 2.
   c. paragraphs 3 to 8.

3. All of the following contributed to the outbreak of war *except*
   a. the Treaty of Versailles.
   b. American participation in the League of Nations.
   c. a worldwide depression.

4. During the thirties, totalitarian governments were able to come to power because
   a. there was widespread political turmoil.
   b. there had been too many years of prosperity.
   c. there had been too many years of peaceful inactivity.

5. According to paragraphs 11 and 12
   a. America remained strictly neutral until it declared war on the Axis.
   b. America joined in the fighting as soon as England became involved.
   c. America was helping the Allies before it officially joined the war.

6. What is the topic of paragraph 13?
   a. the causes of World War II
   b. the home front in America during World War II
   c. the results of World War II

7. According to the information given in paragraph 14,
   a. only the Allied nations suffered many casualties.
   b. the losses among the Axis nations were tremendous.
   c. both sides suffered staggering losses during World War II.

8. How would you describe the tone of the last two paragraphs?
   a. confident and optimistic
   b. despairing and pessimistic
   c. solemn and cautious

9. When he first went to school, Albert Einstein was
   a. disruptive.
   b. frustrated.
   c. fascinated.

10. In his message to the World Congress, why did Einstein say that modern scientists had a tragic destiny?
   a. They were unable to make any significant discoveries.
   b. They had created the tools of total destruction.
   c. Because of intense rivalries, they were unable to work together.

B. **Which Happened First?** Circle the correct answer in the following pairs.

1. a. World War I ended.
   b. The Treaty of Versailles placed bitter penalties upon the German people.
2. a. A worldwide depression developed.
   b. The American stock market collapsed.
3. a. Governments toppled in the aftermath of World War I.
   b. Dictators took advantage of anarchy to set up new regimes.
4. a. Hitler annexed Austria.
   b. Hitler remilitarized the Rhineland.
5. a. Hitler invaded Poland.
   b. Hitler invaded Czechoslovakia.
6. a. Congress passed the Lend-Lease Act.
   b. Churchill sent an urgent plea to Roosevelt.
7. a. American embargoes hurt Japanese trade.
   b. Pearl Harbor was attacked.
8. a. American troops advanced toward Okinawa.
   b. The United States declared war on the Axis coalition.
9. a. British troops won a key victory in Egypt.
   b. Allied soldiers pushed northward into Italy.
10. a. An Allied invasion force landed at Normandy.
    b. The Russians resisted a massive attack on Stalingrad.
11. a. Soviet forces reached Berlin.
    b. The war in Europe ended.
12. a. An atomic bomb was dropped on Hiroshima.
    b. The war in the Pacific ended.

C. **Where Did It Happen?** Place the correct name next to the place described below. **The questions are in chronological order.**

Normandy	*Austria*	*El Alamein*	*Czechoslovakia*
France	*Stalingrad*	*England*	*Pearl Harbor*
Hiroshima	*Versailles*	*Poland*	*Berlin*

1. At the palace here, a disastrous treaty was agreed upon after World War I.
2. In defiance of that treaty, Hitler annexed this nation after remilitarizing the Rhineland.
3. Nazi troops then invaded this nation.
4. England and France declared war on Nazi Germany after this country was invaded.
5. To everyone's surprise, this country—along with most of western Europe—fell quickly.
6. Fighting alone, this nation asked America for strategic assistance.
7. The American navy was crippled by a secret attack on this Pacific island base.
8. British troops won a key victory at this Egyptian battle.
9. Russian troops withstood a massive attack on this city.
10. History's largest water-borne invasion force landed on the beaches here.
11. With Soviet forces advancing westward, and with the Allied troops moving eastward from Normandy, Nazi troops were trapped in this capital.
12. Soon after the devastation of an atomic attack on this city, World War II was over.

D. Answer *true* or *false* to the following statements.

1. The Treaty of Versailles was a major factor in bringing about a second world war.
2. Isolationism was still strong in America after the First World War.
3. The crash on Wall Street did not have a great effect around the world.
4. In the aftermath of World War I, there was worldwide political stability.
5. Totalitarian governments filled many power gaps that had appeared after World War I.
6. Despite their losses in the First World War, France and England were eager to fight again.
7. From 1939 to 1942, the Allied forces triumphed in Europe.
8. Turning points in both Europe and the Pacific came in 1942.
9. From 1942 to 1945, Allied forces reconquered Europe.
10. From 1942 to 1945, American forces moved west across the Pacific.

Vocabulary

A. Fill in the blanks below with an appropriate word from the following list. Make any necessary changes.

dictatorial   sustain   gap   concentration
authorize   declare   perish   instability
breed   neutrality

1. Millions of civilians _____ of starvation, disease, and the unspeakable cruelties of systematic genocide.

2. They died in the countryside, in cities, or at the hands of their captors in _____ camps.

3. Never in Europe's history had people experienced such _____ devastation.

4. Many of the victims of financial collapse were also faced with political _____ .

5. In the aftermath of the First World War, enormous power _____ had appeared.

6. Because of American isolation, La Guardia said, Europe again became a _____ ground for war.

7. In many countries, ambitious leaders seized _____ control.

8. France and England did not _____ war until after Poland was invaded.

9. With the Lend-Lease Act, Roosevelt was _____ to send essential supplies.

10. So in spite of its official _____ , the United States was increasingly committed to the Allies.

B. In the sentences below, the italicized words are false. Correct them by substituting an appropriate word from the following list. Make all necessary changes.

belligerent	*anarchy*	*titanic*	*sanctuary*
strategic	*falter*	*congenial*	*eternal*
hideous	*consolidate*		

1. After World War I, *political stability* seemed to be descending on two continents.
2. In Russia, Stalin *broke up* his totalitarian regime.
3. Throughout eastern Europe, democratic governments *became strong*.
4. Memories of the *pleasant* war years had lingered in England and France.
5. America was separated by two vast oceans from the *friendly* nations.
6. The *very small* struggle between both sides left much of the world in ruins.
7. In spite of its neutrality, America began sending *nonessential* goods to the Allies.
8. In the nuclear age, nonmilitary solutions will have to be found to the world's *temporary* rivalries.
9. Einstein found the Swiss academy *unsuitable*.
10. In America, Einstein found *a dangerous place*.

C. In a complete sentence, answer the following by choosing the correct word.

1. Were the Central Powers *honored* or *humiliated* after World War I?
2. Did dictatorial leaders become *prominent* or *unimportant*?
3. Before World War II, was there a spread of *totalitarianism* or of *democracy*?
4. Did people experience *partial* or *relentless* suffering during the war?
5. Was the war's legacy *awesome* or *unimpressive*?
6. According to Einstein, does modern science have a *happy* or a *poignant* destiny?
7. Have modern methods of destruction become *more gruesome* or *less horrible*?
8. Have people found *sufficient* or *inadequate* solutions to worldwide rivalries?

Structures

A. Following the model, combine the sentences below.

Model: World War I ended. Then international rivalries were immediately renewed.
→ No sooner had World War I ended than international rivalries were immediately renewed.

1. World War I ended. Then isolationism grew strong again throughout the United States.
2. World War I ended. Then a weary pacifism developed in Europe.
3. Europe's dynasties toppled. Then power gaps appeared in many countries.
4. America's stock market collapsed. Then a worldwide depression quickly developed.
5. Churchill asked for assistance. Then Congress passed the Lend-Lease Act.
6. Einstein entered school. Then he experienced increasing frustration.
7. Einstein went to Switzerland. Then he began to feel more comfortable.
8. The atom was split. Then the age of nuclear weapons dawned.

B. Follow the model and combine the sentences below.

Model: There was economic chaos after World War I. There was also political turmoil.

→ Not only was there economic chaos after World War I, but there was also political turmoil.

1. Germany had to sign a hated "war guilt clause." It also had to surrender valuable territory.
2. La Guardia was a liberal reformer. He was also a careful student of international affairs.
3. American soldiers fought in Europe. They were also sent to do battle in the Pacific.
4. Millions of soldiers were killed in the war. There were also tremendous civilian casualties.
5. We will have to prevent political confrontations. We will also have to solve our economic problems.

Composition

Write a paragraph on the topic of one of the following.

A. Reread paragraphs 3–9 in the Historical Background. Then in one brief paragraph, give as many reasons as you can for the breakdown of world peace after World War I.

B. Explain the following statement in one well-developed paragraph, giving as many specific details as you can. (You may wish to reread paragraph 13 in the Historical Background.) "Throughout the United States, there were extensive economic and social changes as a result of World War II ."...

C. "Once bitten, twice shy." According to this famous proverb, people who have undergone a very painful experience will be especially careful to avoid a repetition. Why did France and England respond so slowly to the spread of aggression throughout the thirties? How did this contribute to the titanic struggle of the forties?

D. The careers of Albert Einstein and Thomas Edison offer some striking similarities. Both had comparable childhood experiences. Both went on to make discoveries that changed the modern world completely. Expand on this comparison in a well-developed paragraph. (You may wish to refer back to Unit 4.)

Topics for Class Discussion

Interviewing a partner or a small group of your classmates, talk about the following.

A. Can you remember your earliest experiences at school? Were they happy or unhappy, fulfilling or frustrating? Was there a time in your academic career when these conditions changed significantly? Share these memories with your classmates.

B. Einstein's work in the Swiss patent office was beneficial in some fundamental ways. Have you ever had a job that was important to your social, professional, or personal development? Describe this job and the ways in which it helped you.

C. When Einstein moved to Switzerland, he found himself in new and congenial surroundings. Have you ever moved to a place that proved somehow inspirational? Did it open up new opportunities for you? Did you meet new friends? Were there cultural advantages that you had not had before? Was the physical landscape beautiful or interesting?

D. Do you feel optimistic or pessimistic about the chances for world peace? What can be done to make these chances greater? Please try to offer three suggestions to your classmates.

❈ SOME INTERESTING PLACES TO VISIT ❈

Northeastern Area

United States Coast Guard Academy
New London, Connecticut

Middle Atlantic Area

United States Military Academy
West Point, New York

USS *Intrepid*
New York, New York

Eisenhower National Historic Site
Gettysburg, Pennsylvania

United States Naval Academy
Annapolis, Maryland

Iwo Jima Marine Corps Memorial
Arlington, Virginia

Smithsonian Institution, National Air and
Space Museum, U.S. Navy Museum
Washington, D.C.

South Central and Southeastern Areas

Norfolk Naval Base, Norfolk Naval Air
Station, General Douglas MacArthur
Memorial
Norfolk, Virginia

Marine Corps Air-Ground Museum
Quantico, Virginia

Patton Museum of Cavalry and Armor
Fort Knox, Kentucky

USS Alabama Memorial Park
Mobile, Alabama

Patriots Point Naval and Maritime Museum
Charleston, South Carolina

Midwestern Area

Eisenhower Center
Abilene, Kansas

Rocky Mountain Area

United States Air Force Academy
Colorado Springs, Colorado

Pacific Area

USS *Arizona* Memorial
Pearl Harbor
Oahu, Hawaii

10

After the Holocaust

Nonviolent Imperatives

PREREADING

Look at the photograph below. Then, working in pairs or small groups, answer these questions.

1. For this informal portrait taken in 1962, President John F. Kennedy posed with his family on the porch of their summer house in Hyannis, Massachusetts. Describe this well-known photograph with as much detail as you can. What image do you think it presented of America's first family? Do you think this image reflected values that are important to Americans? Why, or why not?

2. Only forty-three years old at the time of his inauguration, John F. Kennedy was America's youngest elected president. How does this compare with your own country's leaders? Are they generally much older? Younger? About the same age? In what ways do you think Kennedy's youth was an advantage? In what ways might it have been a disadvantage?

President John F. Kennedy, his wife Jacqueline, and their two children, Caroline and John Jr.

1   As we have seen, Americans reacted to the end of World War I with the reckless[1] self-indulgence[2] of the twenties. But in the period following the Second World War, the nation's responses were quite different. People in the fifties were cautious and controlled. Instead of the carefree pleasures of the Jazz Age, they wanted comfort and security. They looked for steady investment, not shaky speculation, to build a new postwar economy. And in their social relationships, instead of the freedom of individualism, they chose the safety of conformity. There was no reappearance of the boisterous[3] excitement that had developed after November 1918. Americans in the fifties became prudent[4] and suspicious.

2   There were several important reasons for this. The Great Depression, for a lot of people, was still a terrible memory. The bread lines, the hunger, and the deep humiliation had left scars that wouldn't heal. Could it happen again, Americans wondered. Could the nation's economy collapse without warning in another sudden panic on the market?

ESCALATION OF THE COLD WAR

3   International politics also created stress. The United States could never return to the comforts of isolationism, for the war had placed America in a new position of leadership. Europe—a leading center of Western development—was a devastated continent. It could offer little resistance to the postwar expansion of a growing Communist Soviet Union. By the middle of the century, in fact, the Soviet Union had stabilized its authority over Poland, eastern Europe, and the Balkan states. Communism was also spreading throughout China and parts of eastern Asia. So in the wake of[5] the war's destruction, two competing power blocks developed. On the one side were the United States and its capitalist allies. On the other stood Russia and additional Communist nations. Though tensions between them had existed before the war, the hostility intensified after 1945. Each side attempted to protect its own interests and rapidly to expand its sphere of influence. Each side was afraid of the other's growing power. By the fifties, therefore, competition had become a cold war—an escalating hatred between Russia and America that defined the foreign policies of each nation.

4   Indeed, for the first time in its history, America was involved in a relentless global rivalry. And for many of its people, it was a difficult adjustment. They had long been accustomed to a simpler isolation. Now, their country was a superpower, a world protector, a nation of enormous responsibilities. Its destiny was linked to the future of its allies. From opponents it faced the pressures of continuous mistrust.

5   Unfortunately, because of these pressures, a dangerous arms race soon developed. The terrible weapon that had ended World War II had left a legacy of fear

---

1. reckless: without care or caution
2. self-indulgence: selfishness
3. boisterous: wild and noisy

4. prudent: very careful
5. in the wake of: as a result of (wake: water that is behind a moving ship)

throughout America. What would happen if the secret were transmitted?[6] What if other nations could manufacture such a bomb? By 1950, the dreaded event had happened: the Soviets had exploded their first atomic bomb. So to regain the lead— in spite of opposition from many of its citizens—America built a hydrogen bomb in 1952. Far more powerful than the deadly atom bomb, the weapon nonetheless gave only a temporary advantage. For within a year, it, too, had been exploded by the Soviets. Since both sides, therefore, had limitless power, both sides were determined to build up their defenses. Awesome new weapons were rapidly stockpiled;[7] sophisticated[8] systems of detection were created; and attack procedures were constantly updated.[9] Of course, as the race continued, the tensions of the cold war became almost unbearable. Was it only a matter of time, asked many people. Would the fear of extinction[10] keep peace upon the planet, or would there be a final confrontation?

FORMATION OF THE UNITED NATIONS

6   One thing was certain. If the chances for peace were to remain alive, the United States could never make the errors it had committed after World War I. Then, it had refused to join the League of Nations. It had also underestimated the desperate needs of Europe. But in the critical years of cold war diplomacy, there could be no miscalculations. Americans had to offer unwavering[11] support to the establishment of a new world organization. And they also had to commit themselves to the rapid rebuilding of Europe.

7   Both of these tasks were quickly undertaken. Toward the end of the war, delegates[12] from the Allied countries met in California. To replace the old League, they created a new organization—the United Nations. Its General Assembly was to include all member nations. In its Security Council, there would be eleven countries represented: five of them—Britain, the Soviet Union, France, China, and the United States— were to be permanent members; the other six would be chosen by the Assembly to serve for two-year terms.

8   The first meetings of the General Assembly were held in London in 1946. But when the decision was made to build headquarters in the United States, New York was chosen as the permanent site. Construction of the principal buildings was finished by 1952. Then, as more and more countries joined the UN, it was fervently[13] hoped that this new organization could encourage international cooperation.

MARSHALL PLAN, EUROPEAN TENSIONS, AND CONFLICT IN KOREA

9   Meanwhile, America was also sponsoring[14] a massive European recovery program. This was the Marshall Plan—first proposed by the United States in 1947. In cooperation with the people of Europe, agencies were established to stimulate production, trade, and financial rehabilitation.[15] America's contribution, by the early

---

6. transmit: send; give over
7. stockpile: store
8. sophisticated: complicated
9. updated: modernized; improved
10. extinction: destruction of an entire species

11. unwavering: without hesitation
12. delegates: representatives
13. fervently: deeply; passionately
14. sponsor: pay for; support
15. rehabilitation: recovery

*Soaring above Manhattan's East River, the United Nations is often
the focus of international plans for peace.*

1950s, amounted to over twelve billion dollars worth of aid. Thus, in contrast to the decade after World War I, Europe was able to avoid the upheavals that had led to the chaos of the thirties.

10   Yet in spite of this recovery—and despite the new United Nations—conditions in Europe as well as Asia continued to cause alarm. Postwar Germany, for instance, was a major source of concern. With its eastern sector under Soviet control, it had remained a divided country. Its traditional capital was also divided, for the city of Berlin lay deep within East Germany. Across the city, therefore, and indeed throughout the country, the power blocs of East and West were in direct and daily competition.

11   In Asia, Korea had also been divided since the war. A Soviet sector had been established north of the thirty-eighth parallel north latitude; to the south, an American-controlled zone had been created. And by the middle of the century—as in Germany—two rival governments had developed from this division.

12   The partition,[16] unfortunately, was an explosive one. In 1950, when North Korean forces invaded the South, the United Nations called for assistance in restoring peace to the area. So, supported by the soldiers of fifteen UN members, American troops under Douglas MacArthur joined the forces of South Korea. Then, after three long years of fighting, national boundaries were once again established near the thirty-eighth parallel.

13   Though South Korean sovereignty[17] was thus reaffirmed,[18] the war was both a costly and debilitating[19] one. American casualties alone totaled almost 160,000; South Korean losses reached well over a million; and the frightening prospect[20] of another confrontation left survivors deeply anxious and disturbed.

RENEWED FOCUS ON CIVIL RIGHTS IN AMERICA

14   It is no wonder, then, that as the fifties progressed, apprehension[21] mounted throughout the United States. To many Americans, it seemed as though the worldwide crises would never end. They felt the cold war was becoming worse. Despite their strong determination, the power of their rivals had not diminished abroad. At home, despite rising national prosperity, there was also cause for concern. Unequal opportunity, racism, and poverty among the nation's African Americans were increasingly evident. Now more than ever, with America supporting democracy on a new global basis, these conditions seemed intolerable. Some people started asking what America was doing wrong; what new directions should their country take, they questioned.

15   One answer was provided by Dr. Martin Luther King, Jr. From December 1955, until his death in April 1968, he committed himself through an ever-expanding struggle to the cause of human rights throughout America. Like Abraham Lincoln, he believed that America's future lay in a realization of Jefferson's vision. But as an African American, he knew this accomplishment[22] could only be achieved after the barriers of discrimination had been eliminated. His days of leadership were tragically short. Yet in little more than a decade, King led his country toward the dream Lincoln

---

16. partition: division
17. sovereignty: independence; rule
18. reaffirm: reestablish; repeat
19. debilitating: exhausting; weakening

20. prospect: possibility
21. apprehension: fear
22. accomplishment: achievement

had spoken of; he revolutionized a nation so that the goals of the country's founders could be fulfilled.

16   King was born in Atlanta, Georgia, on the fifteenth of January, 1929. His father, a graduate of Morehouse College, was pastor of Ebenezer Baptist Church and a respected leader of Atlanta's African-American community. His mother, the daughter of a minister, had attended Hampton Institute and had become a teacher before her marriage. The couple presented a study in contrasts: hot-tempered and dynamic, the elder King was a forceful speaker and a determined supporter of African-American advancement; Mrs. King was thoughtful and reserved.[23] Yet she, too, was a steady opponent of racial injustice and inequality. Her father had helped to establish Atlanta's local chapter[24] of the NAACP;* he had also been instrumental[25] in the building of the city's first African-American public high school. So her family tradition, like her husband's commitment, was one of active civic service and dedication to reform.

17   Though King was born in the year of the stock market crash, his childhood days were comfortable. He never knew the terrible poverty that others experienced throughout the Great Depression. In his solid and pious[26] homelife, he was also fortunate. From his mother he acquired unshakable faith in the worth of the individual; from his father's moving sermons, he developed deep religious feelings and a rich appreciation of the power of the word. Yet in spite of these advantages, King's youth was darkened by an increasing awareness of the powerful discrimination that crushed his people. "You are as good as anyone," his mother once responded when young Martin was rejected by white playmates. He could never lose hope, she insisted; he could never lose his self-respect.

18   But in the Deep South in the first half of this century, it was difficult to remember such encouragement. Though slavery in the United States had ended with the Civil War,** discrimination had continued to oppress the nation's African Americans. This was true in both the North and the South; in the South, however, where slavery had existed until 1865, laws were passed in the 1890s to create a strict and systematic segregation.[27] Schools, hospitals, restaurants, public transportation, and even parks were segregated. Complicated voting requirements had also been established—requirements that many African Americans were unable to fulfill. So in the 1930s and 1940s—the period of King's childhood and youth—African Americans faced almost insurmountable[28] obstacles in the economic, political, and social life of the South.

19   For Martin, Jr., the fullest understanding of the evils of this system came in the summer of 1944. He had gone to Connecticut to find a temporary job. And there, at the age of fifteen, he had suddenly experienced a sense of liberation. In the absence of official segregation, he felt a freedom he had never known before. Unfortunately, this wonderful sensation was all too brief. For on his return to Atlanta, King was forced to take a seat behind a curtained section of the train's dining car. Years later, the bitter

---

23. reserved: quiet; dignified   26. pious: religious
24. chapter: branch; department   27. segregation: racial separation
25. be instrumental: play a contributing role   28. insurmountable: unconquerable
*   National Association for the Advancement of Colored People
**   An analysis of the development of slavery in America is given in *America: Past and Present*, Vol. I, Chapter 11.

Dr. Martin Luther King, Jr.

disappointment of that moment was still vivid. "I felt," King recalled, "as if the curtain had been dropped on my selfhood." Yet despite his indignation,[29] King did not give in to helpless rage.[30] Instead, like La Guardia, he made a youthful resolution:[31] someday, he hoped, he would be able to contribute to the end of discrimination against his people.

20   How, exactly, he was to accomplish this was not yet clear to King. Upon returning to Atlanta, he entered Morehouse College. He had thought of becoming either a doctor or a lawyer; but the brilliant sermons and dedicated leadership of some ministers on campus changed his mind. Like his father, he decided, he would become a minister. So in 1947, King was ordained in the Baptist religion. Then, after graduating from Morehouse, he left Alabama for three more years of study at Pennsylvania's Crozer Theological Seminary.

---

29. indignation: resentment
30. rage: extreme anger

31. resolution: decision

DR. KING AND THE PHILOSOPHY OF NONVIOLENT RESISTANCE

21   One lecture in his seminary years was especially influential. This was a presentation of the Gandhian philosophy of nonviolent resistance to injustice. According to Mohandas Gandhi, nonviolent resistance was a positive—not a negative—technique. It was an attack on social evil with the superior weapon of moral truth. But in order for the technique to be effective, in order for the people to accept this truth, the protestors had to be willing to suffer. They had to take on pain, rather than inflict[32] it. Only by making this sacrifice, only by disobeying an unjust law and accepting the punishment for disobedience, could they truly triumph over their oppressors. For in their courage and determination, they would draw increasing attention to the justice of their cause.

22   Could it work in America? King wondered. Could passive resistance, as Gandhi insisted, change centuries of injustice in the United States? Searching for the answer, King began an intensive analysis of Gandhi's fight for freedom from British rule in India. He also decided to broaden his knowledge by pursuing a doctorate in philosophy. So after graduating from Crozer with the highest class honors, King received a scholarship and enrolled in Boston University.

23   While King was in Boston, a central event of his career took place. He met Coretta Scott, a music student at the New England Conservatory. Like him, she had been born and raised in the Deep South. Also like King, she was the gifted and determined descendant of a strong and proud African-American family. She had graduated, in 1951, from Antioch College in Ohio. Then, with a scholarship, she had entered the conservatory in Boston. In addition to music, she was devoted to the advancement of her people and to the cause of human rights throughout the world. King was attracted to her immediately. And before long, Coretta, too, was deeply in love. They were married in Alabama in 1953.

24   Within a year, with his doctoral thesis well under way,[33] King accepted a challenging offer. He moved with his bride to Montgomery, Alabama, where he took over the leadership of Dexter Avenue Baptist Church. After long and careful preparation, and with a determined wife to help him, he was ready to begin his chosen work.

25   His first year as pastor was quietly spent in fulfillment of the duties of his ministry. But at the end of that year, everything suddenly changed. From one simple incident on the bus lines of Montgomery, the American civil rights crusade began. And for the next twelve years, King remained its extraordinary leader.

26   How did this all come about? First, in 1954, the Supreme Court of the United States made a very important decision. In the case of *Brown v. Board of Education of Topeka,* it declared segregation in the nation's public schools to be unconstitutional. Desegregation, of course, was not immediate, for there was resistance, sometimes in the form of violent confrontations, to many desegregation attempts. But in the months that followed that famous decision, African Americans in the South dared to feel a new kind of hope. Racial injustice might after all be diminished. Resistance, somehow, might achieve results.

---

32. inflict pain: cause someone else to suffer pain   33. under way: already begun

27   King was brought to the forefront of such resistance in this period of tension-filled expectation. On the first of December, 1955, Rosa Parks was returning home from work. Her bus was crowded; and as an African-American woman, she knew she was not entitled[34] to keep her seat if there were not enough places for the white passengers.* Yet when told by the driver to relinquish[35] her seat, Mrs. Parks refused. Quietly, with dignity, she explained that she would remain seated. She realized that she was breaking the law, that she would certainly be arrested, and yet she continued her simple, steady refusal. By nightfall, she had been taken to jail. And by the following day, something dramatic had happened in Montgomery. Rosa Parks had become a symbol, an inspiration to its African-American community. Among the leaders of that community, many people understood that a tremendous opportunity had presented itself. If the spirit of their people could be sustained, if it could be shaped and directed toward meaningful action, then perhaps there was a chance to move toward freedom. What was needed, they decided, was a well-organized boycott—a refusal to ride the buses until discrimination on the lines had been eliminated. After several urgent meetings, King was elected to coordinate this protest. He accepted, and a new age began in American social history.

28   Insisting on nonviolence in spite of any punishment, King directed a supremely[36] effective boycott for a year. In eloquent[37] sermons and powerful speeches, he instructed and supported the weary protestors. As he later explained, "Nonviolent resistance had emerged as the technique of the movement, while love stood as the regulating ideal. In other words, Christ furnished the spirit and motivation, while Gandhi furnished the method." The method, King admitted, was "not … for cowards." Boycotters were threatened; King was arrested; his home in Montgomery was bombed. Yet the resistance continued, and Montgomery became a national symbol of the quest for social justice.

EXPANSION OF THE AMERICAN CIVIL RIGHTS CRUSADE

29   With a Supreme Court decision in November 1956, the famous boycott came to an end, for segregation on Alabama's buses was declared unconstitutional.[38] Yet the civil rights movement had only just begun. King was no longer just a pastor in Montgomery. He had become a national figure, the long-hoped-for leader who had brought about reform. And soon, among African Americans in the North as well as the South, a great hope developed—the sudden realization that a method for change had been tested and proven successful.

30   King understood this better than anyone. He had grown enormously during the Montgomery boycott. He had put all his hopes and the fruits of his education to a public, practical test. And he had not been defeated. Now, there could be no turning

---

34. entitled: permitted
35. relinquish: give up
36. supremely: extremely

37. eloquent: elegantly expressive
38. unconstitutional: against the law of the land

* According to the segregation rules, the front section of buses was reserved for white passengers; the back was reserved for African-American passengers; African Americans could also sit in the middle area, but they had to give up their seats if there was not enough room in the front for the whites. Rosa Parks was sitting in the middle section.

back. He would remain committed to nonviolent activity for the cause of civil rights throughout America.

31   In the decade that remained to him, King's influence and achievements were remarkable. He was a man of great charisma, an electrifying speaker who could impress enormous crowds. He was also courteous and persuasive in more private debates. But most of all, it was his courage, his acceptance of danger, that established King's leadership throughout the sixties. Despite threats on his life, frequent arrests, and the mounting violence of opponents, he continued to organize nonviolent resistance across the Deep South. And as in Montgomery, his Gandhian protests slowly brought results. Laws were passed to protect Americans' voting rights. Segregation was shattered by a series of decisive court decisions. And equal opportunity in housing, employment, and education became a possibility for millions of Americans.

32   Meanwhile, as the champion of reform through peaceful protest, King was increasingly honored both at home and overseas. In 1959, for instance, at the request of Indian Prime Minister Jawaharlal Nehru, he went with his wife for a month-long tour of India. Two years earlier, they had been invited to the new African state of Ghana. Chosen "Man of the Year" by *Time* magazine in 1963, King was in Germany the following year as the guest of West Berlin's mayor. Then in December 1964, he was awarded the Nobel Prize for Peace in Oslo, Norway. As the youngest recipient[39] of this award, King was deeply moved by the international recognition.[40] "I accept this prize," he said, "on behalf of all men who love peace and brotherhood ... for in the depths of my heart I am aware that this prize is much more than an honor to me personally." It was the cause of civil rights that had been honored, he insisted. It was resistance to social injustice that had been applauded around the world.

33   Yet in spite of these honors and his growing renown,[41] King faced new difficulties toward the middle of the decade. Not everyone who wanted reform was willing to follow his methods of nonviolence. "King has promised us justice," some African-American critics thought. "Yet our progress has been too slow. Within the South, and in urban ghettos throughout the North, there are still substandard conditions in housing and education. Discrimination has not been eliminated. And though voting abuses[42] and legal segregation have both been diminishing, there is much that remains to be done. We need new methods—more forceful ones. If necessary, we should even resort to[43] violence."

34   King was opposed to these suggestions of violence. But despite his condemnation, terrible riots began to occur in major cities across the nation. Thirty-five people died in Watts, Los Angeles, during the riots of August 1965. Two years later, hundreds were injured and over sixty persons killed in the riots of Newark and Detroit. This rejection of his principles worried King. The gains of nonviolence, he feared, would be rapidly undone by a repressive[44] counteraction[45] to the riots.

35   He was also worried by his country's involvement in the war in Vietnam. It was a mistake, he insisted, to commit the lives of Americans to the internal struggles of

39. recipient: person who receives
40. recognition: attention; appreciation
41. renown: fame
42. abuses: corrupt conditions

43. resort to: use
44. repress: keep down
45. counteraction: reaction

another nation. It was also a mistake to spend enormous sums on an unjust war when there existed poverty and need within America. Government spokesmen and others disagreed. So after 1965, in addition to criticism of his nonviolent methods, King was faced with determined opposition to his views on Vietnam.

36   Nevertheless, through the difficult years of 1966 and 1967, he held fast to his convictions.[46] He spoke out publicly against the war. He spoke out often against violent protest—even when undertaken in the cause of justice. And to emphasize his convictions, toward the end of 1967, he began to plan a Poor People's Campaign. This was to be a massive march on Washington to demonstrate the needs of disadvantaged[47] Americans. But King never lived to lead the demonstration. On April 4, 1968, he was assassinated on a motel balcony in Memphis, Tennessee. He had gone to Memphis to lead a nonviolent protest in support of striking sanitation workers.[48] Yet the senseless[49] violence that he had always condemned put an end to his determined efforts.

37   Throughout America, millions mourned[50] their terrible loss. Yet King himself on the night before he died had already spoken words of hope and comfort. "We've got some difficult days ahead," he had said to his people. "But it doesn't matter with me now. Because I've been to the mountaintop. And I don't mind. Like anybody, I would like to live a long life. Longevity[51] has its place. But I'm not concerned about that now. I just want to do God's will. And He's allowed me to go up to the mountain. And I've looked over. And I've seen the promised land. I may not get there with you. But I want you to know tonight, that we, as a people will get to the promised land. And I'm happy tonight. I'm not worried about anything. I'm not fearing any man. Mine eyes have seen the glory of the coming of the Lord."

---

46. conviction: strong belief
47. disadvantaged: poor
48. sanitation workers: garbage collectors

49. senseless: without meaning
50. mourn: express deep sorrow for
51. longevity: long life

※ SELECTION I

    In 1960, as King was attaining the summit of international prestige, John F. Kennedy was elected president of the United States. Young, energetic, and attractive (at forty-three, in fact, he was the youngest elected president in America's history), Kennedy was—like King—a symbol of hope and vigorous idealism for many Americans. Born in Massachusetts in 1917, he had attended Harvard College and had served in the navy during World War II. From 1947 to 1953, he had represented Massachusetts in the U.S. Congress. From 1952 to 1960, he had been a U. S. Senator. His parents had given him all the advantages of great wealth and social prestige. They had also taught him to set high goals and to work hard to achieve them. So, as he announced in his eloquent Inaugural Address (January 20, 1961), he hoped that his administration could establish a new commitment to worldwide peace and social justice.

    Here are some excerpts from that famous address.

from
Inaugural Address
January 20, 1961

by PRESIDENT JOHN F. KENNEDY

We observe today not a victory of party but a celebration of freedom, symbolizing an end as well as a beginning, signifying renewal as well as change. For I have sworn before you and Almighty God the same solemn oath[1] our forebears[2] prescribed nearly a century and three-quarters ago.

The world is very different now. For man holds in his mortal hands the power to abolish all forms of human poverty and all forms of human life. And yet the same revolutionary belief for which our forebears fought is still at issue[3] around the globe, the belief that the rights of man come not from the generosity of the state but from the hand of God.

We dare not forget today that we are the heirs of that first revolution. Let the word go forth from this time and place, to friend and foe alike, that the torch has been passed to a new generation of Americans, born in this century, tempered[4] by war, disciplined by a hard and bitter peace, proud of our ancient heritage, and unwilling to witness or permit the slow undoing of those human rights to which this nation has always been committed, and to which we are committed today at home and around the world.

Let every nation know, whether it wishes us well or ill, that we shall pay any price, bear any burden, meet any hardship, support any friend, oppose any foe to assure the survival and the success of liberty.

This much we pledge[5]—and more....

All this will not be finished in the first one hundred days. Nor will it be finished in the first one thousand days, nor in the life of this Administration, nor even perhaps in our lifetime on this planet. But let us begin....

Now the trumpet summons[6] us again—not as a call to bear arms, though arms we need; not as a call to battle, though embattled we are; but a call to bear the burden of a long twilight struggle, year in and year out,[7] "rejoicing in hope, patient in tribulation," a struggle against the common enemies of man: tyranny, poverty, disease and war itself.

Can we forge[8] against these enemies a grand and global alliance, North and South, East and West, that can assure a more fruitful life for all mankind? Will you join in that historic effort? ...

And so, my fellow Americans, ask not what your country can do for you; ask what you can do for your country....

---

1. oath: formal promise
2. forebears: ancestors
3. at issue: a subject of controversy, undecided
4. tempered: made wise by experience; toughened

5. pledge: promise
6. summon: call
7. year in and year out: every year
8. forge: create; shape

As the civil rights crusade expanded during the 1960s, a new group of African-American writers focused attention on the themes of prejudice, racial injustice, and the need for radical social change. Among these American writers was the poet Nikki Giovanni. In her first volumes of poetry—*Black Feeling, Black Talk,* and *Black Judgment*—her dramatic, colloquial verses often expressed anger, impatience, and a daring call to revolutionary defiance. In later poems and essays, published in the 1970s and 1980s, the poet's work included more subdued reflections on the wider themes of love, solitude, children, aging, poverty, and the nature of poetry itself. Even in these later works, though, as the following selection indicates, Giovanni's poetry continued to explore the themes of injustice, inequality, and personal commitment to the cause of civil rights.

The excerpt is from a piece entitled *Harvest,* published in the 1983 collection *Those Who Ride the Night Winds* and dedicated to Rosa Parks, heroine of the Montgomery boycott organized by Dr. King. Through an imaginary monologue, it presents the thoughts and feelings of Rosa Parks as she remembers her famous refusal to give up her seat. The first four stanzas of the monologue center on this refusal and the events that led up to it. In the fifth stanza, the focus shifts to a contemporary scenario and to future possibilities.

from
Harvest (for Rosa Parks) *

by NIKKI GIOVANNI

I guess everybody wants ... to be special ... and pretty ... the boys ... just want to be strong ... or fast ... all the same things ... children want ... everywhere ... It was ordinary ... as far as I can see ... my childhood ... but ... well ... I don't know ... much ... about psychology ... We had a lot of pride ... growing up ... in Tuskegee ... You could easily see ... what our people could do ... if somebody set a mind ... to it ... Father was a carpenter ... Mama taught school ... I got married ... at nineteen ...

You always felt ... you should do something ... It just wasn't right ... what they did to Negroes ... and why Negroes ... let it happen ... Colored people couldn't vote ... couldn't use the bathroom in public places ... couldn't go to the same library they paid taxes for ... had to sit on the back of the buses ... couldn't live places ... work places ... go to movies ... amusement parks ... Nothing ... if you were colored ... Just signs ... always signs ... saying No ... No ... No ...

---

* From *Harvest (for Rosa Parks)* from *Those Who Ride the Night Winds* by Nikki Giovanni. Copyright © by Nikki Giovanni. By permission of William Morrow & Company, Inc.

My husband is a fine man ... a fighting man ... When we were young ... belonging to the N double A C P was radical ... dangerous ... People got killed ... run out of town ... beaten and burned out ... just for belonging ... My husband belonged ... and belonged ... In 1943 ... during the war ... Double Victory was just as important ... one thing without the other was not good ... enough ... I was elected Secretary ... of the Montgomery branch ... I am proud ... of that ... Many people just think History ... just fell on my shoulders ... or at my feet ... 1 december 1955 ... but that's not true ...

Sometimes it seemed it was never going ... to stop ... That same driver ... who had me arrested ... had put me off a bus ... from Maxwell Air Base ... where I had worked ... or maybe they all ... look the same ... I wasn't looking ... for anything ... That Colvin girl had been arrested ... and nobody did anything ... I didn't think ... they would do anything ... when the driver told us ... it was four of us ... to move ... Three people moved ... I didn't ... I couldn't ... it was just so ... wrong ... Nobody offered to go ... with me ... A neighbor ... on the same bus ... didn't even tell ... my husband ... what had happened ... I just thought ... we should let them know ... I should let them know ... it wasn't right ... You have to realize ... I was forty years old ... all my life ... all I'd seen ... were signs ... that everything was getting worse ...

The press people came ... around after ... we won ... I had to reenact ... everything ... I was on the aisle ... the man by the window ... got up ... I don't fault him ... for getting up ... he was just doing ... what he was told ... Across the aisle were two women ... they got up ... too ... There was a lot of violence ... physical and verbal ... I kinda thought ... something might happen ... to me ... I just didn't ... couldn't ... get up ...

They always tell us one ... person doesn't make any difference ... but it seems to me ... something ... should be done ... In all these years ... it's strange ... but maybe not ... nobody asks ... about my life ... If I have children ... why I moved to Detroit ... what I think ... about what we tried ... to do ... somehow ... you want to say things ... are better ... somehow ... they are ... not in many ways ... People ... older people ... are afraid ... younger people ... are too ... I really don't know ... where it will end ... Our people ... can break ... your heart ... so can other ... people ... I just think ... it makes a difference ... what one person does ... young people forget that ... what one person does ... makes a difference ...

❋ EXERCISES

Reading Comprehension

A. Choose the best answer for the following:

1. The years after World War II in America were
   a. more carefree than the years after World War I.
   b. just as carefree as the years after World War I.
   c. more cautious than the years after World War I.

2. "There were several important reasons for *this.*" In paragraph 2, the italicized word refers to
   a. the self-indulgence of the twenties.
   b. the caution of the fifties.
   c. the caution of the twenties.

3. All of the following were causes for the suspicious mood of the fifties except
   a. Europe's recovery.
   b. the Great Depression.
   c. international tensions.

4. In paragraph 4, the author
   a. continues the topic of paragraph 3.
   b. presents a contrast to paragraph 3.
   c. introduces an entirely new topic.

5. According to the information in paragraph 5,
   a. the arms race brought security at last.
   b. the arms race increased international tensions.
   c. the arms race gave America a permanent advantage.

6. Both the United Nations and the Marshall Plan are introduced as examples of
   a. mistakes America made after World War I.
   b. mistakes America made after World War II.
   c. attempts America made to avoid repeating previous errors.

7. From what we are told in paragraph 17, we may assume that
   a. King had a stormy relationship with his parents.
   b. parental support was an important factor in King's development.
   c. King owed more to his mother than to his father.

8. "But in the Deep South in the first half of this century, it was difficult to remember such encouragement." The reasons for this statement in paragraph 18 are given in
   a. paragraph 17.
   b. paragraph 18.
   c. paragraph 19.

9. The main topic of paragraph 21 is
   a. Gandhi's philosophy.
   b. discrimination in America.
   c. the nonviolent movement in America.

10. King and his wife may best be compared because
    a. they were both from the Deep South.
    b. they had both gone to school in the North.
    c. they were both committed to the cause of civil rights.
11. What is the subject of paragraph 31?
    a. King's achievements
    b. the international honors that King received
    c. the problems that King faced in the mid-sixties

B.   **In your own words, complete the sentences below.**

1. Although Americans grew carefree after the First World War, _____

   _____ .

2. Whereas America had refused to join the League of Nations, _____

   _____ .

3. Despite the end of hostilities in Korea,_____

   _____ .

4. Even though America developed a hydrogen bomb during the fifties, _____

   _____ .

5. Since there was a tradition of segregation in the South during the fifties,_____

   _____ .

6. Like both of his parents, Dr. Martin Luther King, Jr., believed _____

   _____ .

7. Unlike supporters of violent revolution, King favored_____

   _____ .

8. Because Coretta Scott King shared her husband's high ideals, _____

   _____ .

C.   **Fill in the following blanks with any appropriate word.**

In contrast to the carefree crowds of Jazz Age high society, Americans in the

fifties were _____ and _____ . Many of them could still remember the

_____ . They often asked themselves if it could happen again. They were also

disturbed by international _____ . They had long been accustomed to a

simpler isolation; now, their nation was a _____ . Its destiny was linked

to the future of its allies. From opponents it faced the pressures of continuous

mistrust.

Unfortunately, because of these pressures, an arms race developed. But as new _____ were stockpiled, the tensions of the Cold War continued to increase. People questioned if there would ever be peace on this planet. They wondered if there would be one final _____ .

One thing was certain. Americans could not repeat the _____ they had committed after World War I. Now, they had to _____ a new world organization; and they also had to try to _____ the devastated nations of Europe.

Both of these tasks were quickly _____ . Yet in spite of these efforts, conditions in Europe as well as Asia continued to cause _____ . Throughout Germany, for example, _____ and _____ were in constant competition. There was also trouble in Korea. It is no wonder, therefore, that as the fifties progressed, _____ also mounted throughout America.

Vocabulary

A.   **Choose the words that are closest in meaning to the italicized words in the following sentences:**

1. Like Abraham Lincoln, he believed that America's future lay in a realization of Jefferson's *vision*.
   a. dreams   b. accusations   c. fears
2. Her family tradition, like her husband's commitment, was one of active *civic* service.
   a. religious   b. community   c. family
3. In Connecticut, he suddenly experienced a sense of *liberation*.
   a. happiness   b. freedom   c. loneliness
4. King was impressed by the Gandhian philosophy of nonviolent *resistance*.
   a. opposition   b. surrender   c. acceptance
5. From one simple *incident* on the bus lines of Montgomery, the civil rights crusade began.
   a. attack   b. event   c. refusal
6. "Love was the *regulating* ideal," said King.
   a. controlling   b. developing   c. expanding
7. It was a mistake, he said, to become involved in another nation's *internal* struggles.
   a. international   b. continuous   c. civil
8. *Courteous* and persuasive, King was an effective leader.
   a. courageous   b. polite   c. well-prepared

B. Antonyms. Choose the italicized word that best completes each sentence below.

1. Jazz Age society was often *(reckless, careful)*.
2. People in the fifties, however, were often *(prudent, careless)*.
3. The *(quiet, boisterous)* excitement of the Roaring Twenties vanished.
4. As the arms race expanded, *(sophisticated, simple)* weapons were developed.
5. Then the mounting anxiety became *(tolerable, unendurable)*.
6. For the sake of world peace, America had to offer *(faltering, unwavering)* support to the establishment of a new world organization.
7. Because of continuous international tension, *(confidence, apprehension)* mounted throughout America.

C. Idioms and Special Expressions.   From the following list, substitute an appropriate phrase for the italicized words in the sentences below. Make all necessary changes.

year after year	*no wonder*	*within a year*
at issue	*hold fast to*	*put an end to*
in the wake of	*well under way*	*resort to*
a matter of time		

1. King insisted that the protestors should not *use* violence.
2. In spite of increasing difficulties, he *remained committed to* his beliefs.
3. When King went to Alabama, his doctoral thesis *had progressed significantly*.
4. *As a result of* World War II's destruction, two competing power blocs had emerged.
5. *It is no surprise that* Americans reacted with increasing suspicion.
6. "Is it *inevitable?*" Americans wondered. "Will there soon be a final confrontation?"
7. *Before the end of one year,* the Soviets, too, had built a hydrogen bomb.
8. The senseless violence King had always condemned *stopped* his determined efforts.
9. The beliefs of our ancestors are still *a subject of controversy*, Kennedy said.
10. He also asked his countrymen to struggle hard *every year*.

Structures

A. Match the clauses in column A with those in column B.

A	B
1. When the armistice ended the First World War,	people felt as though there would never be another confrontation.
2. Because the Depression continued to worsen,	Americans in the fifties became prudent and suspicious.
3. Because postwar Communism spread rapidly abroad,	King felt as if the curtain had been dropped on his selfhood.
4. When he returned from his job in Connecticut,	King's critics felt as though there hadn't been sufficient progress.
5. Since discrimination continued throughout the sixties,	Americans felt as though there would never be prosperity again.

B. Following the model, change the sentences below.

Model: Despite his indignation, King did not give in to helpless rage.
→ *In spite of his indignation,* King did not give in to helpless rage.

1. Despite the heat, enormous crowds had gathered to hear King's speech.
2. Despite King's insistence on nonviolent resistance, riots broke out in urban ghettos.
3. Despite Hoover's efforts, unemployment in America continued to rise.
4. Despite the driver's repeated requests, Rosa Parks refused to leave her seat.
5. Despite his exhaustion, Lindbergh managed to cross the Atlantic.

Composition

Choose one of the following.

A. During the decade that followed the end of the Second World War, many Americans became prudent, controlled, and suspicious of other world powers. Review the information given in paragraphs 1–5 of the Historical Background. Then in your own words, explain why these feelings of insecurity developed.

B. After the First World War, many Americans were opposed to extensive involvement in European affairs. After World War II, however, the situation was very different. In one well-developed paragraph, talk about this difference, showing how America played a key role in the postwar reconstruction. (You may wish to reread paragraphs 6–9 of the Historical Background.)

C. "It was the straw that broke the camel's back." According to this proverb, people who carry many burdens may often reach their level of endurance; so an additional load—no matter how small—may suddenly provoke a rebellion. Rosa Parks had long endured the burden of discrimination. Then, one evening, she refused to accept additional humiliation. Tell the story of Mrs. Parks's refusal and the effect it had on the career of Dr. King.

D. Reread the last paragraph of the historical introduction. What do you think King meant by the "promised land"? From what you have read, do you think King took his people closer to this land? In what ways?

Topics for Class Discussion

Interviewing a partner or a small group of your classmates, talk about the following.

A. Why do you think Dr. King might have enjoyed talking with each of the following? What might they have had in common?

1. Jane Addams
2. Queen Liliuokalani
3. Franklin D. Roosevelt
4. John Steinbeck

B. In your opinion, who overcame the greatest disadvantages?

1. Andrew Carnegie
2. Thomas Edison
3. Martin Luther King, Jr.

C. Does discrimination of any kind exist in your country? Is it social? religious? racial? Has it existed for a long time? Are conditions improving? worsening? What, if anything, do you feel can be done about it?

D. Of the people you have studied in this volume, who, in your opinion, was

the most talented?	the most appealing?
the most determined?	the least appealing?
the most tragic?	the luckiest?
the most unlucky?	the most successful?
the most inspiring?	the most charismatic?
the most energetic?	the most extraordinary?

SOME INTERESTING PLACES TO VISIT

New England Area

Boston African American National Historic Site
Boston, Massachusetts

John F. Kennedy National Historic Site
Brookline, Massachusetts

Museum at the John Fitzgerald Kennedy Library
University of Massachusetts
Boston, Massachusetts

Middle Atlantic Area

United Nations
New York, New York

African American Historical and Cultural
    Museum
Philadelphia, Pennsylvania

National Museum of African Art
Washington, D.C.

Southeastern and South Central Areas

John F. Kennedy Grave Site
Arlington National Cemetery
Arlington, Virginia

Martin Luther King, Jr., National Historic Site
Atlanta, Georgia

Civil Rights Memorial
Montgomery, Alabama

Museum of Science and History
    (Birthplace of Gen. Douglas MacArthur)
Little Rock, Arkansas

Midwestern Area

Museum of African American History
Detroit, Michigan

11

Bicentennial Reflections

Lincoln's Promise Outstanding

PREREADING

Look at the photograph below. Then, working in pairs or small groups, answer these questions.

1. Escorted by hundreds of smaller American boats, tall ships from around the world enter New York City's harbor during the American bicentennial celebration. What kind of ships are they? Why do you think this international parade was chosen as an appropriate way to celebrate? Do you think New York City's harbor was a fitting place for this celebration? Why, or why not?

2. How old is your country? Is there a national day or a day of independence commemorated each year? When is it? What are some of the ways in which people celebrate on this day? Has your country experienced many changes in the last century? What are some of these changes?

New York City's harbor, July 4, 1976

1   July 4, 1976. As Americans celebrated their nation's bicentennial, there were many among them who paused to consider how the country had developed since its centennial festivities.[1] It had been a nation of farmers at the end of the Civil War— a land of wide undeveloped prairies and the promise of opportunity. Then, with the coming of the railroads, this promise had become reality for American settlers. Though Native Americans had encountered relentless devastation, pioneers had prospered on the nation's sun-baked plains. Industrialists had built legendary empires. And the spirit of invention had quickly swept over the continent. So by the turn of the century, rural America had begun to disappear. The United States was emerging as the leader in a modern and mechanized world.

2   But with leadership and prosperity had come new problems and commitments. Toward the end of the nineteenth century, there had been conflicts in the Caribbean as well as the Pacific. Twenty years later, during the world's first total war, American soldiers had fought with their allies in the terrible trenches of Europe. A frantic[2] decade—the Roaring Twenties—had resulted; and then, in quick succession, had come economic chaos, a second world war, and the disturbing anxieties of the nuclear age. Indeed, America's second century had been one of sweeping transformations. Each decade had differed from the one that preceded[3] it. Each generation had looked back in wonder at the passing of old customs and outmoded beliefs.

3   In the midst[4] of this constant change, however, there had been one enduring tradition: from the Gilded Age to the protests of the sixties, Americans had found guidance in the dream of their nation's founders. This had been clear in the career of Jane Addams, in the reforms of Franklin D. Roosevelt, in the dedication of La Guardia, and in the struggles of Dr. Martin Luther King, Jr. They all had represented a return in times of crisis to the democratic visions of the nation's creators.

4   But in the problematic future, would the tradition continue? Would leaders emerge who could take the nation forward toward a fuller realization of those democratic visions? Pessimists had their growing doubts. For in the period preceding the country's bicentennial, there were many disturbing events and developments. In 1963, for example, the promise of John Kennedy's presidency was shattered by an assassin's bullet. And though Kennedy's successor, Lyndon Johnson, expanded his predecessor's social welfare plans, though he sponsored important legislation to wage an aggressive War on Poverty,* the Johnson years were traumatic ones for the American people. They were years when the nation's involvement in Vietnam continued to escalate dramatically.

---

1. festivities: celebration
2. frantic: very excited

3. precede: go before
4. midst: middle

* For example, he supported laws to protect the voting rights of Americans and to decrease discrimination in housing and employment. He also sponsored a Medicare system of health benefits for the elderly, a program of federal assistance to schools and colleges, laws to purify the nation's environment, measures for the rehabilitation of America's cities, and new consumer protection legislation.

VIETNAM, WATERGATE, AND THE COUNTERCULTURE REBELLION

5   Here, as in the area of domestic programs, Johnson continued his predecessors' policies. For in the conflict between South Vietnam and Communist North Vietnam, President Eisenhower had sent military advisors to support South Vietnam, and Kennedy had increased America's presence to sixteen thousand soldiers. But the major escalation took place after Kennedy's death. In 1964, after reports of an attack on American ships near Vietnam, Johnson asked Congress to pass the Tonkin Gulf Resolution—a statement which authorized the president "to repel any armed attack against the forces of the United States and to prevent further aggression." Then, from 1965 to the end of Johnson's administration in 1968, the terrible struggle in Vietnam expanded. Bombing raids against North Vietnam began in 1965; the number of American troops increased to over half a million; the cost of the war, by 1967, was up to twenty-five billion dollars per year; and as the years of guerilla warfare continued, the far greater cost in human lives was staggering. By 1973, the year of America's withdrawal from Vietnam, there had been a total of over 350,000 American casualties, while Vietnamese casualties for both the North and the South were estimated to have reached over four million.

6   In 1968, Johnson chose not to run for reelection, for American opposition to the war had steadily grown. Thus, it was under Richard Nixon, Johnson's successor, that the American withdrawal from Vietnam occurred. Yet the Nixon years (1968 to 1974) brought still another traumatic experience to the American people: the Watergate scandal. On June 17, 1972, five men were arrested as they attempted to break into and wiretap the Watergate* office of Democratic Party National Committee headquarters. Little by little, it was revealed that the break-in had been planned by some high-ranking Republican party members. Extensive investigations uncovered evidence of further illegal activities among presidential advisors. As the scandals multiplied, public confidence in the Nixon administration decreased. Finally, on August 5, 1974, the President admitted that he had cooperated in attempting to cover up the facts about Watergate. Four days later, he resigned from office—the first president in America's history to do so.

7   Thus, in the decade preceding America's bicentennial, the country was rocked repeatedly by a series of long and bitterly painful experiences. In addition to Vietnam, Kennedy's assassination, and Watergate, there occurred the assassination of Dr. Martin Luther King, Jr., in April 1968, and that of Robert Kennedy two months later. Also, as an expression of the unrest that was caused by these experiences, violence spread throughout certain areas of society. On the nation's campuses, at the height of the Vietnam conflict, there was widespread student unrest. In some major cities, in spite of Dr. King's philosophy, explosive tensions led to rioting—confrontations that were supported by militant African-American leaders such as Stokely Carmichael and H. Rap Brown. And across the nation, especially among America's disillusioned youth, a counterculture of rebellion, drug experimentation, and sexual liberation spread.

---

* Watergate: Washington, D.C., apartment complex.

ECONOMIC DOWNTURN OF THE SEVENTIES

8   The economy, too, had become a source of concern by the end of the 1970s. Prices were rising sharply, while productivity was declining. Both at home and abroad—with increasing competition from European, Japanese, and emerging Pacific Rim manufacturers—American companies found themselves settling for[5] a smaller share of key markets. Especially in the automobile industry and in the growing field of electronics, there were signs of a disturbing trade imbalance. As exports fell off and unemployment spiraled, some Americans feared the possibility of another Great Depression.

9   They were also afraid of a growing "energy crunch."[6] Having failed to conserve their own energy resources, they had become more and more dependent on oil from abroad. In 1973, the situation became critical when OPEC* nations, intent upon raising oil prices, imposed an embargo on oil shipments to the United States. Almost immediately, the cost of gasoline, heating oil, and fuel for industry in America soared. It was a sobering[7] experience. For the first time since World War II, America seemed to be surrendering the control of its own economy. It also seemed to be losing international prestige. A new world order was taking shape—one in which American power seemed to be diminishing.

CHANGING POSITION OF THE UNITED STATES ABROAD

10   This was especially clear toward the end of the decade. In 1979, after the shah of Iran was overthrown, President Carter admitted the shah for medical treatment in America. In protest, opponents of the deposed shah seized Americans in the U.S. embassy in Teheran, dealing a blow to the Carter presidency and to American pride. When a rescue attempt to free the hostages failed, American morale[8] hit a new low. People became angry, despondent.[9] After the violence of the 1960s, the Vietnam conflict, the Watergate scandal, and the energy embargo, the long hostage crisis seemed to confirm their worst fears. "These continual upheavals have weakened us badly," they thought. "Even our own security is at risk."

THE PRESIDENCY OF RONALD REAGAN

11   In the elections of 1980, Americans showed their concern by refusing to reelect President Carter. Instead, they chose Ronald Reagan, former governor of California. Almost seventy at the time, Reagan was the oldest man elected president in America's history. Yet to many of the voters, he seemed full of youthful vigor. Time and again, in eloquent speeches, he outlined the changes he felt America needed: a reduction in government social welfare spending, decreased federal regulation of private enterprise, improved military defenses, and a return to traditional values. He was confident and persuasive, expressing hope in the future and unshakable faith in the country's potential. Not surprisingly, to a people tired of economic problems, political humiliations, and social instability, he was enormously appealing.

---

5. settle for: accept
6. energy crunch: lack of fuel
7. sobering: humbling

8. morale: self-confidence
9. despondent: sad; depressed

* OPEC: Organization of Petroleum Exporting Countries

12   Once in office, Reagan worked quickly to put his programs into effect. He cut billions from social welfare spending and added billions to the budget for national defense. Taxes were reduced to stimulate the economy, and federal regulations of private enterprise decreased. Less is more, Reagan believed, when it came to the role of the government in private affairs. Instead of federal interference, he preached aggressive individualism. This, he insisted, would create a new prosperity. It would bring back the frontier spirit. It would also restore pride in the American dream.

13   Toward the middle of the 1980s, as the president had predicted, there were indeed signs of a new prosperity. Unemployment declined, inflation decreased, and consumer spending—fueled by the growing confidence—soared. Reagan's popularity also soared. In the elections of 1984, he was overwhelmingly reelected.[10] America was on the move, it seemed. Once again, after a long period of turbulence,[11] there was a promise of wealth and the possibility of prestige. People everywhere began to focus on these material possibilities, turning away from the idealism of the preceding age. They were exhausted by the conflicts they had faced in the last two decades. Now, even among the young, there was a new preoccupation:[12] to have a share in the land of plenty while the prosperity endured.

THE ROARING EIGHTIES AND A NEW NATION DIVIDED

14   Fortunes were made on Wall Street during this period of expansion. Millions were also made in real estate, banking, and corporate development. Like the Jazz Age of the Twenties, it was a time of frenzied[13] speculation.[14] Also like the Jazz Age, it was a time of conspicuous consumption.[15] Money was spent lavishly on homes, furnishings, cars, clothing, and vacations. Status was eagerly sought and loudly proclaimed.[16] Self-indulgence became the fashion, as extravagant luxuries turned into necessities.

15   Unfortunately, however, not everyone shared equally in the boom of the Roaring Eighties. Those with a good education, social connections, and financial backing were best able to profit from the sudden opportunities. People without these advantages were often excluded. Thus, especially in urban environments, the gap between rich and poor widened. Inner cities were plagued with[17] growing violence and decay. The rapid spread of crack—a powerful, relatively inexpensive drug—victimized neighborhoods that were already coping with poor schools, inadequate housing, and unemployment. Most disturbing of all was the growing AIDS* epidemic. Among drug addicts, for example, the death toll from this disease was steadily rising. Yet money to deal with a problem like AIDS was getting harder to find, for cuts in social welfare expenses had reduced federal, state, and local assistance.

16   Truly, as in the Gilded Age of a century earlier, America in the 1980s seemed to be splitting in two. On the one side was the promise of a luxurious prosperity; on the other was the hopelessness of the permanently poor. Any true picture of the decade,

---

10. overwhelmingly reelected: chosen again in a great victory
11. turbulence: turmoil; confusion
12. preoccupation: constant thought
13. frenzied: frantic; very excited

14. speculation: risky investment
15. conspicuous consumption: money spent on expensive items
16. proclaim: announce
17. plagued with: troubled by

* AIDS: Acquired Immune Deficiency Syndrome

then, must show both of these sides, and no one has done this better than the contemporary writer Tom Wolfe.

FOCUS ON TOM WOLFE

17   Born in Richmond, Virginia, in 1931, Tom Wolfe became a journalist after receiving his doctorate in American Studies from Yale University. As a feature writer and reporter, he became famous for developing New Journalism, a vivid nonfiction style that used techniques normally found only in novels and short stories. Among these techniques were detailed descriptions, realistic dialogues, psychological analyses, and unusual punctuation. Wolfe included them all in his journalism, creating a bold combination of factual reporting and imaginative summary.

18   His first novel, *The Bonfire of the Vanities,* was published in 1987. The book was instantly successful, becoming a national best-seller and the basis for a film released in the fall of 1990. Like Fitzgerald's *The Great Gatsby*—the classic portrayal of Jazz Age corruption—Wolfe's *The Bonfire of the Vanities,* became a true classic of the 1980s. In fact, as one reviewer has written, "No one has portrayed New York Society this accurately[18] and devastatingly since Edith Wharton."* Wolfe's style is very different from Edith Wharton's, to be sure. But his subject is very similar: Manhattan money and its effect on the rich and poor in New York.

19   Written on a grand scale, the story is told with a sweeping realism, recalling the great nineteenth-century European novels of Balzac or Dickens. Its hero, Sherman McCoy, is a young, successful Wall Street bond trader. As the story begins, he is at the top of his profession. He earns a million dollars a year, lives in a Park Avenue duplex, spends all of his money lavishly, and feels vastly superior to the less privileged people around him. Indeed, though he is not yet forty, he thinks of himself as a "Master of the Universe"—powerful, privileged, well-mannered, and well-connected. He is devoted to his small daughter, though he has long since become bored with his socialite wife. Hence he has become involved with Maria Ruskin, a beautiful, young woman married to a wealthy, old businessman.

20   As he is driving Maria home from the airport one night, Sherman takes a wrong turn and finds himself lost in the dark streets of the Bronx. He goes further and further astray,[19] hopelessly confused, until he finally sees a ramp to the Manhattan expressway. Getting out of the car to remove a few tires blocking the ramp, he notices two African-American youths approaching. They want to help him, they say. Sherman panics.[20] Do they really want to help him? He throws a tire in their direction, runs toward the car, and jumps into the passenger seat, just as Maria—now in the driver's seat—steps on the gas. They hear a terrifying sound as they lurch[21] past the tires—the sound of a body falling, the sound of a collision. They do not stop. In a matter of seconds, they are back on the expressway, racing toward Manhattan.

---

18. accurate: correct
19. go astray: become lost
20. panic: become frightened and confused

21. lurch: stagger; move forward unevenly

* Richard Vigilante, "The Truth About Tom Wolfe," *National Review,* 18 Dec. 1987, p. 46.

21   From this isolated event at the beginning of the novel, Wolfe's incredible panorama of New York City unfolds. Characters are introduced from the Wall Street world of high finance, from the Bronx world of the courts, from trendy restaurants, terrifying jail cells, summer clubs, subways, newsrooms, and restrooms. Little by little, these characters become connected, as Sherman's involvement in the hit-and-run accident becomes known. He is arrested for leaving an accident scene—a charge that becomes more serious when his accident victim finally dies.

22   For Sherman McCoy, "Master of the Universe," nothing will ever again be the same. He loses his job, his family, his apartment, his mistress, his friends. In the process, he comes to the realization that his whole life has been a lie. He has allowed his possessions to define his personality, his inner self. Without them—without all the money and the status—he is spiritually bankrupt. Alone, and very frightened, he finds himself trapped in the alien[22] world of criminal justice. He is brutalized,[23] victimized, and stripped of all illusions. He learns to resort to violence, as the poor in the ghettos must do. He also learns, as they do, never to trust anyone. For even among the authorities—among church leaders, politicians, community officials, and attorneys— greed and ambition have replaced honor and faith. Wolfe has brilliantly captured the flavor of the prosperous eighties—"the decade of money fever," as he once called it in an interview. He has also captured the horrors faced by the underprivileged in those years. Thus, though filled with humorous incidents, *The Bonfire of the Vanities* is a very chilling novel. Like millions of others who are condemned to live in the inner cities, Sherman McCoy finds a nightmare—not the American dream.

23   There is a glimmer[24] of hope, though, toward the close of the novel. As he prepares for the trial he must face, with no possessions to give him any identity, Sherman slowly begins to develop a new self-esteem. "In an odd way I feel liberated," he confesses at the end. He has found inner strength through suffering. He has also discovered a new connection to others. No longer the "master" of his universe, he is finally *part* of the city—equal to everyone, superior to none. His destiny is forever tied to that of the great urban world around him.

24   For many readers of Wolfe's novel, Sherman McCoy's transformation offers a commentary on America's cities as the twenty-first century dawns. Through a connection to others, there is the promise of renewal. Through the discovery of a shared destiny, there is a chance of rebirth.

---

22. alien: foreign
23. brutalize: treat with cruelty
24. glimmer: tiny light

The following selection from *The Bonfire of the Vanities* is deservedly[1] famous. Filled with realistic details, repetitions, unusual punctuation, italics, foreign phrases, and amusing exaggerations, it is a perfect example of Wolfe's well-known style. It is also a brilliant interior monologue—a passage that shows the flow of a character's thoughts. In this case, they are the thoughts of Sherman McCoy as he waits nervously during the second day after the hit-and-run accident.

To Sherman's relief, there has been no mention of the accident in any of the papers. Yet, as he struggles to pay attention to the financial deals in his office, he continues to worry. What would happen, he wonders, if his role in the accident were ever discovered? What would happen to his latest international money scheme—the Giscard deal—that promised millions of dollars profit from gold-backed French bonds? It would collapse, Sherman decides. And he would lose status as well as a hefty[2] commission. He might even be forced to move into a modest one-million-dollar apartment—an impossible humiliation. Of course, what Sherman doesn't even imagine is the far greater suffering that awaits him in the future.

from
The Bonfire of the Vanities

by TOM WOLFE

—his spirits plunged[3] even lower. *One* breath of scandal, and not only would the Giscard scheme collapse but *his very career* would be finished! And what would he do then? *I'm already going broke on a million dollars a year!* The appalling figures came popping up into his brain. Last year his income had been $980,000. But he had to pay out $21,000 a month for the $1.8 million loan he had taken out to buy the apartment. What was $21,000 a month to someone making a million a year? That was the way he had thought of it at the time—and in fact, it was merely a *crushing, grinding burden*—that was all! It came to $252,000 a year, none of it deductible,[4] because it was a personal loan, not a mortgage. (The cooperative boards in Good Park Avenue Buildings like his didn't allow you to take out a mortgage on your apartment.) So, considering the taxes, it required $420,000 in income to pay the $252,000. Of the $560,000 remaining of his income last year, $44,400 was required for the apartment's monthly maintenance fees;[5] $116,000 for the house on Old Drover's Mooring Lane in Southampton ($84,000 for mortgage payment and interest, $18,000 for heat, utilities, insurance, and repairs, $6,000 for lawn and hedge cutting, $8,000 for taxes). Entertaining at home and in restaurants had come to $37,000. This was a modest sum compared to what other people spent; for example, Campbell's birthday party in Southampton had had only one carnival ride (plus, of

---

1. deservedly: with good reason
2. hefty: large; heavy
3. plunge: drop suddenly
4. deductible: constituting a tax reduction permitted by the government
5. maintenance fee: money for repairs and services

course, the obligatory[6] ponies and the magician) and had cost less than $4,000. The Taliaferro School, including the bus service, cost $9,400 for the year. The tab[7] for furniture and clothes had come to about $65,000; and there was little hope of reducing that, since Judy was, after all, a decorator and had to keep things up to par. The servants (Bonita, Miss Lyons, Lucille the cleaning woman, and Hobie the handyman in Southampton) came to $62,000 a year. That left only $226,200, or $18,850 a month, for additional taxes and this and that, including insurance payments (nearly a thousand a month, if averaged out), garage rent for two cars ($840 a month), household food ($1,500 a month), club dues (about $250 a month)—the abysmal[8] truth was that he had spent *more* than $980,000 last year. Well, obviously he could cut down here and there—but not nearly enough—*if the worst happened!* There was no getting out from under the $1.8 million loan, the crushing $21,000-a-month nut[9] without paying it off or selling the apartment and moving into one far smaller and more modest —an *impossibility!* There was no turning back! Once you had lived in a $2.6 million apartment on Park Avenue—it was impossible to live in a $1 million apartment! Naturally, there was no way to explain this to a living soul. Unless you were a complete fool, you couldn't even make the words come out of your mouth. Nevertheless—*it was so!* It was ... *an impossibility!* Why, his building was one of the great ones built just before the First World War! Back then it was still not entirely proper for a good family to live in an apartment (instead of a house). So the apartments were built like mansions, with eleven-, twelve-, thirteen-foot ceilings, vast entry galleries, staircases, servants' wings, herringbone-parquet[10] floors, interior walls a foot thick, exterior walls as thick as a fort's, and fireplaces, fireplaces, fireplaces, even though the buildings were all built with central heating. A mansion!—except that you arrived at the front door via an elevator (opening upon your own private vestibule) instead of the street. That was what you got for $2.6 million, and anyone who put one foot in the entry gallery of the McCoy duplex on the tenth floor knew he was in ... *one of those fabled[11] apartments that the world,* le monde,[12] *died for!* And what did a million get you today? At most, at most, at *most:* a three-bedroom apartment—no servants' rooms, no guest rooms, let alone dressing rooms and a sunroom—in a white-brick high-rise built east of Park Avenue in the 1960s with 8 ½-foot ceilings, a dining room but no library, an entry gallery the size of a closet, no fireplace, skimpy[13] lumberyard moldings,[14] if any, plasterboard walls that transmit whispers, and no private elevator stop. Oh no; instead, a mean[15] windowless elevator hall with at least five pathetically[16] plain bile-beige[17] metal-sheathed[18] doors, each protected by two or more ugly drop locks, opening upon it, one of these morbid[19] portals[20] being *yours.*

　　Patently,[21] ... *an impossibility!*

---

6. obligatory: necessary
7. tab: bill
8. abysmal: terrible
9. nut: expense (slang)
10. herringbone parquet: diagonal wood floor pattern
11. fabled: well-known; legendary
12. *le monde:* French for "the world"
13. skimpy: too small

14. molding: wood trim at the top or bottom of a wall
15. mean: poor; unattractive
16. pathetic: pitiful; very sad
17. bile-beige: greenish-tan
18. sheathed: covered
19. morbid: gloomy; depressing
20. portal: door
21. patently: obviously

Though very different from *The Bonfire of the Vanities,* another book of the eighties—*The Dream of the Earth*—has a similar theme. Its author, Thomas Berry, is a well-respected American historian and conservationist. He is also, like Tom Wolfe, a careful observer of contemporary trends. He, too, has described the quest for power and profit that typified the 1980s, and he has vividly portrayed its catastrophic results.

In the reckless pursuit of gain, Berry insists, there is a double danger: a threat to the spiritual health of humanity, and an ever-increasing danger to the balance of nature. Uncontrolled industrialization has depleted[1] the earth's richness, he writes, while technological advancements have contaminated our air. Yet the quest for profit continues. In the name of progress, human technologies still ravage our planet's technologies—a process that endangers *all* of the earth's inhabitants.

To reverse this trend, Berry concludes, we need a new global philosophy. Instead of proudly assuming we are the masters of our universe, we must begin to see ourselves as humble participants. Instead of greedily taking as much as we can from the earth, we must respect its delicate balance and cherish its nourishing grandeur. It is a philosophy that has long been central to Native American traditions. Now, as the following selection indicates, human survival may depend on just how well people learn what the Native Americans have to teach.

from
The Dream of the Earth *

by THOMAS BERRY

The Indian people of this hemisphere will soon be ending their first five centuries of contact with the European peoples who have been occupying this region of the world since the early sixteenth century. While there was a certain historical inevitability[2] in this meeting, no adequate interpretation of this event is yet available. It remains, however, one of the most significant events in the total history of the earth. At first glance it was pure tragedy on one side, unmeasured gain on the other, but this is too simple a view. The final evaluation has not yet been made. Just now there is a deeply tragic aspect on the human level for all concerned.

The effects of this meeting have varied in South America, in Mexico and Central America, in the United States, in Canada. The Spanish, Portuguese, French, English, and Dutch were the earliest to occupy the North American continent. Other peoples of Europe came later. Peoples from Africa were brought here. Then, more recently,

---

1. deplete: reduce   2. inevitable: cannot be avoided

peoples of Asia arrived. Among all these newcomers the Indian peoples maintain their unique status as the original dwellers in this region of the world. They have this position of honor not merely by their temporal[3] priority, but also by their mystical understanding and communion with the continent.... Even those desolate[4] regions assigned to the Indian tribes by the white peoples seem to become sources of strength. This has become true particularly for the Navajo. After having been removed from their original land and placed in starving conditions for years, the Navajo were given back a desolate part of their former territory. Despite their displacement,[5] they survived in communion with this territory to become the most populous[6] of all the tribal peoples of the continent. What is profoundly impressive is the subjective[7] communion that takes place between the Indian and the North American continent.

This communion with the natural world, understood with a certain instinctive awareness by tribal peoples, is something that we, with all our science and technology, seem unable to appreciate, even when our very existence is imperiled.[8] As Europeans on this continent, we have had a certain sense of ourselves as above all other living forms, as the lordly rulers of the continent. We see the North American continent as divinely presented to us to do with as we please. We were the bearers of that mystical something that we call "civilization." The continent was simply there as an abiding[9] reality that would by some inevitable law not only provide our basic needs, but also endure whatever affliction[10] we might lay upon it. It would sustain any amount of damage as an inexhaustible store[11] of nourishment and of energy for carrying out our divine mission. With supreme shock we discover that our historic mission is not what we thought it was. Beyond that we discover that this continent is a delicate balance of life systems, that the fuels for our machines are limited, that defacing[12] the earth defiles[13] ourselves and destroys the divine voice that speaks so powerfully through every phase of cosmic activity.

The Indian now offers to the Euroamerican a mystical sense of the place of the human and other living beings. This is a difficult teaching for us since we long ago lost our capacity for being present to the earth and its living forms in a mutually[14] enhancing[15] manner. This art of communion with the earth we can relearn from the Indian. Thus a reverse dependence is established. Survival in the future will likely depend more on our learning from the Indian than the Indian's learning from us. In some ultimate sense we need their mythic capacity for relating to this continent more than they need our capacity for mechanistic exploitation of the continent.

---

3. temporal: pertaining to time
4. desolate: lifeless
5. displacement: removal from home
6. most populous: largest in population
7. subjective: personal
8. imperil: endanger
9. abiding: permanent

10. affliction: trouble; pain
11. store: supply
12. deface: make ugly; destroy
13. defile: deface
14. mutual: pertaining to both
15. enhance: improve; make more beautiful

❈ EXERCISES

Reading Comprehension

A.　Choose the best answer for the following:

1.　Paragraphs 1 and 2 of the Historical Background present
   a.　a summary of America's development in the first century.
   b.　a summary of America's development in its first two centuries.
   c.　a summary of America's development in its second century.

2.　Paragraph 3 presents
   a.　a continuation of paragraph 2.
   b.　a contrast to paragraph 2.
   c.　an entirely new topic.

3.　In paragraph 5, the Vietnam conflict is introduced as an example of
   a.　another cold war confrontation.
   b.　a traumatic experience of the sixties and seventies.
   c.　Johnson's war on poverty.

4.　From what we are told in paragraphs 4–6, we may infer that Johnson chose *not* to run for reelection because
   a.　he was exhausted from the strain of the Vietnam conflict.
   b.　he was afraid he might not win reelection.
   c.　he wanted to expand his war on poverty.

5.　All of the following were associated with Nixon except
   a.　America's withdrawal from Vietnam.
   b.　the assassination of Dr. Martin Luther King, Jr.
   c.　the Watergate scandal.

6.　"The economy, too, had become a source of concern by the end of the 1970s." The reasons for this statement in paragraph 8 are given in
   a.　paragraph 8.
   b.　paragraphs 8 and 9.
   c.　paragraphs 8, 9, and 10.

7.　"*This* was especially clear toward the end of the decade." In paragraph 10, the italicized word refers to
   a.　the rise in American fuel prices.
   b.　the decline in American prestige abroad.
   c.　the decline in American productivity.

8.　From what we are told in paragraph 11, we may assume that one of Reagan's greatest advantages was
   a.　his experience as former governor of California.
   b.　his age.
   c.　his ability to express himself forcefully.

9.　In paragraph 14, the author
   a.　continues the topic of paragraph 13.
   b.　presents a contrast to paragraph 13.
   c.　introduces an entirely new topic.

10. Tom Wolfe and F. Scott Fitzgerald may best be compared because
    a. they were both American novelists.
    b. they both wrote about Manhattan.
    c. their novels were classic reflections of the eras in which they lived.
11. What was unique about New Journalism?
    a. It used techniques that had not been used before in nonfiction.
    b. It consisted of simple, straightforward reporting.
    c. It was used only by Tom Wolfe.

B.   Match the presidents in column A with the events, periods, or developments in column B.

A	B
William McKinley	World War I
Theodore Roosevelt	war on poverty
Woodrow Wilson	stock market crash
Warren G. Harding	Watergate
Herbert Hoover	the Roaring Eighties
Franklin D. Roosevelt	World War II
Richard Nixon	Spanish-American War
Lyndon Johnson	Iran hostage crisis
Jimmy Carter	the Roaring Twenties
Ronald Reagan	Progressivism

C.   Complete the following equations.

1. Edith Wharton: New York = Willa Cather: _____

2. World War I: League of Nations = World War II: _____

3. New Deal: United States = Marshall Plan: _____

4. Dr. Martin Luther King, Jr.: Montgomery = Jane Addams: _____

5. John Steinbeck: Nobel Prize for Literature = Dr. Martin Luther King, Jr. =

   _____

6. Johnson: Vietnam = Carter: _____

7. John F. Kennedy: America's youngest elected president = Ronald Reagan:

   _____

8. The Roaring Twenties: F. Scott Fitzgerald = The Roaring Eighties:

   _____

	1492	Columbus arrives in America
	1776	Declaration of Independence—a new nation is born
	1848	Andrew Carnegie arrives in America
America Civil War	⌈1861	
	⌊1865	
	1869	First transcontinental railroad route complete in Utah
America's Centennial	1876	
	1879	Edison invents the light bulb
	1883	Willa Cather moves to Nebraska
	1889	Jane Addams opens Hull House
Native American confrontation at Wounded Knee, South Dakota	1890	
Spanish-American War	1898	
Teddy Roosevelt becomes president	1901	
	1905	*The House of Mirth* published
	1913	*O Pioneers!* published
World War I	⌈1914	
	1917	America enters World War I
	⌊1918	
Prohibition goes into effect	1920	Commercial radio broadcasting develops
	1925	*The Great Gatsby* published
Stock market crashes: Depression begins	1929	*A Farewell to Arms* published
	1931	Death of Thomas Edison
Franklin Roosevelt becomes president	1932	
Prohibition repealed	1933	La Guardia becomes mayor of New York
Depression		
	1939	*The Grapes of Wrath* published
World War II	1941	America enters World War II
	⌊1945	
	1946	First meeting of UN held in London
Korean War	⌈1950	
	⌊1953	
	1955	Dr. Martin Luther King, Jr., begins to lead Montgomery boycott
Hawaii and Alaska become states	1959	
Assassination of President Kennedy	1963	Johnson administration
Assassination of Dr. King	1968	
Nixon administration	1969	American astronauts first land on moon
	1973	OPEC oil embargo
	⌊1974	
America's Bicentennial	1976	
Hostage crisis	1979	
Reagan administration	⌈1980	
	1987	*The Bonfire of the Vanities* published
	⌊1988	
	1992	500th anniversary of the European discovery of America

D. **Study the time line on p. 194. Then answer the following:**

1. Did the Civil War take place in America's first century or in its second?

2. How long after the Civil War ended was the first transcontinental railroad line completed?

3. After Willa Cather moved to Nebraska, how many years elapsed before *O Pioneers!* was published?

4. How long was World War I? World War II?

5. After Teddy Roosevelt became president, how many years elapsed before his cousin Franklin took office?

6. How long was Prohibition in effect?

7. Did Hemingway write *A Farewell to Arms* immediately after World War I? If not, why do you suppose there was a time lag?

8. How long did the Great Depression last?

9. How many years elapsed between the publication of Edith Wharton's *House of Mirth* and Tom Wolfe's *The Bonfire of the Vanities*? Would you say that New York City, the subject of both novels, changed a great deal during those years? Please explain your answer.

10. What happened one hundred years after the first transcontinental railroad was completed? Why were both of these events of major significance in the history of the United States? Can you see any connection between them?

Vocabulary

A. 1. **Word Formation.** In the sentences below, form nouns by adding *-ation, -ance, -ism, -ity,* or *-ment* to the italicized verb. Be sure to drop silent *e* before adding the suffix.

a. *(confront)* In spite of Dr. King's philosophy, violent _____ developed in the 1960s.

b. *(involve)* During President Johnson's term of office, American _____ in the Vietnam war grew.

c. *(escalate)* This _____ worried many Americans.

d. *(secure)* American _____ seemed threatened as the 1970s progressed.

e. *(prosper)* Toward the middle of the 1980s, there were indeed signs of a new _____ .

f. *(assist)* As government _____ decreased, funds for social welfare programs became harder to find.

g. *(realize)* Slowly, Sherman McCoy came to the _____ that his whole life had been a lie.

2. The following words have the prefix *re-* (meaning *again*); from the list, choose a word that best completes each sentence below.

   restore   *recall*   *reelection*   *rebirth*   *resign*

   a. As the Watergate scandal unfolded, many people hoped that the president would _____ .

   b. In spite of the long hostage crisis, President Carter made the decision to run for _____ .

   c. Reagan was sure his new programs could _____ pride in America.

   d. Written on a grand scale, Wolfe's novel _____ the great classics of nineteenth-century realism.

   e. Through a new community spirit, there might be a chance for _____ in American cities.

B.   **Idioms and Special Expressions.**   From the following list, choose the phrase that best substitutes for the italicized words below. Make any necessary changes.

   up to par   *in office*   *get out from under*   *here and there*
   go astray   *go broke*   *time and again*   *deal a blow*

   1. Once *elected*, Reagan worked quickly to put his programs into effect.
   2. Opponents of the shah seized Americans abroad, *damaging* the Carter presidency and American pride.
   3. There was no way that Sherman McCoy could *escape* all the crushing debt.
   4. His wife was a decorator, so she had to keep everything *at its best*.
   5. He was already *spending all his money* on an income of a million dollars a year!
   6. Perhaps she could reduce her expenses *in a few areas*.
   7. They *got lost* in the Bronx.
   8. *Repeatedly*, Reagan outlined the changes he felt America needed.

C.   **Two-Word Verbs.**   Substitute a verb phrase from the following list for the italicized words below. Make any necessary changes.

   come to   *cut down*   *settle for*   *fall off*   *cover up*

   1. American companies in the 1970s had to *accept* smaller shares of key markets.
   2. As exports *declined* and unemployment spiraled, some Americans were afraid of another Great Depression.
   3. After the Watergate scandal, President Nixon was accused of *hiding* the facts.
   4. Sherman McCoy's bills for clothes and furniture *totaled* almost $65,000.
   5. It was unlikely that Mrs. McCoy would *reduce* her expenses.

D. **Antonyms.** Choose the italicized word that best completes each sentence below.

1. During the long hostage crisis, many Americans became *(enthusiastic, despondent)*.
2. Truly, the decade preceding America's bicentennial was a time of great *(peace, turbulence)*.
3. After his arrest, Sherman McCoy became trapped in the *(alien, familiar)* world of criminal justice.
4. As a result of the scandal, he lost a *(hefty, small)* commission.
5. His spirits *(rose, plunged)* when he thought about his problems.
6. After all, ponies were *(obligatory, optional)* at the best parties for children.
7. Apartments with *(generous, skimpy)* moldings were not as elegant as Sherman's great duplex.
8. Like Edith Wharton, Tom Wolfe portrayed Manhattan society *(incorrectly, accurately)*.

Structure

A. Follow the model and complete the sentences below.

Model: *(direct)* If Martin Luther King, Jr., had lived longer, he *would have directed* a great Poor People's March.

1. *(be)* If Americans had conserved their own fuel supplies, there _____ no energy crunch.

2. *(improve)* If the rescue attempt had been successful, Carter's image _____ .

3. *(feel)* If the economy had improved during the 1970s, Americans _____ more secure.

4. *(develop)* If the government had reduced spending, Reagan said, people _____ more self-reliance.

5. *(avoid)* If Sherman McCoy had reported the accident, he _____ the awful nightmare.

B. Following the model, change the sentences you completed in Exercise A.

Model: *If Martin Luther King, Jr., had lived longer, he would have directed a great Poor People's March.*
   → *Had Martin Luther King, Jr., lived longer, he would have directed a great Poor People's March.*

Composition

Choose one of the following.

A. Review the information given in paragraphs 4–10 of the Historical Background. Then in one well-developed paragraph, explain why the decade preceding the bicentennial of the United States was a time of increasing frustration for many Americans.

B. In a well-constructed paragraph, describe Ronald Reagan's philosophy and some of the effects that it had on America in the 1980s. You may wish to reread paragraphs 11–16 of the Historical Background.

C. "To the victor belong the spoils." According to this English proverb, those who compete successfully are entitled to the rewards of victory; those who cannot win, of course, cannot claim any prize. Do you think this proverb reflects the way America developed in the 1980s? Please explain your answer in one well-organized paragraph.

D. Imagine you are one of the most successful financiers in your country. Your salary is one million dollars a year. Instead of saving part of this money, you spend it all every year maintaining your life style. How do you do it? Describe the luxuries you have and the monthly expenses they cost.

Topics for Class Discussion

Interviewing a partner or a small group of your classmates, talk about the following.

A. The 1970s in America were years of stress and insecurity. People had serious doubts about the future and unsettling fears about the past. It was a time of transition, a difficult period of adjustment for the nation. Has your nation ever experienced such a challenge? Were the changes political, social, economic, or a combination of forces?

B. Reagan and Carter were a study in contrasts. In their solutions for America's problems, they offered opposing interpretations. Pick two leaders in your nation who have opposing political views. How are their ideas different? Who is more popular? Who is more experienced? Are they both very different in personality? In age? In looks? Please give as much information as you can.

C. The following pairs would probably have enjoyed talking to each other and sharing their experiences. Why?
   1. Franklin D. Roosevelt/Andrew Carnegie
   2. Thomas Edison/Albert Einstein
   3. Queen Liliuokalani/Dr. Martin Luther King, Jr.
   4. John Steinbeck/Jane Addams
   5. Edith Wharton/Tom Wolfe
   6. Charles Lindbergh/Ronald Reagan

D. Name one of your country's well-known journalists. Does this person write for the newspapers? For magazines? Is he or she also a media personality? Please share as many details as you can about this person.

SOME INTERESTING PLACES TO VISIT

Middle Atlantic Area

Vietnam Veterans Memorial
Washington, D.C.

Southeastern Area

Jimmy Carter Library and Museum
Atlanta, Georgia

South Central Area

American Museum of Science and Energy
Oak Ridge, Tennessee

Lyndon Baines Johnson Library and Museum
Austin, Texas

Pacific Area

Richard Nixon Library and Birthplace
Yorba Linda, California

The Ronald Reagan Presidential Library
Simi Valley, California

12

America's Third Century

The Continuing Quest

PREREADING

Look at the photograph below. Then, working in pairs or small groups, answer these questions.

1. Pictured with the great humanitarian[1] Mother Teresa is Robert Macauley, founder and chairman of AmeriCares. Describe the scene with as much detail as you can. What do you think Robert Macauley might have in common with Mother Teresa? Why do you think she might be interested in his organization?

2. Turn to the photograph on p. 211. Pictured is Dr. Sally K. Ride, America's first woman astronaut, together with fellow crew members of the space shuttle's seventh mission. What special qualities might have enabled Dr. Ride to achieve this high goal? What special training? In becoming an astronaut, what obstacles, if any, do you think she might have faced as a woman?

Mother Teresa and Robert Macauley

---

1. humanitarian: person devoted to helping all people

1   Quietly, but with pride in the pioneer spirit that had defined much of their history, Americans celebrated another important anniversary on July 24, 1989. Twenty years earlier, American astronauts had returned from their first lunar[1] landing—perhaps the most memorable event in the nation's aerospace program. Pausing to reflect on that extraordinary achievement, President Bush urged a new commitment to further research and exploration. America's space program, he insisted, should continue throughout the 1990s, expanding in scope and significance as the twenty-first century dawned. Although some people disagreed, citing urban renovation, environmental conservation, and educational improvements as greater national priorities, most Americans shared in this moment of pride as they looked back on the highlights of American space exploration.

2   This program had its origins in the competition of the cold war. For on October 4, 1957, Soviet scientists astounded[2] the world with the launching of *Sputnik*, earth's first artificial satellite. Less than one month later, a second Russian satellite was encircling the earth. So to equal these dramatic achievements, American scientists intensified their efforts in the new astrophysical technology. Within three months, *Explorer I*—America's first satellite—was launched. And soon a race to the new frontiers of outer space began.

3   Both superpowers were quickly involved in ambitious long-range plans to reach the moon. Here again, as they had with their *Sputniks,* the Soviets scored an initial triumph. On April 12, 1961, Soviet Cosmonaut Yuri Gagarin completed one full circuit in orbit around the earth. Thus, in a mission that lasted just under two hours, he became the first person to travel in outer space. The age of human space flight had suddenly dawned. Could a three-day journey to the moon become reality?

4   In response to this challenge, President John F. Kennedy addressed his fellow Americans on May 25, 1961. "I believe this nation should commit itself," he said, "to achieving the goal, before this decade is out, of landing a man on the moon and returning him safely to earth." Space exploration had to become a priority, he insisted. It was time for the United States to take the lead. "We go into space because whatever mankind must undertake, free men must fully share," he concluded. And throughout America, many people agreed. Thus, there was widespread support for a new aggressive program to explore—and possibly conquer—the mysteries of space.

PROJECT APOLLO AND THE AMERICAN LUNAR LANDINGS

5   Because of this extensive support—and the growing sense of urgency that had followed each Soviet victory—Project Apollo, the planned lunar voyage, became a major American goal throughout the sixties. Enormous Saturn rockets were developed, while a series of piloted spacecraft was also tested and improved. First, from 1961 to 1963, Mercury spacecraft carried American astronauts in suborbital and orbital space flights. Then, toward the middle of the sixties, new spacecraft were

---

1. lunar: pertaining to the moon   2. astound: surprise

developed: the Gemini series. As their name indicates,* Gemini spacecraft were designed to carry two astronauts. (Only one had traveled in each Mercury flight.) They were also intended for extended missions of up to fourteen days in length. During these missions, astronauts practiced EVA (extra-vehicular activity, i.e., spacewalks), docking maneuvers, and other procedures that would be essential to a moon landing. Their reactions to longer space flights were also carefully observed.

6   Toward the end of the sixties, a third type of spacecraft—the Apollo series—was developed. It was a tripartite[3] spacecraft, having a command module[4] to transport three astronauts on a round-trip lunar voyage, a service module to contain the flight's mechanical systems, and a lunar module to land two astronauts on the surface of the moon. Unfortunately, just before Apollo's piloted test flights began, America's first tragedy in space exploration occurred. A flash fire[5] developed while *Apollo 1* stood at the launching pad, and three astronauts—Virgil Grissom, Edward White, and Roger Chaffee—perished instantly inside. The terrible accident was a setback for America, and Project Apollo was temporarily delayed until new fireproofing measures could be adopted.

7   At last, in October 1968, the first piloted Apollo mission—*Apollo 7*—was launched. Though it did not travel to the moon, it provided an opportunity to test essential equipment. Over the next several months, there were similar test flights. And finally, on July 16, 1969, *Apollo 11* began its historic mission. Aboard the spacecraft were astronauts Neil Armstrong, Edwin Aldrin, and Michael Collins. Three days later, they were in lunar orbit—more than 200,000 miles from the earth. While circling the moon, they checked their systems and equipment. Then in the afternoon of July 20— after detaching the lunar module *Eagle* from the command module *Columbia*— Armstrong and Aldrin made a careful descent. Over five hundred million viewers— nearly twenty percent of the world's total population—watched their TVs tensely as the voices of the astronauts described the slow approach. At 4:17 P.M. EDT, there was news of a touchdown. "Houston," said Armstrong, "Tranquillity Base here. The *Eagle* has landed."

8   Almost seven hours later, after checking *Eagle's* systems and putting on their spacesuits, the astronauts were ready to make the first human appearance in an alien world. Jumping from *Eagle's* ladder to the rocky, barren[6] landscape, Armstrong spoke to the viewers on his distant home planet. "That's one small step for a man," he announced; "one giant leap for mankind." It was a moment of unforgettable inspiration—a chance to share with determined explorers in a brave and brilliant discovery.

9   Armstrong and Aldrin continued their lunar exploration for over two hours. Then after returning to *Eagle,* they prepared for the critical lunar lift-off. Would they leave the moon safely, everyone wondered. Or would the courageous explorers be stranded[7] in space? The answer came at 1:55 P.M. on the following day: *Eagle* lifted

---

3. tripartite: having three parts
4. module: section
5. flash fire: sudden blaze

6. barren: lifeless
7. stranded: abandoned

* *Gemini*—Latin name for twins; also a constellation in the sky and one of the signs of the zodiac.

off from the surface of the moon and soared into lunar orbit to rejoin *Columbia*. Three days later, on July 24, 1969, *Apollo 11* splashed down in the Pacific—the triumphant conclusion to a decade of sustained scientific effort.

10   Though *Apollo 11* was perhaps the most memorable of America's space achievements, there were other exciting missions and new discoveries to come. For example, from November 1969 to December 1972, there were six more lunar missions: *Apollo 12* to *Apollo 17*. Of these only one—*Apollo 13*—had to return to earth before its astronauts could attempt the scheduled lunar exploration. The other five were successful piloted missions to the surface of the moon and back to earth.

EXPLORING THE DISTANT PLANETS

11   In addition to these Apollo missions, America's program has also included some remarkable unpiloted planetary probes. A series of *Mariner* spacecraft, launched in the 1960s and early 1970s, followed a carefully planned course past Mercury, Mars, and Venus, sending photographs and information back to scientists on earth. *Voyagers I* and *II* were then launched to explore the outer planets of the solar system. *Voyager I* flew past Jupiter in 1979. A year later, still returning data to scientists on earth, the probe flew past Saturn on its continuing path toward interstellar[8] space. Finally, in 1990, at a distance of almost four billion miles from the sun, *Voyager I* took its last photographs—a wondrous[9] set of images that displayed almost the entire planetary system.

12   *Voyager II* meanwhile, soaring out into space on its own spectacular mission, flew past Jupiter, Saturn, and Uranus between 1979 and 1986. Incredibly, still on course twelve years after its launching from earth, and still sending back information, *Voyager II* flew past Neptune in the summer of 1989. It encountered the huge outer planet at a remarkably close range—about three thousand miles—and returned photographic proof of multiple rings and new moons that had never before been discovered.

13   More recently, probes like the radar-mapping *Magellan* have returned detailed images of the surface of Venus, while the spacecraft *Galileo,* gaining power on a complicated path around Venus and Earth, set out for a two-year orbital exploration of the largest planet, Jupiter. Unlike earlier *Mariner* and *Voyager* probes, these spacecraft were not launched from earth, but from outer space itself. They were released by an earth-orbiting space shuttle—one of America's newest and most versatile[10] spacecraft.

THE SPACE SHUTTLE

14   Designed to blast off into orbit, remain in space for observation and experiment, and return to earth in a normal runway landing, the reusable shuttle is very different from the "one-time-only" spacecraft of the 1960s and 1970s. Thus it was a thrilling moment indeed when the first round-trip shuttle flight, on the orbiter *Columbia,* took place in April 1981—the twentieth anniversary of Yuri Gagarin's famous flight.

---

8. interstellar: among the stars beyond our solar system
9. wondrous: splendid; wonderful
10. versatile: capable of doing many things

15   Over the next few years, more exciting shuttle missions followed, until suddenly, on January 28, 1986, the second terrible tragedy in American space exploration occurred. Shortly after liftoff, the shuttle *Challenger* exploded, ignited[11] by flames from a defective solid-fuel booster[12] rocket. All seven crew members aboard *Challenger* died, and the space shuttle program was immediately halted. After intense national mourning, a complete examination of the shuttle program began. Improvements were made in the design of *Discovery, Atlantis,* and *Columbia*—the remaining shuttle orbiters—and NASA* was thoroughly reorganized. Finally, almost three full years after the *Challenger* disaster, the shuttle *Discovery* was launched, with a five-member crew, on September 29, 1988. To the relief of the many people who watched *Discovery* lift off, and to the credit of the brave crew, it was a near-perfect five-day mission. The American shuttle was back in operation. More flights were completed in the late 1980s and into the 1990s, providing countless opportunities for medical, industrial, and astrophysical experiments. Thus the shuttle remained a key part of American space exploration and became a national symbol for the fortitude[13] of pioneers.

THE CONTINUING QUEST

16   So at the dawn of America's third century, the quest continues—not in sailing ships and wagon trains but in spacecraft soaring through the heavens. Distant stars are tomorrow's frontiers—stars that sparkle with the visions of glory that burned once, intensely, in the soul of Columbus. Is there another new world waiting to be discovered? Or will the promise of the future remain the noble dreams of justice that inspired the early founders of America? One thing is certain. Tomorrow's challenges will be immense ones. Those who respond will be the true heirs to America's heritage— a past that has inspired explorers and idealists as well. Both have always been central to the American experience. Both discoverers and reformers have shaped the nation's traditions. In shaping its future, both, perhaps, will make even greater contributions. Astronauts will yearn, as Columbus once did, for the irresistible horizons of vast, unknown worlds. And despite the problems that continue as the twenty-first century begins, reformers will dream still of a brave new world here.

FOCUS ON ROBERT MACAULEY

17   Reformers will find no better model than the humanitarian Robert Macauley. Entrepreneur,[14] businessman, and unabashed[15] idealist, Macauley has shown, even in the decade of greed, that a vigorous generosity can still play a key role in contemporary America. "Idealism is alive and well here," he insists. As proof, he points to the thousands of volunteers who have turned AmeriCares, the agency he founded, into the world's largest private humanitarian organization. When asked about this success, Macauley's response is straightforward. "You're not in this world alone," he says, quoting the words of Albert Schweitzer. "Your brothers are here too." Recently

---

11. ignite: set on fire
12. boost: push upward
13. fortitude: courageous determination

14. entrepreneur: financier; business manager
15. unabashed: unashamed

* NASA: National Aeronautics and Space Administration

awarded the national Jefferson award—a prize founded by Jacqueline Kennedy Onassis, Senator Robert Taft, Jr., and Samuel Beard to honor outstanding public service performed by a private citizen—Macauley protested at once that it was his small staff of thirty-five and his thousands of worldwide volunteers who really deserved the prestigious honor. True enough. Yet it is his own faith and energy that have remained their inspiration.

18   Macauley remembers his parents as early role models in humanitarian commitment, but his own career in public service began many years after his childhood. Before graduating from Yale University, he flew air cargo planes for the army during the Second World War. Handsome and charming, like Lindbergh, he was *not,* like Lindbergh, unassuming[16] and shy. Macauley was incurably sociable—an accomplished musician, high-rolling gambler, sportsman, yachtsman, and hard-drinking friend. At war's end, before completing his studies, he drifted back home, playing barroom pianos to pay for his fast-paced existence. It was at this point that he met Leila Lindgren, a young schoolteacher, war widow, and mother of a small boy. Macauley fell promptly in love and proposed on the spot.[17] Leila was charmed by the dashing[18] pilot but afraid of the playboy. She refused him and later remarried; he returned to his studies, then to the nightlife of Europe. Finally, growing tired of a barroom pianist's life, he returned to New York, where he accepted a job in sales for $35 a week.

19   It was the perfect career start for a born salesman like Macauley. In time, with soaring earnings from sales commissions, he started his own company, Virginia Fibre Corporation, now a multimillion dollar business. Meanwhile, in 1965—two decades after his first impetuous[19] proposal—he married the twice-widowed, still beloved Leila. Calling their love "the greatest seven that I ever rolled,"[20] Macauley movingly acknowledged his wife's ongoing support as he accepted the Jefferson Award on behalf of AmeriCares. A fitting tribute indeed, for it was shortly after their marriage, that Macauley's extraordinary career in public service began.

20   It started simply enough with a newspaper report. Reading about an actor, Richard Hughes, who was helping the orphaned[21] children of war-torn Vietnam, Macauley pledged $5,000 to establish the Shoeshine Foundation. (The agency took its name from the way the orphans had earned their money.) Several years later, after the Shoeshine Foundation had provided care and new housing for thousands of Vietnamese orphans, another news report caught Macauley's attention. A jet carrying Vietnamese children had crashed on takeoff from Tan Son Nhut. Half of the 243 children were dead, and the others were seriously injured; it would be almost two weeks before any survivors could be rescued.

21   For the impatient Macaulcy, such a delay seemed intolerable. Offering his house as collateral to secure a quarter-million-dollar loan, he privately chartered a jet to rescue the children. Within forty-eight hours (and with his home now heavily mortgaged), Macauley's jet was back in the States, along with the Vietnamese survivors.

---

16. unassuming: quiet; modest
17. on the spot: at once
18. dashing: stylish; very charming
19. impetuous: impatient; spontaneous

20. rolling a seven: getting a lucky combination with dice, as in a game of chance or gambling
21. orphaned: left without parents

A NEW GLOBAL HUMANITARIANISM

22   It was the first of many dramatic air rescues to come, for in 1982, after an urgent papal[22] request for medical aid to Poland, Macauley founded a new organization, AmeriCares. "At the time, AmeriCares consisted of a staff of one—me," Macauley recalls. He knew nothing about pharmaceuticals,[23] but with encouragement from corporate colleagues and the help of determined volunteers, he began contacting business leaders throughout the pharmaceutical industry. As always, he was both eloquent and relentless, begging for medicines, supplies, and related equipment. Soon, his hard-hitting salesmanship produced incredible results. "To our utter amazement," he remembers, "in less than two months we had received approximately two and one half million dollars worth of pharmaceuticals, which we airlifted to Poland (on borrowed money) on the 10th of March 1982."

23   AmeriCares had accomplished its first international mission. Could he do it again, Macauley wondered. If he kept right on asking, would his friends in the business world keep right on giving? Would more volunteers want to help? Could he coordinate it all? Never a man to hesitate, Macauley plunged ahead that year. More and more people, he found, were willing to donate their time, supplies, services, and support. Soon a second airlift of medicines reached Afghanistan's borders, and a third reached the inhabitants of war-torn Beirut.

24   Cries for help then began reaching Macauley from the needy worldwide, and AmeriCares grew quickly. Its volunteers brought aid to India after the Bhopal chemical spill. After an earthquake destroyed Mexico, they were again on the scene. They rushed directly to the Caribbean, airlifting food and pharmaceuticals, after hurricane winds devastated Puerto Rico.

25   To these and other disaster victims, minutes often spelled the difference between survival and death. So speed and efficiency became priorities at AmeriCares. After Chernobyl's nuclear disaster, Macauley immediately had over a million pounds of milk, food, and medicines en route to Eastern Europe. The first private relief plane to reach Armenia, destroyed by a massive earthquake, carried AmeriCares volunteers and thousands of pounds of donated medical supplies. After an even greater earthquake hit Iran, AmeriCares volunteers were again ready to go. With a cargo of desperately needed medicine, their jet was the first American aircraft to land in Teheran since the tense hostage situation of the late 1970s.

26   In the 1990s, a long-term global challenge developed, for in 1989, with unexpected swiftness, the cold war between Communism and the Western world came to an end. Throughout Eastern Europe and the Soviet Union, as the controlled economies of Communist countries verged on[24] total collapse, totalitarian regimes were replaced by more democratic forms of government. Plans for competitive market economies, social reforms, and political freedom replaced repression, fear of capitalism, and dictatorial authority. The Berlin Wall—long a symbol of cold war tensions—crumbled; then, after almost fifty years of division into Communist and non-Communist parts, East and West Germany moved swiftly toward reunification. Ethnic groups demanded autonomy within the Soviet Union and

---

22. papal: pertaining to the Pope   24. verge on: approach
23. pharmaceuticals: medicines

Yugoslavia. A bloody rebellion ended the rule of Romania's tyrant, Nicolae Ceausescu.

27   After such sweeping transformations, cooperation—not confrontation—marked emerging new relationships between the United States and former Communist foes. Impatient as ever, Macauley was eager to participate. Hearing of severe shortages of food and medicine throughout Eastern Europe, he organized airlifts to Romania, Czechoslovakia, and Poland. Hearing of similar problems in Russia, he sent over a million pounds of food and medicine to Moscow—the first private American airlift to respond to Russia's post–cold-war needs. With a new AmeriCares program, Doctors to All Peoples, a permanent rehabilitation clinic was established in Armenia. It will be followed, Macauley hopes, by clinics in other countries—including those within the former Communist bloc.

28   Truly, in just one brief decade, Macauley's leadership has inspired astonishing efforts. Both at home and abroad, AmeriCares is credited with having saved almost ten million lives. It has managed to ship over four hundred million dollars worth of food and medicine to the needy worldwide. By the middle of the 1990s, Macauley projects, he can increase that figure to a billion.

29   With only a barebones[25] staff of thirty people or so, how does he do it, people ask. First and foremost, as he admits, he is beholden to the efforts of "those unsung[26] heroes around the world, volunteers all, of the AmeriCares effort." And secondly, as he is also quick to point out, he keeps efficiency high by keeping his overhead low. "We avoid the four B's," he explains, "—big buildings and bloated[27] bureaucracies." Instead of complicated procedures and multiple committees, he favors rapid decision making and a streamlined[28] chain of command. In well under two hours, he can mobilize a crew of determined volunteers. He also remains a master of networking[29] skills. "I'm a beggar," he says. When disaster occurs—no matter where—he'll contact anyone he can think of who might pledge food or supplies. He'll plead for free transportation. He'll even ask old pilot friends to help land his planes.

30   What he won't do, however, is take "no" for an answer. "Get the job done," he tells his staff. "Make things happen." Indeed, Robert Macauley *is* "making things happen." With irrepressible[30] energy, into a world in need of caring, he is pouring much of the good fortune he found in his own crowded life. Realists remind him, sometimes, that he can never solve *all* of the world's problems. In response, he tells a favorite tale. "Along an endless sun-baked beach somewhere—one filled with millions of starfish washed up on the sand—a boy once walked slowly, picking the starfish up gently and returning them, one by one, into the safety of the sea. An old man who was watching questioned the boy. Since there were millions upon millions of starfish, said the man, what was the boy trying to do? He couldn't possibly make a difference. The boy looked at the man, then at the starfish he had just returned to the security of the waves. 'I made a difference to this one,' he replied." It is a tale to be remembered—a worthy challenge for the United States as its third century begins.

---

25. barebones: minimal
26. unsung: not having received public praise
27. bloated: swollen

28. streamlined: efficient; uncomplicated
29. network: maintain contact with colleagues
30. irrepressible: very enthusiastic

On June 18, 1983, America's seventh shuttle mission was launched. Among the *Challenger*'s five-member crew was Dr. Sally K. Ride, America's first spacewoman. Born in California in 1951, Dr. Ride graduated from Stanford University with a double English/Physics major. In 1977, while completing her Ph.D. studies in Physics, she applied—along with over eight thousand other candidates—for admission to NASA's astronaut program. She was accepted in 1978—one of six women among the thirty-five people who were finally chosen.

Following are excerpts from an interview which the author had with Dr. Ride on July 27, 1983.

Q. Dr. Ride, you have often said that your interest in science was sparked in high school.

A. That's probably right. In junior high I was interested in science and knew that that was something that I wanted to pursue—at least through high school; and then, in high school, I had two really excellent science teachers who encouraged me to continue pursuing it....

Q. You pursued your interest in science by taking a physics major, I believe, in college; and you also took an English major.... Do you think this helped you as an astronaut?

A. I'm not sure that it helped me as an astronaut. But I think that one of the things the astronaut program was looking for in its applicants was not necessarily a diversity but a willingness to diversify. You know, they don't want someone who is a specialist only in x-ray astrophysics. They want someone who's willing to learn other fields....

Q. I know you were a ranked[1] tennis player in college and also in high school. Do you think this helped you as an astronaut?

A. I think that it did.... For one thing, it gave me a chance to travel a lot; and it gave me a chance to meet a lot of people that I wouldn't have met otherwise. It also gave me a sense of competition—but I think in a good sense—competition as a part of the team.

Q. Learning to win and maybe even learning to lose?

A. Learning to win, learning to lose, learning to get along with your doubles partner. That's important.

Q. This brings me to a question—I'll call it an epiphany for lack of anything else—a moment when a person feels a communion with nature and one's fellow man in a moment of beauty and joy and peace.... Did you feel that? Did you have, as an explorer, a mystical moment?

---

1. ranked: numbered among the nation's best

A. I don't think that I would call the moment mystical. But we certainly did have some exhilarating moments ... just being up there in an entirely new environment—an environment that can't be duplicated on earth. And the weightlessness is something we can't even come close to on the ground. Being weightless, being in that environment and then looking back down at the earth, was very exhilarating for all of us—almost euphoric.[2]

Q. What was the most exciting moment during this flight? Can you pinpoint anything that was ...

A. Well, the launch is exciting. And the first moment that you're weightless—that you realize that you're weightless.

Q. When is that?

A. It's about eight minutes into the flight—right after the main engines cut off you're weightless. And although you're strapped into the seat you can let go of your pencil and it doesn't fall.

Q. How far up are you eight minutes into the flight?

A. 60 miles....

Q. What was the least pleasant aspect?

A. There really weren't any unpleasant aspects of the entire flight....

Q. When you returned, did you have a letdown?

A. No I haven't yet.... I don't know whether they've kept us busy since we've been back ... or whether we're all so excited about getting a chance to go again that we haven't had a letdown. But I honestly haven't experienced one.

Q. Did you find a week too long?

A. No. We could have stayed up a lot longer and enjoyed every minute of it.

Q. I've read that NASA would hope to use the shuttle to build a space station. Do you see this as a reality in the near future—a place where crews could work for a couple of months in outer space?

A. I hope so. The space station isn't funded yet but that's really the next logical step in a space program—a space exploration or a space usage program. And staying up in space for two months or three months or four months is no problem physiologically; it's no problem for people to do that and it's something that's very important to establish if we're going to make full use of space either for industrialization purposes or as a kind of a stepping stone for further space exploration....

Q. I've read that a weightless environment is advantageous for some industrial and medical research....

---

2. euphoric: extremely pleasant

Aboard the spacecraft Challenger *on America's seventh shuttle mission were astronauts Robert Crippen, mission commander* (center); *Frederick Hauck, mission pilot* (lower right); *and mission specialists Sally Ride* (lower left), *John Fabian* (upper left)*, and Norman Thagard* (upper right).

A. That's right…. There are a lot of raw materials that can only be produced by heating them to extremely high temperatures…. The problem with trying to heat materials to very high temperatures on the ground is that any container that you've got also starts to melt and contaminates what you're trying to combine; … While up in a weightless environment, you don't need a container. In fact, one of the experiments that we carried out was something that's called an acoustic levitator. That is really just a box that has essentially a lot of sound waves to go through it. You can stabilize a sample in the middle and just hold it right there in the middle of the box touching nothing just by the sound waves. And you keep it stable so that you can heat that sample to an extremely high temperature and not contaminate it and do whatever you want to with it, which allows for much purer materials that we can't produce here.

Q. And vaccines and serums that we can't make—that's a possibility too?

A. One of the other experiments that we carried out was designed to produce pharmaceuticals that can't be produced on the ground because we can't separate them from their normal tissue culture environment.... Any separation process on the ground is basically clouded by gravity. The way that we did it is to take a syringe[3] of the serum[4] and inject it into a solution[5] that's basically flowing up the column, and then as it flows up the column put an electric field across it, and the electric field separates what you want from what you don't want....

Q. May I ask you, do you think we're going to go to Mars?

A. *(emphatically)* Yes!

Q. And do you think we'll have a tug that'll launch itself out of the space shuttle and go to the moon and back?

A. *(emphatically, again)* Yes!

Q. And how about starships?

A. *(slowly, with a broadening smile)* Starships are going to be a little longer.

---

3. syringe: needle
4. serum: blood fluids

5. solution: liquid

Following are excerpts from an interview which the author had with Robert Macauley on June 20, 1991.

Q.   Mr. Macauley, in spite of the "money hunger" of the eighties, you've maintained that idealism is alive and well in our country.

A.   Oh, it's alive and well, all right! *(heartily)* All you have to do is bring it out in people. We have a long waiting list here of volunteers—highly qualified people— people who just want to come and join us…. We must have 50,000 to 100,000 volunteers in foreign countries. We don't pay them any money. We're out to save lives, and there are a lot of people out there who just want to save lives.

Q.   Is there a "typical" volunteer at AmeriCares—a common profile of the person who works for your organization?

A.   You mean, is there a quintessential[1] volunteer? — No. *(with a smile, pointing to the hall beyond his office)* Just look outside. There's a guy out there who's eighty-three years old. He hasn't missed a day of work since about a week after I started. We have people here in their seventies, youngsters who work through the summer, people with physical disabilities…. You can't say they're young or they're old. You can't say they're black or they're white. You can't say they're male or they're female…. They just want to serve humanity. College graduates, for example, who want to give a year, two years, three years of their lives. They're very serious about it.

Q.   Like the people who go on relief missions for you?

A.   Yes. And some of the trips we send our people on are very, very difficult—going into war zones, bearing up under extremely difficult circumstances, … hunger. They're not very comfortable existences. You go on any of the flights that we take—we have two going to Ethiopia next week—and you can almost freeze to death for one thing. They're cargo planes. I used to give everybody bottles of Murine to use when they returned, because after a long tough trip—twenty or thirty hours on an airplane like that—you'll generally have red eyes. You're pretty tired. *(another smile)* Then a guy complained to me about it: "Bob, I went to use the Murine when we landed, but it was frozen in the bottle."

Q.   You've always been quick to credit the generosity of your volunteers. What about you? What motivates you?

A.   Well, if I had to pick one guy in this world who rolled sevens all his life, it must have been me. *(after a moment)* I used to be a piano player … in Europe … in some not so respectable places. And when I think of the good luck that I've had, when I look at my wife and my children, I know they're the greatest inspiration I've ever had…. I go into refugee camps very frequently—I'll go in there and I'll see five, ten, fifteen thousand people—and I look at the expressions on the faces of those

---

1. quintessential: ideal

children and I look in their eyes—every night—and I see the eyes of my own children and I think, there but for the grace of God go I. *I* could be that parent.... Yet all *I've* ever done is roll sevens. *(another moment)* When you roll sevens all the time, it's your *obligation* to put some back. You've just got to help those who are less fortunate.

Q. I've read that the supplies you send worldwide are often labeled, "With love, from the people of the United States."

A. We do that on the outside of every container. We'll be doing it tonight and tomorrow on containers for Ethiopia, in Amharik, the native language of Ethiopia. We'll be printing up great big signs—eighteen feet long on each container of medicine—and they'll say, "From the people of the United States, to the people of Ethiopia," and then, in great big letters—"WITH LOVE."

Q. So that's the bottom line? That's what it's all about?

A. It's all about love. How else are you going to solve the problems of the world? Not by political agreements. You can tear up political agreements and throw the pieces away. No political agreements have ever held up in the last two thousand years. The one thing that *does* last is love.... And the one thing that's going to bring peace to this world is compassion.

Q. A last question, Mr. Macauley.... If you had a chance to say a few words to the young people of today—those who are just starting out, those who aren't sure yet, perhaps, about which path to choose—what would you tell them about the role they might play in the twenty-first century?

A. I guess I would ask them to imagine their last hour and what they might see as they reflected on their lives. I would tell them that the greatest joy they're ever going to have will come from giving to others. It's not going to come from making ninety million dollars a year. It's not going to come from seeing their name in print. "So don't look back," I'd remind them, "and say I made a million dollars. Look back on the fact that maybe the world is a little better place for your having been there. Or at least, if you can't attribute to yourself the value of having lit one candle for humanity, at least don't blow any out. That's the greatest satisfaction you can get.... Put some back.... Leave the world finer than when you found it.... It all comes down to one word: *(steadily)* love."

✕ EXERCISES

Reading Comprehension

A.   Choose the best answer for the following:

1. All of the following were Soviet space triumphs *except*
   a. landing the first astronaut on the moon
   b. launching the first earth-orbiting satellite
   c. sending the first astronaut into outer space

2. What is the subject of paragraphs 7 to 9?
   a. risks involved in space exploration
   b. the development of the Apollo series
   c. the first lunar landing of American astronauts

3. In all, how many American missions involved successful lunar landings?
   a. six   b. five   c. seven

4. What is unique about the space shuttle?
   a. It does not go into orbit.
   b. It can return to earth in a normal runway landing.
   c. It can remain in space for an extended period of time.

5. From what we are told in paragraph 21, we can assume that Macauley risked losing his home
   a. because he was very wealthy.
   b. because he felt human life was more important that the structure he lived in.
   c. because he was still an imprudent gambler.

6. In paragraph 27, AmeriCares' airlift to Moscow is introduced as an example of
   a. aid to Russia in a new age of cooperation.
   b. aid to Russia in spite of ongoing confrontation.
   c. aid to Russia in place of help to Iran.

7. Paragraph 28 offers
   a. a summary of the preceding paragraphs.
   b. a contrast to the preceding paragraphs.
   c. an entirely new topic.

8. As noted in the interview on p. 209, participation in sports was helpful to Dr. Ride for all of the following reasons *except*:
   a. It helped her acquire a team spirit.
   b. It taught her never to lose.
   c. It gave her an opportunity to travel.

9. As noted in the interview on p. 213, relief missions for AmeriCares could often be difficult because
   a. the volunteers did not receive any salary.
   b. the aircraft were unsafe.
   c. the destinations might be unsafe.

10. Sally Ride and Robert Macauley may best be compared because of
    a. their great faith in the power of individual effort.
    b. their extensive flight experience.
    c. their excellence in sports.

B. **Look at the map on p. 217. Then answer the following.**

1. Which planet is closest to the sun?
2. What two planets are closest to earth?
3. Which is the largest planet?
4. Which is the smallest?
5. Which planet is farthest from the sun?
6. How many days does it take the earth to go around the sun? How many days does it take Venus? How long does it take Pluto?
7. How many miles is Earth from the sun?
8. How far is Pluto from the sun?
9. What galaxy is our solar system in?
10. Locate "Tranquillity Base" where *Eagle* landed on July 20, 1969.

C. **What qualities do you think an astronaut should have? Below, place the number 1 next to those you consider absolutely essential. Place the number 2 next to those you consider advisable, but not essential. Whatever you consider unnecessary should be marked with the number 3. Place the number 4 next to anything unacceptable.**

_____ courage	_____ youth
_____ athletic ability	_____ health
_____ musical talent	_____ dependability
_____ poise	_____ jealousy
_____ a sense of humor	_____ a quick wit
_____ generosity	_____ a large ego
_____ medical training	_____ a short temper
_____ determination	_____ scientific training

D. **Who Am I?** **Identify the following by choosing from the list below.**

Herbert Hoover	Douglas MacArthur
Franklin D. Roosevelt	Albert Einstein
Edith Wharton	Dr. Sally K. Ride
Fiorello La Guardia	Dr. Martin Luther King, Jr.
John Steinbeck	Mohandas Gandhi

1. My discoveries in science helped to bring about the nuclear age.
2. Born and raised in California, I immortalized the struggles of its migrant workers.
3. It was my fate to be America's president when Wall Street collapsed in 1929.
4. I entered the White House when the depression was at its worst. I remained the country's president throughout most of World War II.
5. Athlete, scientist, and literature student, I was also an experienced astronaut.
6. In Italian, my first name meant "Little Flower"; but the press compared me to a package of explosives.
7. I was commander of the UN military forces during the war in Korea.
8. Born and raised in Manhattan, I immortalized the struggles of women in New York's Gilded Age society.
9. Dedicated to the cause of human rights, I directed a nonviolent campaign to end discrimination in America.
10. I was influenced by the works of Thoreau, an American; later my own work influenced another American, Dr. Martin Luther King, Jr.

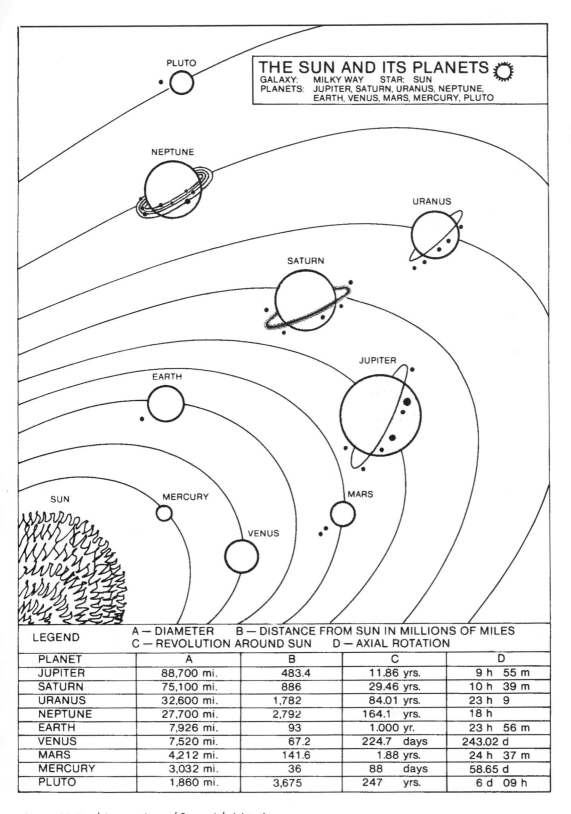

THE SUN AND ITS PLANETS

GALAXY: MILKY WAY   STAR: SUN
PLANETS: JUPITER, SATURN, URANUS, NEPTUNE,
EARTH, VENUS, MARS, MERCURY, PLUTO

LEGEND	A — DIAMETER B — DISTANCE FROM SUN IN MILLIONS OF MILES C — REVOLUTION AROUND SUN D — AXIAL ROTATION			
PLANET	A	B	C	D
JUPITER	88,700 mi.	483.4	11.86 yrs.	9 h 55 m
SATURN	75,100 mi.	886	29.46 yrs.	10 h 39 m
URANUS	32,600 mi.	1,782	84.01 yrs.	23 h 9
NEPTUNE	27,700 mi.	2,792	164.1 yrs.	18 h
EARTH	7,926 mi.	93	1.000 yr.	23 h 56 m
VENUS	7,520 mi.	67.2	224.7 days	243.02 d
MARS	4,212 mi.	141.6	1.88 yrs.	24 h 37 m
MERCURY	3,032 mi.	36	88 days	58.65 d
PLUTO	1,860 mi.	3,675	247 yrs.	6 d 09 h

Source: *National Aeronautics and Space Administration*

217

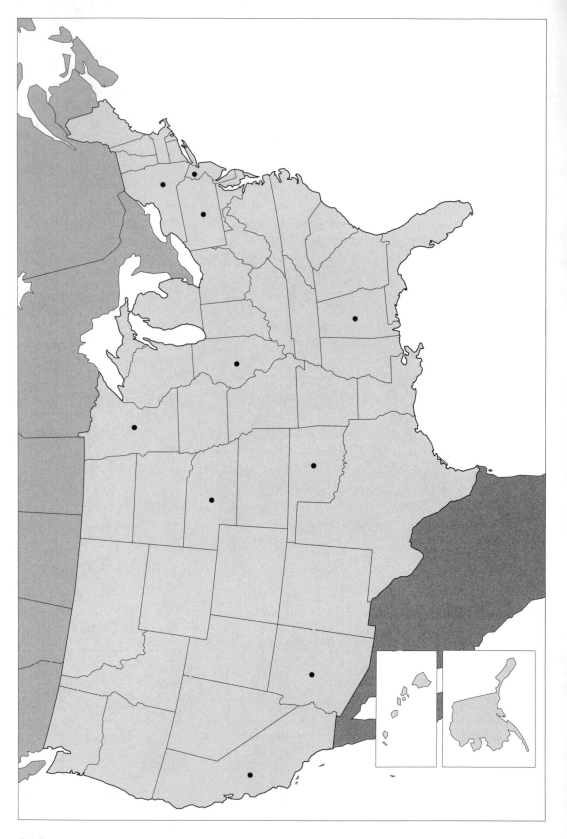

E. **Where Did It Happen?** **From the following list, select the state that best corresponds to each description below.**

Pennsylvania   California
Nebraska   New Jersey
Illinois   Alabama
New York   Minnesota
Oklahoma   Arizona

1. Astounding the world with his extraordinary inventions, Edison worked tirelessly at his laboratory here.
2. Charles A. Lindbergh spent a happy and rugged childhood on a farm in this state.
3. Carnegie arrived here as a poor but spirited immigrant; later, as a millionaire, he supported many projects in the state.
4. Terrible dust storms swept across this state in the thirties; so its farmers struggled west in search of employment.
5. Only the hardiest pioneers could survive on this state's treeless plains.
6. America's financial capital is located in this state; a crash here collapsed the nation's economy in 1929.
7. In this state's largest city, Jane Addams established Hull House, a famous American settlement.
8. Desperate for employment, thousands of migrant workers arrived here in the 1930s.
9. In this state, Dr. King led a nonviolent boycott that changed the course of civil rights in America.
10. Far away from New York's confusion, Fiorello La Guardia spent his formative years in the open spaces of this southwestern state.

F. **On page 218 is a map of the American states. Markers have been added to indicate the ten places described in exercise E above. Put the correct number next to each marker.**

Vocabulary

A. **In your own words, define the italicized words below.**

1. In 1957, Soviet scientists *astounded* the world by launching earth's first artificial satellite.
2. Millions of viewers watched the astronauts land on the moon's *barren* surface.
3. Would they be *stranded* in space, people wondered.
4. The probe continued directly on its path to *interstellar* space.
5. Finally, it sent back a *wondrous* set of pictures of the solar system.
6. *Ignited* by flames from a defective solid booster rocket, the orbiter exploded.
7. The shuttle has remained a symbol for the *fortitude* of pioneers.
8. It is an extremely *versatile* spacecraft.
9. Macauley knew little about *pharmaceuticals* at first.
10. He had been trying to help the *orphaned* children of war-torn Vietnam.
11. In managing AmeriCares, he favors a *streamlined* operation.
12. *Entrepreneur* and humanitarian, he remains an idealist.

B. Fill in the blanks below with an appropriate adjective from the following list.

dashing   irrepressible   impetuous   unassuming   unabashed

1. In spite of the world's problems, he remains an _____ believer in the power of love.

2. He was certainly not, like Lindbergh, _____ and shy.

3. Though she was attracted to the _____ pilot, she was afraid of the playboy.

4. Twenty years after his first _____ proposal, she accepted.

5. He continues to work with _____ energy.

Structures

A. In the paragraph below, add the correct prepositions.

At last, _____ October 1968, the first piloted Apollo mission—*Apollo 7*—was launched. Though it did not travel _____ the moon, it provided an opportunity _____ test essential equipment. _____ the next several months, there were similar test flights. And finally, _____ July 16, 1969, *Apollo 11* began its historic mission. _____ the spacecraft were astronauts Neil Armstrong, Edwin Aldrin, and Michael Collins. Three days later, they were _____ lunar orbit—more than two hundred thousand miles from the earth. While circling the moon, they checked their systems and equipment. Then _____ the afternoon _____ July 20th—after detaching the lunar module *Eagle* _____ the command module *Columbia*—Armstrong and Aldrin made a careful descent. Over five hundred million viewers—nearly twenty percent of the world's total population—watched their TVs tensely as the voices _____ the astronauts described the slow approach. _____ 4:17 P.M. EDT, there was news _____ a touchdown. "Houston," said Armstrong, "Tranquility Base here. The *Eagle* has landed."

B. In the following paragraph, add *the, a,* or *an* where necessary. If no marker is necessary, leave the space blank.

Both superpowers were quickly involved in ambitious long-range plans to reach _____ moon. Here again, as they had with their *Sputnik,* _____ Soviets scored _____ initial triumph. On April 12, 1961, _____ Soviet cosmonaut Yuri Gagarin completed one full orbit around _____ earth. Thus, in _____ mission that lasted just under two hours, he was _____ first person to travel in _____ outer space. _____ age of human space flight had suddenly dawned. Could _____ three-day journey to _____ moon become reality?

Composition

Choose one of the following.

A. Reread paragraphs 11–14 in the Historical Background. Then in one well-developed paragraph, describe some of the highlights of America's unpiloted planetary exploration.

B. "Rome wasn't built in a day." According to this familiar proverb, great achievements take time. They are not accomplished overnight. They usually require long preparation, determined effort, and well-organized gradual expansion. Do you think this was true of the American project to land a person on the moon? Give as many specific details as possible.

C. Reread the author's interview with Sally Ride on pp. 209–212. Then in your own words, tell how the various different interests that Dr. Ride pursued as a student later became useful to her as an astronaut.

D. Reread the author's interview with Robert Macauley on pp. 213–214. What does Macauley mean by "putting some back?" Do you think Jane Addams would have agreed with this philosophy? Why, or why not? (You may wish to review information given in Unit 5, pp. 72–76.)

Topics for Class Discussion

Interviewing a partner or a small group of your classmates, talk about the following.

A. *The High Frontier,* a popular book by Gerard K. O'Neill, offers a fascinating proposal for the building of space colonies in the near future. These colonies, as described by Dr. O'Neill, would be enclosed earth-like environments. Their inhabitants would work in the many space industries that would have research and development centers in orbit. Transportation to and from the colonies, in shuttle-type craft, would be on a regularly scheduled basis. Would you want to visit—or even live for a while—in a space colony? Why, or why not?

B. Imagine that you are in Washington to gather support for America's space program. You are speaking to several senators. Within a week, they will vote on a proposal to increase the funds available for shuttle operations. What arguments would you use—that is, what, in your opinion, are the benefits to be gained from exploration into outer space?

C. Pretend you are one of the senators who has just heard the arguments in Topic B above for expanded space exploration. You now hear the following opposing view, as presented by an environmentalist.

"It is foolish to spend taxpayers' money on further space exploration. We should be concentrating on improving our own planet's environment. We should be developing alternate forms of energy, as our supplies of oil, coal, and gas decrease. We should be reducing the pollution that threatens our earth's protective atmosphere. In the United States alone, as a result of industrial development, millions of pounds of toxic wastes are released yearly into the air. Our coastal waters are being contaminated by trash and raw sewage. Our parklands are filled with litter, our forests are being depleted, and the habitats for our wildlife are being destroyed by overdevelopment. Forget space stations and probes and trips to the moon; we should be spending our time and energy repairing the damage to this planet."

Which position would you, as an American senator, agree with? Give reasons for your answer.

D. Choose the person who most appealed to you in this volume. Please give a brief oral summary of this person's life. Conclude by explaining why this life story especially interested or appealed to you.

SOME INTERESTING PLACES TO VISIT

New England Area

AmeriCares World Headquarters
New Canaan, Connecticut

Middle Atlantic Area

American Museum—Hayden Planetarium
New York, New York

National Air and Space Museum
Smithsonian Institution
Washington, D.C.

Southeastern Area

Air Force Space Museum
NASA Kennedy Space Center Tours
Cape Canaveral, Florida

South Central Area

NASA Lyndon B. Johnson Space Center
Clear Lake City, Texas

Appendix A

The Declaration of Independence, July 4, 1776

THE UNANIMOUS DECLARATION OF THE
THIRTEEN UNITED STATES OF AMERICA,

When in the Course of human events, it becomes necessary for one people to dissolve the political bands which have connected them with another, and to assume among the powers of the earth, the separate and equal station to which the Laws of Nature and of Nature's God entitle them, a decent respect to the opinions of mankind requires that they should declare the causes which impel them to the separation.

We hold these truths to be self-evident, that all men are created equal, that they are endowed by their Creator with certain unalienable Rights, that among these are Life, Liberty and the pursuit of Happiness. That to secure these rights, Governments are instituted among Men, deriving their just powers from the consent of the governed. That whenever any Form of Government becomes destructive of these ends, it is the Right of the People to alter or abolish it, and to institute new Government, laying its foundation on such principles and organizing its powers in such form, as to them shall seem most likely to effect their Safety and Happiness. Prudence, indeed, will dictate that Governments long established should not be changed for light and transient causes; and accordingly all experience hath shewn, that mankind are more disposed to suffer, while evils are sufferable, than to right themselves by abolishing the forms to which they are accustomed. But when a long train of abuses and usurpations, pursuing invariably the same Object evinces a design to reduce them under absolute Despotism, it is their right, it is their duty, to throw off such Government, and to provide new Guards for their future security. Such has been the patient sufferance of these Colonies; and such is now the necessity which constrains them to alter their former Systems of Government. The history of the present King of Great Britain is a history of repeated injuries and usurpations, all having in direct object the establishment of an absolute Tyranny over these States. To prove this, let Facts be submitted to a candid world.

He has refused his Assent to laws, the most wholesome and necessary for the public good.

He has forbidden his Governors to pass Laws of immediate and pressing importance, unless suspended in their operation till his Assent should be obtained; and when so suspended, he has utterly neglected to attend to them.

He has refused to pass other Laws for the accommodation of large districts of people, unless those people would relinquish the right of Representation in the Legislature, a right inestimable to them and formidable to tyrants only.

He has called together legislative bodies at places unusual, uncomfortable, and distant from the depository of their public Records, for the sole purpose of fatiguing them into compliance with his measures.

He has dissolved Representative Houses repeatedly, for opposing with manly firmness his invasions on the rights of the people.

He has refused for a long time, after such dissolutions, to cause others to be elected; whereby the Legislative powers, incapable of Annihilation, have returned to the People at large for their exercise; the State remaining in the mean time exposed to all the dangers of invasion from without, and convulsions within.

He has endeavoured to prevent the population of these States; for that purpose obstructing the Laws for Naturalization of Foreigners; refusing to pass others to encourage their migration hither, and raising the conditions of new Appropriations of Lands.

He has obstructed the Administration of Justice, by refusing his Assent to Laws for establishing Judiciary powers.

He has made Judges dependent on his Will alone, for the tenure of their offices, and the amount and payment of their salaries.

He has erected a multitude of New Offices, and sent hither swarms of Officers to harrass our people, and eat out their substance.

He has kept among us, in times of peace, Standing Armies without the Consent of our legislatures.

He has affected to render the Military independent of and superior to the Civil power.

He has combined with others to subject us to a jurisdiction foreign to our constitution, and unacknowledged by our laws; giving his Assent to their Acts of pretended Legislation:

For quartering large bodies of armed troops among us:

For protecting them, by a mock Trial, from punishment for any Murders which they should commit on the Inhabitants of these States:

For cutting off our Trade with all parts of the world:

For imposing Taxes on us without our Consent:

For depriving us in many cases of the benefits of Trial by Jury:

For transporting us beyond Seas to be tried for pretended offences:

For abolishing the free System of English Laws in a neighbouring Province, establishing therein an Arbitrary government, and enlarging its Boundaries so as to render it at once an example and fit instrument for introducing the same absolute rule into these Colonies:

For taking away our Charters, abolishing our most valuable Laws, and altering fundamentally the Forms of our Governments:

For suspending our own Legislatures, and declaring themselves invested with power to legislate for us in all cases whatsoever.

He has abdicated Government here, by declaring us out of his Protection and waging War against us.

He has plundered our seas, ravaged our Coasts, burnt our towns, and destroyed the Lives of our people.

He is at this time transporting large Armies of foreign Mercenaries to compleat the works of death, desolation and tyranny, already begun with circumstances of Cruelty and perfidy scarcely paralleled in the most barbarous ages, and totally unworthy the Head of a civilized nation.

He has constrained our fellow Citizens taken Captive on the high Seas to bear Arms against their Country, to become the executioners of their friends and Brethren, or to fall themselves by their Hands.

He has excited domestic insurrections amongst us, and has endeavoured to bring on the inhabitants of our frontiers, the merciless Indian Savages, whose known rule of warfare, is an undistinguished destruction of all ages, sexes and conditions.

In every stage of these Oppressions We have Petitioned for Redress in the most humble terms: Our repeated Petitions have been answered only by repeated injury. A Prince, whose character is thus marked by every act which may define a Tyrant, is unfit to be the ruler of a free people.

Nor have We been wanting in attention to our British brethren. We have warned them from time to time of attempts by their legislature to extend an unwarrantable jurisdiction over us. We have reminded them of the circumstances of our emigration and settlement here. We have appealed to their native justice and magnanimity, and we have conjured them by the ties of our common kindred to disavow these usurpations, which, would inevitably interrupt our connections and correspondence. They too have been deaf to the voice of justice and of consanguinity. We must, therefore, acquiesce in the necessity, which denounces our separation, and hold them, as we hold the rest of mankind, Enemies in War, in Peace Friends.

We, therefore, the Representatives of the United States of America, in General Congress, Assembled, appealing to the Supreme Judge of the world for the rectitude of our intentions, do, in the Name, and by the authority of the good People of these Colonies, solemnly publish and declare, That these United Colonies are, and of Right ought to be Free and Independent States; that they are Absolved from all Allegiance to the British Crown, and that all political connection between them and the State of Great Britain, is and ought to be totally dissolved; and that as Free and Independent States, they have full Power to levy War, conclude Peace, contract Alliances, establish Commerce, and to do all other Acts and Things which Independent States may of right do. And for the support of this Declaration, with a firm reliance on the protection of divine Providence, we mutually pledge to each other our Lives, our Fortunes, and our sacred Honor.

Appendix B

The Constitution of the United States of America

PREAMBLE

We the People of the United States, in Order to form a more perfect Union, establish Justice, insure domestic Tranquility, provide for the common defence, promote the general Welfare, and secure the Blessings of Liberty to ourselves and our Posterity, do ordain and establish this Constitution for the United States of America.

ARTICLE I

Section 1. All legislative Powers herein granted shall be vested in a Congress of the United States, which shall consist of a Senate and House of Representatives.

Section 2. The House of Representatives shall be composed of Members chosen every second Year by the People of the several States, and the Electors in each State shall have the Qualifications requisite for Electors of the most numerous Branch of the State Legislature.

No Person shall be a Representative who shall not have attained to the Age of twenty-five Years, and been seven Years a Citizen of the United States, and who shall not, when elected, be an inhabitant of that State in which he shall be chosen.

Representatives and direct Taxes shall be apportioned among the several States which may be included within this Union, according to their respective Numbers, [which shall be determined by adding to the whole Number of free Persons, including those bound to Service for a Term of Years, and excluding Indians not taxed, three fifths of all other Persons.][1] The actual Enumeration shall be made within three Years after the first Meeting of the Congress of the United States, and within every subsequent Term of ten Years, in such Manner as they shall by law direct. The Number of Representatives shall not exceed one for every thirty Thousand, but each State shall have at Least one Representative; and until such enumeration shall be made, the State of New Hampshire shall be entitled to chuse three, Massachusetts eight, Rhode-Island and Providence Plantations one, Connecticut five, New York six, New Jersey four, Pennsylvania eight, Delaware one, Maryland six, Virginia ten, North Carolina five, South Carolina five, and Georgia three.

When vacancies happen in the Representation from any State, the Executive Authority thereof shall issue Writs of Election to fill such Vacancies.

The House of Representatives shall chuse their Speaker and other Officers; and shall have the sole Power of Impeachment.

Section 3. The Senate of the United States shall be composed of two Senators from each State, [chosen by the Legislature thereof,][2] for six Years; and each Senator shall have one Vote.

Immediately after they shall be assembled in Consequence of the first Election, they shall be divided as equally as may be into three Classes. The Seats of the Senators of the first Class

---

1. Superseded by the Fourteenth Amendment.

2. Superseded by the Seventeenth Amendment.

shall be vacated at the Expiration of the second Year, of the second Class at the Expiration of the fourth Year, and of the third Class at the Expiration of the sixth Year, so that one third may be chosen every second Year; [and if Vacancies happen by Resignation, or otherwise, during the Recess of the Legislature of any State, the Executive thereof may make temporary Appointments until the next Meeting of the Legislature, which shall then fill such Vacancies.][3]

No Person shall be a Senator who shall not have attained to the age of thirty Years, and been nine Years a Citizen of the United States, and who shall not when elected, be an Inhabitant of that State for which he shall be chosen.

The Vice President of the United States shall be President of the Senate, but shall have no Vote, unless they be equally divided.

The Senate shall chuse their other Officers, and also a President pro tempore, in the Absence of the Vice President, or when he shall exercise the Office of President of the United States.

The Senate shall have the sole Power to try all Impeachments. When sitting for that Purpose, they shall be on Oath or Affirmation. When the President of the United States is tried, the Chief Justice shall preside: and no person shall be convicted without the Concurrence of two thirds of the Members present.

Judgment in Cases of Impeachment shall not extend further than to removal from office, and disqualification to hold and enjoy any Office of honor, Trust or Profit under the United States: but the Party convicted shall nevertheless be liable and subject to Indictment, Trial, Judgment and Punishment, according to Law.

Section 4. The Times, Places and Manner of holding Elections for Senators and Representatives, shall be prescribed in each State by the Legislature thereof; but the Congress may at any time by Law make or alter such Regulations, except as to the Places of chusing Senators.

[The Congress shall assemble at least once in every Year, and such Meeting shall be on the first Monday in December, unless they shall by Law appoint a different Day.][4]

Section 5. Each House shall be the Judge of the Elections, Returns and Qualifications of its own Members, and a Majority of each shall constitute a Quorum to do Business; but a smaller Number may adjourn from day to day, and may be authorized to compel the Attendance of absent Members, in such Manner, and under such Penalties as each House may provide.

Each House may determine the Rules of its Proceedings, punish its Members for disorderly Behaviour, and, with the Concurrence of two thirds, expel a Member.

Each House shall keep a Journal of its Proceedings, and from time to time publish the same, excepting such Parts as may in their Judgment require Secrecy; and the Yeas and Nays of the Members of either House on any question shall, at the Desire of one fifth of those Present, be entered on the Journal.

Neither House, during the Session of Congress, shall, without the Consent of the other, adjourn for more than three days, nor to any other Place than that in which the two Houses shall be sitting.

Section 6. The Senators and Representatives shall receive a Compensation for their Services, to be ascertained by Law, and paid out of the Treasury of the United States. They shall in all Cases except Treason, Felony and Breach of the Peace, be privileged from Arrest during their Attendance at the Session of their respective Houses, and in going to and returning from the same; and for any Speech or Debate in either House, they shall not be questioned in any other Place.

No Senator or Representative shall, during the Time for which he was elected, be appointed to any civil Office under the Authority of the United States, which shall have been created, or the Emoluments whereof shall have been increased during such time; and no Person holding any Office under the United States, shall be a Member of either House during his Continuance in Office.

---

3. Changed by the Seventeenth Amendment.

4. Superseded by the Twentieth Amendment.

Section 7. All bills for raising Revenue shall originate in the House of Representatives; but the Senate may propose or concur with Amendments as on other Bills.

Every Bill which shall have passed the House of Representatives and the Senate, shall, before it become a Law, be presented to the President of the United States; If he approve he shall sign it, but if not he shall return it, with his Objections to that House in which it shall have originated, who shall enter the Objections at large on their Journal, and proceed to reconsider it. If after such Reconsideration two thirds of that House shall agree to pass the Bill, it shall be sent, together with the Objections, to the other House, by which it shall likewise be reconsidered, and if approved by two thirds of that House, it shall become a Law. But in all such Cases the Votes of both Houses shall be determined by Yeas and Nays, and the Names of the Persons voting for and against the Bill shall be entered on the Journal of each House respectively. If any Bill shall not be returned by the President within ten Days (Sundays excepted) after it shall have been presented to him, the Same shall be a Law, in like Manner as if he had signed it, unless the Congress by their Adjournment prevent its Return, in which Case it shall not be a Law.

Every Order, Resolution, or Vote to which the Concurrence of the Senate and House of Representatives may be necessary (except on a question of Adjournment) shall be presented to the President of the United States; and before the Same shall take Effect, shall be approved by him, or being disapproved by him, shall be repassed by two thirds of the Senate and House of Representatives, according to the Rules and Limitations prescribed in the Case of a Bill.

Section 8. The Congress shall have Power To lay and collect Taxes, Duties, Imposts and Excises, to pay the Debts and provide for the common Defence and general Welfare of the United States; but all Duties, Imposts and Excises shall be uniform throughout the United States;

To borrow Money on the credit of the United States;

To regulate Commerce with foreign Nations, and among the several States, and with the Indian Tribes;

To establish a uniform Rule of Naturalization, and uniform Laws on the subject of Bankruptcies throughout the United States;

To coin Money, regulate the Value thereof, and of foreign Coin, and fix the Standard of Weights and Measures;

To provide for the Punishment of counterfeiting the Securities and current Coin of the United States;

To establish Post Offices and post Roads;

To promote the Progress of Science and useful Arts, by securing for limited Times to Authors and Inventors the exclusive Right to their respective Writings and Discoveries;

To constitute Tribunals inferior to the supreme Court;

To define and punish Piracies and Felonies committed on the high Seas, and Offences against the Law of Nations;

To declare War, grant Letters of Marque and Reprisal, and make Rules concerning Captures on Land and Water;

To raise and support Armies, but no Appropriation of Money to that Use shall be for a longer Term than two Years;

To provide and maintain a Navy;

To make Rules for the Government and Regulation of the land and naval Forces;

To provide for calling forth the Militia to execute the Laws of the Union, suppress Insurrections and repel Invasions;

To provide for organizing, arming, and disciplining, the Militia, and for governing such Part of them as may be employed in the Service of the United States, reserving to the States respectively, the Appointment of the Officers, and the Authority of training the Militia according to the discipline prescribed by Congress;

To exercise exclusive Legislation in all Cases whatsoever, over such District (not exceeding ten Miles square) as may, by Cession of particular States, and the Acceptance of Congress, become the Seat of the Government of the United States, and to exercise like Authority over all Places purchased by the Consent of the Legislature of the State in which the Same shall be, for the Erection of Forts, Magazines, Arsenals, dock-Yards, and other needful Buildings;— And

To make all Laws which shall be necessary and proper for carrying into Execution the foregoing Powers, and all other Powers vested by this Constitution in the Government of the United States, or in any Department or Officer thereof.

Section 9. The Migration or Importation of such Persons as any of the States now existing shall think proper to admit, shall not be prohibited by the Congress prior to the Year one thousand eight hundred and eight, but a Tax or duty may be imposed on such Importation, not exceeding ten dollars for each Person.

The Privilege of the Writ of Habeas Corpus shall not be suspended, unless when in Cases of Rebellion or Invasion the public safety may require it.

No Bill of Attainder or ex post facto Law shall be passed.

No Capitation, or other direct, Tax shall be laid, unless in Proportion to the Census or Enumeration herein before directed to be taken.[5]

No tax or Duty shall be laid on Articles exported from any State.

No Preference shall be given by any Regulation of Commerce or Revenue to the Ports of one State over those of another; nor shall Vessels bound to, or from, one State, be obliged to enter, clear, or pay Duties in another.

No money shall be drawn from the Treasury, but in Consequence of Appropriations made by Law; and a regular Statement and Account of the Receipts and Expenditures of all public Money shall be published from time to time.

No Title of Nobility shall be granted by the United States: And no Person holding any Office of Profit or Trust under them, shall, without the Consent of the Congress, accept any present, Emolument, Office, or Title, of any kind whatever, from any King, Prince, or foreign State.

Section 10. No State shall enter into any Treaty, Alliance, or Confederation; grant Letters of Marque and Reprisal; coin Money; emit Bills of Credit; make any Thing but gold and silver Coin a Tender in Payment of Debts; pass any Bill of Attainder, ex post facto Law, or Law impairing the Obligation of Contracts, or grant any Title of Nobility.

No State shall, without the Consent of the Congress, lay any Imposts or Duties on Imports or Exports, except what may be absolutely necessary for executing its inspection laws; and the net Produce of all Duties and Imposts, laid by any State on Imports or Exports, shall be for the Use of the Treasury of the United States; and all such Laws shall be subject to the Revision, and Control of the Congress.

No State, shall, without the Consent of Congress, lay any Duty of Tonnage, keep Troops, or Ships of War in time of Peace, enter into any Agreement or Compact with another State, or with a foreign Power, or engage in War, unless actually invaded, or in such imminent Danger as will not admit of delay.

ARTICLE II

Section 1. The executive Power shall be vested in a President of the United States of America. He shall hold his Office during the Term of four Years, and, together with the Vice President, chosen for the same Term, be elected, as follows.

Each State shall appoint, in such Manner as the Legislature thereof may direct, a Number of Electors, equal to the whole Number of Senators and Representatives to which the State may be entitled in the Congress: but no Senator or Representative, or Person holding an Office of Trust or Profit under the United States, shall be appointed an Elector.

[The Electors shall meet in their respective States, and vote by Ballot for two Persons, of whom one at least shall not be an Inhabitant of the same State with themselves. And they shall make a List of all the Persons voted for, and the Number of Votes for each; which list they shall sign and certify, and transmit sealed to the Seat of the Government of the United States, directed

---

5. Changed by the Sixteenth Amendment.

to the President of the Senate. The President of the Senate shall, in the Presence of the Senate and House of Representatives, open all the Certificates, and the Votes shall then be counted. The person having the greatest Number of Votes shall be the President, if such Number be a Majority of the whole Number of Electors appointed; and if there be more than one who have such Majority, and have an equal Number of Votes, then the House of Representatives shall immediately chuse by Ballot one of them for President; and if no Person have a Majority, then from the five highest on the List the said House shall in like Manner chuse the President. But in chusing the President, the Votes shall be taken by States, the Representation from each State having one Vote; A quorum for this purpose shall consist of a Member or Members from two-thirds of the States, and a Majority of all the States shall be necessary to a Choice. In every Case, after the Choice of the President, the Person having the greatest Number of Votes of the Electors shall be the Vice President. But if there should remain two or more who have equal Votes, the Senate shall chuse from them by Ballot the Vice President.][6]

The Congress may determine the Time of chusing the Electors, and the Day on which they shall give their Votes; which Day shall be the same throughout the United States.

No Person except a natural born Citizen, or a Citizen of the United States, at the time of the Adoption of this Constitution, shall be eligible to the Office of President; neither shall any Person be eligible to that Office who shall not have attained to the Age of thirty-five Years, and been fourteen Years a Resident within the United States.

[In Case of the Removal of the President from Office, or of his Death, Resignation, or Inability to discharge the Powers and Duties of the said Office, the Same shall devolve on the Vice President, and the Congress may by law provide for the Case of Removal, Death, Resignation or Inability, both of the President and Vice President, declaring what Officer shall then act as President, and such Officer shall act accordingly, until the Disability be removed, or a President shall be elected.][7]

The President shall, at stated Times receive for his Services, a Compensation, which shall neither be encreased nor diminished during the Period for which he shall have been elected, and he shall not receive within that Period any other Emolument from the United States, or any of them.

Before he enter on the Execution of his Office, he shall take the following Oath or Affirmation:—"I do solemnly swear (or affirm) that I will faithfully execute the Office of President of the United States, and will to the best of my Ability, preserve, protect and defend the Constitution of the United States."

Section 2. The President shall be Commander in Chief of the Army and Navy of the United States, and of the Militia of the several States, when called into the actual Service of the United States; he may require the Opinion, in writing, of the principal Officer in each of the executive Departments, upon any Subject relating to the Duties of their respective Offices, and he shall have Power to grant Reprieves and Pardons for Offenses against the United States, except in Cases of Impeachment.

He shall have Power, by and with the Advice and Consent of the Senate, to make Treaties, provided two thirds of the Senators present concur; and he shall nominate, and by and with the Advice and Consent of the Senate, shall appoint Ambassadors, other public Ministers and Consuls, Judges of the supreme Court, and all other Officers of the United States, whose Appointments are not herein otherwise provided for, and which shall be established by Law: but the Congress may by Law vest the Appointment of such inferior Officers, as they think proper, in the President alone, in the Courts of Law, or in the Heads of Departments.

The President shall have Power to fill up all Vacancies that may happen during the Recess of the Senate, by granting Commissions which shall expire at the End of their next Session.

Section 3. He shall from time to time give to the Congress Information of the State of the Union, and recommend to their Consideration such Measures as he shall judge necessary and expedient; he may, on extraordinary Occasions, convene both Houses, or either of them, and in Case of Disagreement between them, with Respect to the Time of Adjournment, he may

---

6. Superseded by the Twelfth Amendment.   7. Changed by the Twenty-fifth Amendment.

adjourn them to such Time as he shall think proper; he shall receive Ambassadors and other public Ministers; he shall take Care that the Laws be faithfully executed, and shall Commission all Officers of the United States.

Section 4. The President, Vice President and all civil Officers of the United States, shall be removed from Office on Impeachment for, and Conviction of, Treason, Bribery, or other high Crimes and Misdemeanors.

ARTICLE III

Section 1. The judicial Power of the United States, shall be vested in one supreme Court, and in such inferior Courts as the Congress may from time to time ordain and establish. The Judges, both of the supreme and inferior Courts, shall hold their Offices during good Behaviour, and shall, at stated Times, receive for their Services, a Compensation, which shall not be diminished during their Continuance in Office.

Section 2. The judicial Power shall extend to all Cases, in Law and Equity, arising under this Constitution, the Laws of the United States, and Treaties made, or which shall be made, under their Authority;—to all Cases affecting Ambassadors, other public Ministers and Consuls;—to all Cases of admiralty and maritime Jurisdiction;—to Controversies to which the United States shall be a party;—to Controversies between two or more States;—between a State and Citizens of another State;—between Citizens of different States,—between Citizens of the same State claiming Lands under Grants of different States, and between a State, or the Citizens thereof, and foreign States, Citizens or Subjects.[8]

In all cases affecting Ambassadors, other public Ministers and Consuls, and those in which a State shall be Party, the supreme Court shall have original Jurisdiction. In all the other Cases before mentioned, the supreme Court shall have appellate Jurisdiction, both as to Law and fact, with such Exceptions, and under such Regulations as the Congress shall make.

The Trial of all Crimes, except in Cases of Impeachment, shall be by Jury; and such Trial shall be held in the State where the said Crimes shall have been committed; but when not committed within any State, the Trial shall be at such Place or Places as the Congress may by Law have directed.

Section 3. Treason against the United States, shall consist only in levying War against them, or in adhering to their Enemies, giving them Aid and Comfort. No Person shall be convicted of Treason unless on the Testimony of two Witnesses to the same overt Act, or on Confession in open Court.

The Congress shall have Power to declare the Punishment of Treason, but no Attainder of Treason shall work Corruption of Blood, or Forfeiture except during the Life of the Person attainted.

ARTICLE IV

Section 1. Full Faith and Credit shall be given in each State to the public Acts, Records, and judicial Proceedings of every other State. And the Congress may by general Laws prescribe the Manner in which such Acts, Records and Proceedings shall be proved, and the Effect thereof.

Section 2. The Citizens of each State shall be entitled to all Privileges and Immunities of Citizens in the several States.

A Person charged in any State with Treason, Felony, or other Crime, who shall flee from Justice, and be found in another State, shall on Demand of the executive Authority of the State from which he fled, be delivered up, to be removed to the State having Jurisdiction of the Crime.

[No Person held to Service or Labour in one State, under the Laws thereof, escaping into another, shall, in Consequence of any Law or Regulation therein, be discharged from such Service or Labour, but shall be delivered up on Claim of the Party to whom such Service or Labour may be due.][9]

---

8. Changed by the Eleventh Amendment.   9. Superseded by the Thirteenth Amendment.

Section 3. New States may be admitted by the Congress into this Union; but no new State shall be formed or erected within the Jurisdiction of any other State; nor any State be formed by the Junction of two or more States, or Parts of States, without the Consent of the Legislatures of the States concerned as well as of the Congress.

The Congress shall have Power to dispose of and make all needful Rules and Regulations respecting the Territory or other Property belonging to the United States; and nothing in this Constitution shall be so construed as to Prejudice any Claims of the United States, or of any particular State.

Section 4. The United States shall guarantee to every State in this Union a Republican Form of Government, and shall protect each of them against Invasion; and on Application of the Legislature, or of the Executive (when the Legislature cannot be convened) against domestic Violence.

ARTICLE V

The Congress, whenever two thirds of both Houses shall deem it necessary, shall propose Amendments to this Constitution, or, on the Application of the Legislatures of two thirds of the several States, shall call a Convention for proposing Amendments, which, in either Case, shall be valid to all Intents and Purposes, as Part of this Constitution, when ratified by the Legislatures of three fourths of the several States, or by Conventions in three fourths thereof, as the one or the other Mode of Ratification may be proposed by the Congress; Provided that no Amendment which may be made prior to the Year One thousand eight hundred and eight shall in any Manner affect the first and fourth Clauses in the Ninth Section of the first Article; and that no State, without its Consent, shall be deprived of its equal Suffrage in the Senate.

ARTICLE VI

All Debts contracted and Engagements entered into, before the Adoption of this Constitution, shall be as valid against the United States under this Constitution, as under the Confederation.

This Constitution, and the Laws of the United States which shall be made in Pursuance thereof; and all Treaties made, or which shall be made, under the Authority of the United States, shall be the supreme Law of the Land; and the Judges in every State shall be bound thereby, any Thing in the Constitution or Laws of any State to the Contrary notwithstanding.

The Senators and Representatives before mentioned, and the Members of the several State Legislatures, and all executive and judicial Officers, both of the United States and of the several States, shall be bound by Oath or Affirmation, to support this Constitution; but no religious Test shall ever be required as a Qualification to any Office or public Trust under the United States.

ARTICLE VII

The Ratification of the Conventions of nine States, shall be sufficient for the Establishment of this Constitution between the States so ratifying the Same.

[Signatures omitted.]

[Amendments]

ARTICLES in addition to, and Amendment of the Constitution of the United States of America, proposed by Congress, and ratified by the Legislatures of the several States, pursuant to the fifth Article of the original Constitution.

ARTICLE I

Congress shall make no law respecting an establishment of religion, or prohibiting the free exercise thereof; or abridging the freedom of speech, or of the press; or the right of the people peaceably to assemble, and to petition the Government for a redress of grievances.

ARTICLE II

A well regulated Militia, being necessary to the security of a free State, the right of the people to keep and bear Arms, shall not be infringed.

ARTICLE III

No Soldier shall, in time of peace be quartered in any house, without the consent of the Owner, nor in time of war, but in a manner to be prescribed by law.

ARTICLE IV

The right of the people to be secure in their persons, houses, papers, and effects, against unreasonable searches and seizures, shall not be violated, and no Warrants shall issue, but upon probable cause, supported by Oath or affirmation, and particularly describing the place to be searched, and the persons or things to be seized.

ARTICLE V

No person shall be held to answer for a capital, or otherwise infamous crime, unless on a presentment or indictment of a Grand Jury, except in cases arising in the land or naval forces, or in the Militia, when in actual service in time of War or public danger; nor shall any person be subject for the same offense to be twice put in jeopardy of life or limb; nor shall be compelled in any criminal case to be a witness against himself, nor be deprived of life, liberty, or property, without due process of law; nor shall private property be taken for public use, without just compensation.

ARTICLE VI

In all criminal prosecutions, the accused shall enjoy the right to a speedy and public trial, by an impartial jury of the State and district wherein the crime shall have been committed, which district shall have been previously ascertained by law, and to be informed of the nature and cause of the accusation; to be confronted with the witnesses against him; to have compulsory process for obtaining witnesses in his favor, and to have the Assistance of Counsel for his defense.

ARTICLE VII

In Suits at common law, where the value in controversy shall exceed twenty dollars, the right of trial by jury shall be preserved, and no fact tried by a jury, shall be otherwise re-examined in any Court of the United States, than according to the rules of the common law.

ARTICLE VIII

Excessive bail shall not be required, nor excessive fines imposed, nor cruel and unusual punishments inflicted.

ARTICLE IX

The enumeration in the Constitution, of certain rights, shall not be construed to deny or disparage others retained by the people.

ARTICLE X

The powers not delegated to the United States by the Constitution, nor prohibited by it to the States, are reserved to the States respectively, or to the people.

ARTICLE XI [adopted in 1798]

The Judicial power of the United States shall not be construed to extend to any suit in law or equity, commenced or prosecuted against one of the United States by Citizens of another State, or by Citizens or Subjects of any Foreign State.

ARTICLE XII [adopted in 1804]

The Electors shall meet in their respective states, and vote by ballot for President and Vice-President, one of whom, at least, shall not be an inhabitant of the same state with themselves; they shall name in their ballots the person voted for as President, and in distinct ballots the person voted for as Vice-President, and they shall make distinct lists of all persons voted for as President, and of all persons voted for as Vice-President, and of the number of votes for each, which lists they shall sign and certify, and transmit sealed to the seat of the government of the United States, directed to the President of the Senate;—The President of the Senate shall, in the presence of the Senate and House of Representatives, open all certificates and the votes shall then be counted;—The person having the greatest number of votes for President, shall be the President, if such number be a majority of the whole number of Electors appointed; and if no person have such majority, then from the persons having the highest numbers not exceeding three on the list of those voted for as President, the House of Representatives shall choose immediately, by ballot, the President. But in choosing the President, the votes shall be taken by states, the representation from each state having one vote; a quorum for this purpose shall consist of a member or members from two-thirds of the states, and a majority of all the states shall be necessary to a choice. [And if the House of Representatives shall not choose a President whenever the right of choice shall devolve upon them, before the fourth day of March next following, then the Vice-President shall act as President, as in the case of the death or other constitutional disability of the President.][10] The person having the greatest number of votes as Vice-President, shall be the Vice-President, if such number be a majority of the whole number of Electors appointed, and if no person have a majority, then from the two highest numbers on the list, the Senate shall choose the Vice-President; a quorum for the purpose shall consist of two-thirds of the whole number of Senators, and a majority of the whole number shall be necessary to a choice. But no person constitutionally ineligible to the office of President shall be eligible to that of Vice-President of the United States.

---

10. Superseded by the Twentieth Amendment.

ARTICLE XIII [adopted in 1865]

Section 1. Neither slavery nor involuntary servitude, except as a punishment for crime whereof the party shall have been duly convicted, shall exist within the United States, or any place subject to their jurisdiction.

Section 2. Congress shall have power to enforce this article by appropriate legislation.

ARTICLE XIV [adopted in 1868]

Section 1. All persons born or naturalized in the United States, and subject to the jurisdiction thereof, are citizens of the United States and of the State wherein they reside. No State shall make or enforce any law which shall abridge the privileges or immunities of citizens of the United States; nor shall any State deprive any person of life, liberty, or property, without due process of law; nor deny to any person within its jurisdiction the equal protection of the laws.

Section 2. Representatives shall be apportioned among the several States according to their respective numbers, counting the whole number of persons in each State, excluding Indians not taxed. But when the right to vote at any election for the choice of electors for President and Vice President of the United States, Representatives in Congress, the Executive and Judicial officers of a State, or the members of the Legislature thereof, is denied to any of the male inhabitants of such State, being twenty-one years of age, and citizens of the United States, or in any way abridged, except for participation in rebellion, or other crime, the basis of representation therein shall be reduced in the proportion which the number of such male citizens shall bear to the whole number of male citizens twenty-one years of age in such State.

Section 3. No person shall be a Senator or Representative in Congress, or elector of President and Vice President, or hold any office, civil or military, under the United States, or under any State, who, having previously taken an oath, as a member of Congress, or as an officer of the United States, or as a member of any State legislature, or as an executive or judicial officer of any States, to support the Constitution of the United States, shall have engaged in insurrection or rebellion against the same, or given aid and comfort to the enemies thereof. But Congress may by a vote of two-thirds of each House, remove such disability.

Section 4. The validity of the public debt of the United States, authorized by law, including debts incurred for payment of pensions and bounties for services in suppressing insurrection or rebellion, shall not be questioned. But neither the United States nor any state shall assume or pay any debt or obligation incurred in aid of insurrection or rebellion against the United States, or any claim for the loss or emancipation of any slave; but all such debts, obligations, and claims shall be held illegal and void.

Section 5. The Congress shall have power to enforce, by appropriate legislation, the provisions of this article.

ARTICLE XV [adopted in 1870]

Section 1. The right of citizens of the United States to vote shall not be denied or abridged by the United States or by any State on account of race, color, or previous condition of servitude.

Section 2. The Congress shall have power to enforce this article by appropriate legislation.

ARTICLE XVI [adopted in 1913]

The Congress shall have power to lay and collect taxes on incomes, from whatever source derived, without apportionment among the several States, and without regard to any census or enumeration.

ARTICLE XVII [adopted in 1913]

The Senate of the United States shall be composed of two Senators from each State, elected by the people thereof, for six years; and each Senator shall have one vote. The electors in each State shall have the qualifications requisite for electors of the most numerous branch of the State legislatures.

When vacancies happen in the representation of any State in the Senate, the executive authority of such State shall issue writs of election to fill such vacancies: *Provided,* That the legislature of any State may empower the executive thereof to make temporary appointments until the people fill the vacancies by election as the legislature may direct.

This amendment shall not be so construed as to affect the election or term of any Senator chosen before it becomes valid as part of the Constitution.

ARTICLE XVIII [adopted in 1919; repealed by the 21st Amendment]

Section 1. After one year from the ratification of this article the manufacture, sale, or transportation of intoxicating liquors within, the importation thereof into, or the exportation thereof from the United States and all territory subject to the jurisdiction thereof for beverage purposes is hereby prohibited.

Section 2. The Congress and the several States shall have concurrent power to enforce this article by appropriate legislation.

Section 3. This article shall be inoperative unless it shall have been ratified as an amendment to the Constitution by the legislatures of the several States, as provided in the Constitution, within seven years from the date of the submission hereof to the States by the Congress.

ARTICLE XIX [adopted in 1920]

The right of citizens of the United States to vote shall not be denied or abridged by the United States or by any State on account of sex.

Congress shall have power to enforce this article by appropriate legislation.

ARTICLE XX [adopted in 1933]

Section 1. The terms of the President and Vice President shall end at noon on the 20th day of January, and the terms of Senators and Representatives at noon on the 3d day of January, of the years in which such terms would have ended if this article had not been ratified; and the terms of their successors shall then begin.

Section 2. The Congress shall assemble at least once in every year, and such meeting shall begin at noon on the 3d day of January, unless they shall by law appoint a different day.

Section 3. If, at the time fixed for the beginning of the term of the President, the President elect shall have died, the Vice President elect shall become President. If a President shall not have been chosen before the time fixed for the beginning of his term, or if the President elect shall have failed to qualify, then the Vice President elect shall act as President until a President shall have qualified; and the Congress may by law provide for the case wherein neither a President elect nor a Vice President elect shall have qualified, declaring who shall then act as President, or the manner in which one who is to act shall be selected, and such person shall act accordingly until a President or Vice President shall have qualified.

Section 4. The Congress may by law provide for the case of the death of any of the persons from whom the House of Representatives may choose a President whenever the right of choice shall have devolved upon them, and for the case of the death of any of the persons from whom the Senate may choose a Vice President whenever the right of choice shall have devolved upon them.

Section 5. Sections 1 and 2 shall take effect on the 15th day of October following the ratification of this article.

Section 6. This article shall be inoperative unless it shall have been ratified as an amendment to the Constitution by the legislatures of three-fourths of the several States within seven years from the date of its submission.

ARTICLE XXI [adopted in 1933]

Section l. The Eighteenth article of amendment to the Constitution of the United States is hereby repealed.

Section 2. The transportation or importation into any State, Territory, or possession of the United States for delivery or use therein of intoxicating liquors, in violation of the laws thereof, is hereby prohibited.

Section 3. This article shall be inoperative unless it shall have been ratified as an amendment to the Constitution by conventions in the several States, as provided in the Constitution, within seven years from the date of the submission hereof to the States by the Congress.

ARTICLE XXII [adopted in 1951]

Section 1. No person shall be elected to the office of the President more than twice, and no person who has held the office of President, or acted as President, for more than two years of a term to which some other person was elected President shall be elected to the Office of the President more than once. But this Article shall not apply to any person holding the office of President when this Article was proposed by the Congress, and shall not prevent any person who may be holding the Office of President, or acting as President, during the term within which this Article becomes operative from holding the office of President or acting as President during the remainder of such term.

Section 2. This article shall be inoperative unless it shall have been ratified as an amendment to the Constitution by the legislatures of three-fourths of the several States within seven years from the date of its submission to the States by the Congress.

ARTICLE XXIII [adopted in 1961]

Section 1. The District constituting the seat of Government of the United States shall appoint in such manner as the Congress may direct:

A number of electors of President and Vice President equal to the whole number of Senators and Representatives in Congress to which the District would be entitled if it were a State, but in no event more than the least populous state; they shall be in addition to those appointed by the States, but they shall be considered, for the purposes of the election of President and Vice President, to be electors appointed by a State; and they shall meet in the District and perform such duties as provided by the twelfth article of amendment.

Section 2. The Congress shall have power to enforce this article by appropriate legislation.

ARTICLE XXIV [adopted in 1964]

Section 1. The right of citizens of the United States to vote in any primary or other election for President or Vice President, for electors for President or Vice President, or for Senator or Representative in Congress, shall not be denied or abridged by the United States or any State by reason of failure to pay any poll tax or other tax.

Section 2. The Congress shall have power to enforce this article by appropriate legislation.

ARTICLE XXV [adopted in 1967]

Section 1. In case of removal of the President from office or of his death or resignation, the Vice President shall become President.

Section 2. Whenever there is a vacancy in the office of the Vice President, the President shall nominate a Vice President who shall take office upon confirmation by a majority vote of both Houses of Congress.

Section 3. Whenever the President transmits to the President pro tempore of the Senate and the Speaker of the House of Representatives his written declaration that he is unable to discharge the powers and duties of his office, and until he transmits to them a written declaration to the contrary, such powers and duties shall be discharged by the Vice President as Acting President.

Section 4. Whenever the Vice President and a majority of either the principal officers of the executive departments or of such other body as Congress may by law provide, transmit to the President pro tempore of the Senate and the Speaker of the House of Representatives their written declaration that the President is unable to discharge the powers and duties of his office, the Vice President shall immediately assume the powers and duties of the Office as Acting President.

Thereafter, when the President transmits to the President pro tempore of the Senate and the Speaker of the House of Representatives his written declaration that no inability exists, he shall resume the powers and duties of his office unless the Vice President and a majority of either the principal officers of the executive department or of such other body as Congress may by law provide, transmit within four days to the President pro tempore of the Senate and the Speaker of the House of Representatives their written declaration that the President is unable to discharge the powers and duties of his office. Thereupon Congress shall decide the issue, assembling within forty-eight hours for that purpose if not in session. If the Congress, within twenty-one days after receipt of the latter written declaration, or, if Congress is not in session, within twenty-one days after Congress is required to assemble, determines by two-thirds vote of both Houses that the President is unable to discharge the powers and duties of his office, the Vice President shall continue to discharge the same as Acting President; otherwise, the President shall resume the powers and duties of his office.

ARTICLE XXVI [adopted in 1971]

Section 1. The right of citizens of the United States, who are eighteen years of age or older, to vote shall not be denied or abridged by the United States or by any State on account of age.

Section 2. The Congress shall have power to enforce this article by appropriate legislation.

Appendix C
American Presidents

	Term of Office
George Washington	1789–1797
John Adams	1797–1801
Thomas Jefferson	1801–1809
James Madison	1809–1817
James Monroe	1817–1825
John Quincy Adams	1825–1829
Andrew Jackson	1829–1837
Martin Van Buren	1837–1841
William Henry Harrison	March 4–April 4, 1841
John Tyler	1841–1845
James K. Polk	1845–1849
Zachary Taylor	1849–July 9, 1850
Millard Fillmore	1850–1853
Franklin Pierce	1853–1857
James Buchanan	1857–1861
Abraham Lincoln	1861–April 14, 1865
Andrew Johnson	1865–1869
Ulysses S. Grant	1869–1877
Rutherford B. Hayes	1877–1881
James A. Garfield	March 4–September 19, 1881
Chester A. Arthur	1881–1885
Grover Cleveland	1885–1889, 1893–1897
Benjamin Harrison	1889–1893
William McKinley	1897–September 14, 1901
Theodore Roosevelt	1901–1909
William Howard Taft	1909–1913
Woodrow Wilson	1913–1921
Warren Harding	1921–August 2, 1923
Calvin Coolidge	1923–1929
Herbert Hoover	1929–1933
Franklin D. Roosevelt	1933–April 12, 1945
Harry S. Truman	1945–1953
Dwight D. Eisenhower	1953–1961
John F. Kennedy	1961–November 22, 1963
Lyndon B. Johnson	1963–1969
Richard M. Nixon	1969–1974
Gerald R. Ford	1974–1977
Jimmy Carter	1977–1981
Ronald Reagan	1981–1989
George Bush	1989–1993
Bill Clinton	1993–

Appendix D

American States and Their Abbreviations

AL	Alabama	MT	Montana
AK	Alaska	NE	Nebraska
AZ	Arizona	NV	Nevada
AR	Arkansas	NH	New Hampshire
CA	California	NJ	New Jersey
CO	Colorado	NM	New Mexico
CT	Connecticut	NY	New York
DE	Delaware	NC	North Carolina
FL	Florida	ND	North Dakota
GA	Georgia	OH	Ohio
HI	Hawaii	OK	Oklahoma
ID	Idaho	OR	Oregon
IL	Illinois	PA	Pennsylvania
IN	Indiana	RI	Rhode Island
IA	Iowa	SC	South Carolina
KS	Kansas	SD	South Dakota
KY	Kentucky	TN	Tennessee
LA	Louisiana	TX	Texas
ME	Maine	UT	Utah
MD	Maryland	VT	Vermont
MA	Massachusetts	VA	Virginia
MI	Michigan	WA	Washington
MN	Minnesota	WV	West Virginia
MS	Mississippi	WI	Wisconsin
MO	Missouri	WY	Wyoming

America: Past and Present
Volume III: The Continuing Quest
Answer Key

UNIT 1: *Money and Magnificence:* **The Gilded Age**

Reading Comprehension
A. 1. c, 2. b, 3. c, 4. c, 5. a, 6. a, 7. b, 8. b, 9. b,c,a, 10. c
B. 1. f, 2. t, 3. t, 4. f, 5. t, 6. t, 7. f, 8. f, 9. t, 10. f
C. 1. b, 2. a, 3. b, 4. c
D. 1. b, 2. b, 3. a, 4. b, 5. a

Vocabulary
A. 1. a. conflict, b. conflicted, c. conflicting; 2. a. prosperity, b. prosperous, c. to prosper;
    3. a. assistant, b. to assist, c. assistance; 4. a. capable, b. capably, c. capacity;
    5. a. symbolic, b. symbolized, c. symbol; 6. a. thrilling, b. thrilled, c. thrill;
    7. a. destination, b. destined, c. destiny; 8. a. convert, b. converted, c. conversion
B. horrible, load, powerful, destroy, encourage, plan, change, extraordinary, dishonesty,
    huge
C. 1. brilliant, 2. traumatic, 3. cherished, 4. heritage, 5. abbey, 6. odor, 7. frightful,
    8. vanished, 9. vivid, 10. fraud

Structures
A. of, from, about, for, to, in, of, by, of, upon, of, for, with, to, of
B. larger, more powerful; richer, greedier; harder, fewer; more, wealthier; older, more

UNIT 2: *Conquest of the Prairies:* **One Last Frontier**

Reading Comprehension
A. 1. b, 2. c, 3. b, 4. a, 5. a, 6. b, 7. c, 8. c, 9. a, 10. c
B. free land for Americans on the plains; land grants and subsidies for cross-country
    transportation; source of life's essentials for the Plains people; scene of final confronta-
    tion with Native Americans; place where first cross-country railroad was finished;
    houses of dried earth on the prairies; scene of Willa Cather's childhood memories;
    classic American novel
C. 1. Central Pacific Railroad, Union Pacific Railroad; 2. Southern Pacific Railroad;
    3. Atchison, Topeka & Santa Fe Railroad; 4. Northern Pacific Railroad; 5. Great
    Northern Railroad

Vocabulary
A. 1. a. dreaded, b. dreadful, c. to dread; 2. a. to resist, b. irresistible, c. resistance;
    3. a. unpredictable, b. predict, c. predictions; 4. a. respected, b. respectful, c. to respect;
    5. a. resigned, b. to resign, c. resignation; 6. a. to defy, b. defiance, c. defiant
B. 1. hostility, 2. provincial, 3. themes, 4. linked, 5. plows, 6. cultivate, 7. adopt, 8. prose,
    9. grants, 10. savage
C. scarce, weak, remain, flexible, pleasant, increase, unimpressive, surrender, flood,
    crowded
D. 1. c, 2. b, 3. a, 4. b, 5. b, 6. a, 7. a, 8. b, 9. c, 10. a

Structures

A. a, the, a, the, a, the, a, a, a, an, the, the, the

B. 1. a. will be finishing, b. will be attacking, c. will be returning, d. will be trying, e. will be visiting; 2. a. whether the workers would be finishing, b. whether the Indians would be attacking, c. whether Emil would be returning, d. whether Alexandra would be trying, e. whether Marie would be visiting

UNIT 3: *International Dimensions:* Will Expansionism Triumph?

Reading Comprehension

A. 1. b, 2. c, 3. a, 4. b, 5. b, 6. c, 7. a, 8. b, 9. a, 10. b

B. 1. Captain Cook, 2. *Maine,* 3. Yellow Journalism, 4. Kamehameha I, 5. Liliuokalani, 6. McKinley, 7. Puerto Rico, 8. Oahu, 9. Alaska, 10. Manifest Destiny

C. 1. Georgia, South Carolina, North Carolina, Virginia, Maryland, Delaware, New Jersey, Pennsylvania, New York, Connecticut, Rhode Island, Massachusetts, New Hampshire; 2. Tennessee, Kentucky; 3. yes; 4. yes; 5. yes; 6. Great Plains; 7. Oklahoma, New Mexico, Arizona; 8. Alaska, Hawaii

D. 1. Hawaii, Hawaiian volcanoes; 2. Kauai; 3. Oahu; 4. Molokai

Vocabulary

A. 1. a. reliant, b. to rely, c. reliance; 2. a. to replace, b. replacement, c. irreplaceable; 3. a. temptation, b. tempting, c. tempted; 4. a. opponents, b. opposition, c. to oppose; 5. a. exceedingly, b. exceeded, c. excessive; 6. a. extends, b. extensive, c. extensively; 7. a. scarcely, b. scarce, c. scarcity; 8. a. aggressive, b. aggression, c. aggressively

B. 1. took a strong stand, 2. embarked on, 3. coup d'état, 4. at all costs, 5. come to a head, 6. had come to rely, 7–8. In time, elite, 9. Before the year was out, 10. high-ranking posts

C. 1. bountiful, 2. escalating, 3. jeopardize, 4. outspoken, 5. tawdry, 6. controversy, 7. ceded, 8. lavishly, 9. incautious, 10. enrage

Structures

A. such effective opposition, such beautiful islands, such a continuous eruption, such a tremendous explosion, such lavish hospitality

B. 1. McKinley was the person to whom the advisors spoke. 2. Captain Cook was the person in whom the sailors put their faith. 3. Liliuokalani was the person with whom the rebels had a meeting. 4. Grover Cleveland was the person from whom the isolationists got support. 5. Kamehameha was the person for whom the natives had great respect.

UNIT 4: *American Inventors:* The New Pioneers

Reading Comprehension

A. 1. a, 2. b, 3. c, 4. b, 5. c, 6. c, 7. b, 8. b, 9. c, 10. b

B. 1. a, 2. b, 3. b, 4. c, 5. a

C. 1. b, 2. c, 3. b, 4. b, 5. b

D. 1. Hawaii, 2. telephone, 3. automobile, 4. Cuba, 5. peace

Vocabulary

A. 1. a. investigation, b. to investigate, c. investigative; 2. a. avail, b. availability, c. available; 3. a. achievements, b. to achieve, c. achiever; 4. a. appeal, b. appealed, c. appealing; 5. a. schemes, b. scheme, c. schematic; 6. a. procedures, b. proceed, c. procedural; 7. a. amazement, b. amazed, c. amazing; 8. a. dimmed, b. dim, c. dimly

B. 1. unappealing, 2. unaffected, 3. inaudible, 4. infinite, 5. unavailable
C. boring, ignore, unimportant, willing, pleased, simple, sturdy, small, casual, sad
D. 1. hearing-impaired, 2. rigorous, 3. fruitful, 4. bypassed, 5. manpower, 6. dunce,
    7. vagabond, 8. buoyed, 9. intrigued, 10. lodged

Structures
A. 1. for separating, 2. for recording, 3. for cutting, 4. for transmitting, 5. for storing
B. 1. have, 2. come, 3. help, 4. give, 5. be done, 6. be kept

UNIT 5: *A Vision of Justice:* Progressive Reformers

Reading Comprehension
A. 1. a, 2. b, 3. a, 4. c, 5. b, 6. a, 7. b, 8. b, 9. c, 10. a
B. 1. t, 2. t, 3. f, 4. f, 5. t, 6. t, 7. t, 8. f, 9. t, 10. t
D. 1. 37 million; 2. 0.1 million; 3. 4 million, 6 million, 1.5 million; 5. 56 million

Vocabulary
A. 1. a. defective, b. defectively, c. defects; 2. a. excluded, b. exclusive, c. exclusively;
    3. a. legislative, b. legislators, c. legislation; 4. a. fulfillment, b. fulfilling, c. to fulfill;
    5. a. consulted, b. consultation, c. consultants
B. 1. c, 2. c, 3. b, 4. b, 5. c, 6. a, 7. c, 8. a
C. 1. take up, 2. carry on, 3. managed to, 4. looked ahead, 5. gave up, 6. set up,
    7. brought out, 8. counting on
D. combine, impure, horrible, self-reliant, extensive, dishonest, crowded, careful,
    supporter, danger

Structures
A. 1. traveling, 2. leaving, 3. trying, 4. arguing, 5. selling, 6. raising, 7. refusing,
    8. copying, 9. working, 10. building
B. 1. winning, 2. working, 3. organizing, 4. calling, 5. cheating, 6. selling, 7. losing,
    8. winning, 9. sending, 10. being

UNIT 6: *An Old Order Passes:* World War I

Reading Comprehension
A. 1. c, 2. a, 3. b, 4. a, 5. a, 6. b, 7. b, 8. c, 9. b, 10. b
B. Francis Ferdinand, Sarajevo, Central Powers, Allies, eastern theater, western front,
    Russia, Czar, Lenin, United States, Germany, armistice
C. 1. acb; 2. acb; 3. bca; 4. acb; 5. acb
D. 1. Austria-Hungary; 2. Serbia; 3. Germany, Austria-Hungary, Bulgaria, Ottoman
    Empire; 4. Denmark, the Netherlands, Norway, Sweden, Switzerland, Spain; 5. Great
    Britain, Belgium, France, Italy, Serbia, Montenegro, Albania, Greece, Romania, Russia;
    6. France; 7. Russia
E. eastern theater, western front, Lenin, Central Powers, Armistice, Allied Powers, Bosnia,
    Sarajevo, *Lusitania,* Francis Ferdinand, Czar Nicholas II, Serbia

Vocabulary
A. 1. gracious, 2. alternative, 3. framework, 4. imperial gardens, 5. cellar, 6. sacred,
    7. in vain, 8. assurance, 9. network, 10. protests
B. 1. c, 2. b, 3. a, 4. b, 5. c, 6. b, 7. a, 8. b, 9. c, 10. a
C. destroy, fall, slide, escape from, guns, movement, cease-fire, effect, everlasting,
    uncivilized

Structures
A. 1. a. terrified, b. terrifying; 2. a. devastated, b. devastating; 3. a. appalled, b. appalling; 4. a. shattering, b. shattered; 5. a. exhausted, b. exhausting
B. 1. Many of the Serbians must have been horrified by the plot. 2. Secret information may have been received by Lord Grey. 3. The ship's passengers should have been warned by enemy submarines. 4. The British embargo might have been broken by submarine warfare. 5. The war could have been continued by Lenin.

UNIT 7: *The Roaring Twenties:* Explosive Reaction

Reading Comprehension
A. 1. b, 2. b, 3. acb, 4. c, 5. a, 6. c, 7. a, 8. a, 9. c, 10. a
B. 1. b, 2. c, 3. a, 4. b, 5. a
C. 1. t, 2. f, 3. t, 4. t, 5. f, 6. f, 7. f, 8. t, 9. f, 10. t
D. 1. Thomas Edison, 2. Captain Cook, 3. Ernest Hemingway, 4. Andrew Carnegie, 5. Jacob Riis, 6. Queen Liliuokalani, 7. Willa Cather, 8. Jane Addams, 9. F. Scott Fitzgerald, 10. Charles Lindbergh

Vocabulary
A. 1. a. harmony, b. harmonious, c. to harmonize; 2. a. significant, b. significance, c. significantly; 3. a. rebellion, b. rebellious, c. rebels, d. rebelled; 4. a. deception, b. deceived, c. deceptive; 5. a. immensely, b. immensity, c. immense
B. 1. unconventional, 2. irreverent, 3. unchaperoned, 4. unconcerned, 5. irresistible
D. 1. c, 2. b, 3. a, 4. b, 5. c, 6. a, 7. c, 8. c, 9. b, 10. a
E. liberated woman; a wild and exuberant dance; secret bar; illegal manufacturer or distributor of liquor; smuggling intoxicating beverages into America

Structures
A. to enter, to approach, to convince, to provide, to try, to take off, to keep, to get, to give in, to stay
B. 1. "This dress needs to be shortened ...", 2. "This car needs to be polished ...", 3. "Does this story need to be rewritten ...", 4. "I think the characters need to be developed ...", 5. "Postwar Europe needs to be rebuilt ...".

UNIT 8: *Financial Collapse:* The Depression

Reading Comprehension
A. 1. b, 2. c, 3. b, 4. bca, 5. b, 6. c, 7. a, 8. a, 9. b, 10. b
B. Sales, inventories, production, Wall Street, down, brokers, loans, clients, stocks, banks, depositors, savings
C. 1. about four percent, 2. no, 3. a steep climb, 4. almost twenty-five percent, 5. no, 6. Unemployment rose again. , 7. no, 8. yes, yes, 9. lower, very eventful
D. 1. stem the tide of, 2. at a loss for, 3. fair and foul, 4. weather the storm, 5. let alone, 6. opened the door to

Vocabulary
A. 1. stood out, 2. presided over, 3. wore on, 4. complied with, 5. hold on, 6. cope with, 7. tapered off, 8. bring about, 9. couldn't stand to, 10. take part in
B. 1. fundamental, 2. tolerate, 3. supervision, 4. severe, 5. remedy, 6. spiral, 7. condemned, 8. minimal, 9–10. retired, pension
C. reduce, fierce, enormous, approximately, talented, soften, poor, tight, categories

Structures

A. 1. dropping, 2. closing, 3. producing, 4. resenting, 5. causing, 6. staying, 7. writing, 8. describing
B. 1. will have been flying, 2. will have been standing, 3. will have been speaking, 4. will have been working, 5. will have been living

UNIT 9: *Toward the Unthinkable:* A Second World War

Reading Comprehension

A. 1. a, 2. c, 3. b, 4. a, 5. c, 6. b, 7. c, 8. c, 9. b, 10. b
B. 1. a, 2. b, 3. a, 4. b, 5. b, 6. b, 7. a, 8. b, 9. a, 10. b, 11. a, 12. a
C. 1. Versailles, 2. Austria, 3. Czechoslovakia, 4. Poland, 5. France, 6. England, 7. Pearl Harbor, 8. El Alamein, 9. Stalingrad, 10. Normandy, 11. Berlin, 12. Hiroshima
D. 1. t, 2. t, 3. f, 4. f, 5. t, 6. f, 7. f, 8. t, 9. t, 10. t

Vocabulary

A. 1. perished, 2. concentration, 3. sustained, 4. instability, 5. gaps, 6. breeding, 7. dictatorial, 8. declare, 9. authorized, 10. neutrality
B. 1. anarchy, 2. consolidated, 3. faltered, 4. hideous, 5. belligerent, 6. titanic, 7. strategic, 8. eternal, 9. congenial, 10. sanctuary
C. 1. humiliated, 2. prominent, 3. totalitarianism, 4. relentless, 5. awesome, 6. poignant, 7. more gruesome, 8. inadequate

Structures

A. 1. No sooner had World War I ended than ..., 2. No sooner had World War I ended than ..., 3. No sooner had Europe's dynasties toppled than ..., 4. No sooner had America's stock market collapsed than ..., 5. No sooner had Churchill asked for assistance than ..., 6. No sooner had Einstein entered school than ..., 7. No sooner had Einstein gone to Switzerland than ..., 8. No sooner had the atom been split than ....
B. 1. Not only did Germany have to sign ..., but it also ..., 2. Not only was La Guardia ..., but he was also ..., 3. Not only did American soldiers fight ..., but they were also ..., 4. Not only were millions of soldiers killed ..., but there were also ..., 5 . Not only will we have to ..., but we will also....

UNIT 10: *After the Holocaust:* Nonviolent Imperatives

Reading Comprehension

A. 1. c, 2. b, 3. a, 4. a, 5. b, 6. c, 7. b, 8. b, 9. a, 10. c, 11. a

Vocabulary

A. 1. a, 2. b, 3. b, 4. a, 5. b, 6. a, 7. a, 8. b
B. 1. reckless, 2. prudent, 3. boisterous, 4. sophisticated, 5. unendurable, 6. unwavering, 7. apprehension
C. 1. resort to, 2. held fast to, 3. was well under way, 4. In the wake of, 5. No wonder, 6. a matter of time, 7. Within a year, 8. put an end to, 9. at issue, 10. year after year

Structures

A. 1. people felt as though ..., 2. Americans felt as though ..., 3. Americans in the fifties ..., 4. King felt as if the curtain ..., 5. Dr. King's critics felt ...
B. 1. In spite of the heat ..., 2. In spite of King's insistence ..., 3. In spite of Hoover's efforts ..., 4. In spite of the driver's ..., 5. In spite of his exhaustion ...

UNIT 11: *Bicentennial Reflections:* Lincoln's Promise Outstanding

Reading Comprehension
A. 1. b, 2. a, 3. b, 4. b, 5. b, 6. a, 7. b, 8. c, 9. a, 10. c, 11. a
B. 1. first, 2. four, 3. thirty, 4. four years; six years, 5. twenty-one, 6. thirteen years, 7. no, 8. ten years, 9. eighty-six years, 10. American astronauts land on the moon
C. Spanish-American War, Progressivism, World War I, the Roaring Twenties, stock market crash, World War II, Watergate, War on Poverty, Iran hostage crisis, the Roaring Eighties
D. 1. Nebraska, 2. United Nations, 3. Europe, 4. Chicago, 5. Nobel Peace Prize, 6. Iran, 7. oldest elected president, 8. Tom Wolfe

Vocabulary
A. 1. a. confrontation, b. involvement, c. escalation, d. security, e. prosperity, f. assistance, g. realization; 2. a. resign, b. reelection, c. restore, d. recalled, e. rebirth
B. 1. in office, 2. dealing a blow, 3. get out from under, 4. up to par, 5. going broke, 6. here and there, 7. went astray, 8. Time and again
C. 1. settle for, 2. fell off, 3. covering up, 4. came to, 5. cut down
D. 1. despondent, 2. turbulence, 3. alien, 4. hefty, 5. plunged, 6. obligatory, 7. skimpy, 8. accurately

Structures
A. 1. would have been, 2. would have improved, 3. would have felt, 4. would have developed, 5. would have avoided
B. 1. Had Americans conserved, 2. Had the rescue attempt been, 3. Had the economy improved, 4. Had the government reduced, 5. Had Sherman McCoy reported

UNIT 12: *America's Third Century:* The Continuing Quest

Reading Comprehension
A. 1. a, 2. c, 3. a, 4. b, 5. b, 6. a, 7. a, 8. b, 9. c, 10. a
B. 1. Mercury, 2. Venus, Mars; 3. Jupiter, 4. Mercury, 5. Pluto, 6. 365, 7. 224.7, 247 years; 8. 93 million, 9. 3,675 million, 10. Milky Way
C. 1. Albert Einstein, 2. John Steinbeck, 3. Herbert Hoover, 4. Franklin D. Roosevelt, 5. Dr. Sally K. Ride, 6. Fiorello La Guardia, 7. Douglas MacArthur, 8. Edith Wharton, 9. Dr. Martin Luther King, Jr., 10. Mohandas Gandhi
D. 1. New Jersey, 2. Minnesota, 3. Pennsylvania, 4. Oklahoma, 5. Nebraska, 6. New York, 7. Illinois, 8. California, 9. Alabama, 10. Arizona

Vocabulary
B. 1. unabashed, 2. unassuming, 3. dashing, 4. impetuous, 5. irrepressible

Structures
A. on, to, for, over, on, aboard, in, on, of, from, of, at, of
B. the, the, an, the, a, the, the, a, the